Also Available from Williams Genealogy

Nelson Williams and his Descendants
Three Generations from Maine, USA to New Brunswick, Canada
and Beyond

Jacob Williams
& Joanna Dean Williams
and their Descendants

Volume I

The First Three Generations

Compiled by

Jeffrey Nelson Williams

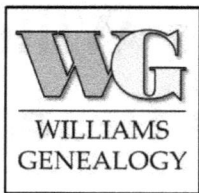

Published by Williams Genealogy
San Jose, California
www.wmsgen.com

Printed by CreateSpace

First Printing December 2018

Forward

Around 1635/1636, the date is not exactly known, my eighth great-grandparents Richard Williams and Frances Deighton emigrated from England to Massachusetts, thus establishing my Williams family line in America.

Flash forward 140 years to the year 1781 when the pioneering family of Jacob Williams, Joanna Dean Williams and their son Caleb moved north from Massachusetts and homesteaded an area along the Kennebec River just north of the Caratunk Falls in what is now Somerset County, Maine. Besides their bravery in moving to an uninhabited and remote area, another interesting point about Jacob and Joanna Dean is that they were distant cousins, both had the last name of Williams before their marriage, and both were direct descendants of Richard Williams and Frances Deighton. Jacob was a great-great-great-grandson and Joanna Dean was a great-great-great-great-granddaughter.

As Jacob and Joanna Dean had the unique qualities of both being direct descendants of the first persons in my Williams family line to come to America and being the first of my family to inhabit Somerset County, I thought they would be a great place to start researching my family history.

In compiling this book my journey has been one of great discovery, meeting family members whom I might not have otherwise met, making new friends and seeing new places. It has been a true labor of love.

There are so many that I need to thank. First, I must thank my children Justin and Aimée whose elementary school homework assignment to draw their family tree let me know how much I didn't know about the Williams family roots and thus inspiring my curiosity. Many thanks to my cousin Ronald Johnson for sharing an incredible amount of family research that let me know the task in front of me was possible. Thank you to Lena Arno from the Madison Historical Society, Emily Quint from the Embden Historical Society, Gloria and Dale Walker caretakers of the North New Portland Cemetery, Rose Hendrick caretaker of the West New Portland Cemetery and Larry Lightbody caretaker of the Sunset Cemetery in North Anson who generously gave of their time to help me in my quest. And a special thank you to my distant cousin Rod Headington and to the members of Find A Grave, especially Gail Kelly, who generously allowed me to use their photographs in this book.

And most importantly, thank you to my wife Jackie for her infinite support and patience with the many, many hours I spent "in the graveyard" doing my research and for occasionally reminding me to "stop and rejoin the living".

November 2018

About this Book

ORGANIZATION - This book has been organized in sections by generation. "Section I – The First Generation" documents the lives of Jacob Williams and Joanna Dean Williams, "Section II – The Second Generation" addresses the children of Jacob Williams and Joanna Dean Williams and "Section III – The Third Generation" covers the grand-children of Jacob Williams and Joanna Dean Williams.

At the beginning of each Section, as shown in the example below, there is an index that allows the reader to follow the line of descendants from Jacob Williams and Joanna Dean Williams to which page their biography is located in that section.

FORMAT – Each section contains a biographical and historical summary of the descendant's life from birth to death, as the available information available allows. Wherever possible anecdotal information has been added to the historical facts listed.

NAMES – Throughout this book when preparing their biographical sketch, I have used an individual's legal given first and middle name, or middle initial. It should also be noted that a person's legal name may occasionally differ from the name they were most commonly known as. Examples of this could be for a woman with the legal name of Elizabeth who was commonly known as Betsey or Eliza. Or for someone who was commonly known by their middle name such as Daniel Prescott who was known by many as Prescott. Legal names have been obtained from birth, marriage and death records.

USE OF *ITALICS* - When listing the children of a family member you will notice that some of their names are in *italics* as seen in the example below.

Francis Llewellyn	b. August 27, 1798	d. December 7, 1868
Suky	*b. February 19, 1801*	*d. March 1, 1801*
Jacob, Jr.	b. March 16, 1802	d. January 6, 1854
Chandler Nason	b. June 6, 1804	d. March 10, 1888
Leonard	*b. November 2, 1806*	*d. May 14, 1830*
Susan	b. July 24, 1809	d. May 29, 1837

For those individuals whose name is listed in *italics*, such as Suky and Leonard in the example above, you will find that information for them will stop in the section where they are first listed. The reason behind this is (a) they died in their youth, (b) they died as young adults and were never married and/or were without issue, or (c) sufficient information regarding their life and death could not be found to support writing an individual biography.

SOURCES - At the end of each person's biography the source documents used to support the individual's life history are listed. All source documents have been reviewed by the author prior to inclusion. If a document, or an independent verifiable source, has not been found to support a "Birth" or a "Marriage" fact, that source area will be left blank. If the "Death" and/or "Graveyard" source area is blank it can mean one of two things (a) a document or independent verifiable source has not been found or (b) the person is still living.

PERSON INDEX - As given names may often be repeated across generations, next to each person's name their year of birth and death has been listed to make it easier for the reader to find the summary for a specific individual.

CORRECTIONS – I have done my best to transcribe and interpret an individual's information from the available documentation. However, the reader may find that unintentional errors or omissions have been made. Reader feedback is always welcome. Please send any corrections you may have to editor@wmsgen.com.

Table of Contents

I

The First Generation:
Jacob Williams and Joanna Dean Williams

Jacob Williams
(1760 - 1814)
&
Joanna Dean Williams
(1764 – 1844)

Jacob Williams was born in Easton, Bristol, Massachusetts on January 18, 1760 to Ebenezer Williams and Anna Keith. Jacob was the great-great-great grandson of Richard Williams and Frances Deighton through their son Benjamin's family line. Richard and Frances, who emigrated from Gloucester, England to Taunton, Bristol, Massachusetts around 1635/1636, were the first to establish their Williams family line in America.

On January 1, 1776, at the age of sixteen, Jacob enlisted as a Private in the Continental Army serving in Captain Crocker's Company of Colonel Baily's Regiment during the American Revolutionary War. He initially served at Dorchester Heights, an area of South Boston in Boston, Suffolk, Massachusetts, and was later deployed to the State of New York.

Additionally, as described by William L. Chaffin in his book "History of the Town of Easton", Jacob had several other deployments as a member of the Easton Militia. In June and July of 1776 Jacob served in Captain Matthew Randall's Company first at Hull, Plymouth, Massachusetts and then later at Castle Island in Boston. On December 8, 1776 he marched with Captain Josiah Keith's Company, which was part of Colonel John Daggett's Regiment, to prevent an invasion from two English and two Hessian brigades that had taken possession of Newport in Newport County, Rhode Island the previous day.

Jacob was again deployed to Rhode Island on July 24, 1777 where he served for one month and four days in Captain Abiel Clapp's Company, which was part of Colonel Carpenter's Regiment. He served there again, on June 21, 1778 with Captain Samuel Robinson, of Colonel Wade's Regiment.

At the age of nineteen, on August 12, 1779, Jacob was married to Joanna Dean Williams, age fifteen, in Easton by the Reverend Archibald Campbell, a Minister of the Church of Christ. Joanna Dean, born on February 4, 1764 in Easton, was the daughter, and first child, of Daniel Williams and Rhoda Lathrop and a distant cousin of Jacob. Her great-great-great grandfather Samuel Williams was the brother of Jacob's great-great grandfather Benjamin Williams, both being sons of Richard Williams and Frances Deighton.

Jacob and Joanna Dean had large family of fifteen children.

Caleb	b. July 10, 1780	d. March 9, 1856
Daniel	b. July 22, 1782	d. July 18, 1874

John	b. August 20, 1784	d. October 8, 1867
Richard	b. February 4, 1787	d. August 30, 1876
Isaac Otis	b. June 15, 1789	d. April 16, 1860
Elsa	b. August 6, 1791	d. March 20, 1862
Ebenezer	b. July 17, 1793	d. April 15, 1870
Kezia	*b. April 27, 1795*	*d. July 15, 1795*
Cyrus	b. April 21, 1796	d. September 16, 1864
Francis Llewellyn	b. August 27, 1798	d. December 7, 1868
Suky	*b. February 19, 1801*	*d. March 1, 1801*
Jacob, Jr.	b. March 16, 1802	d. January 6, 1854
Chandler Nason	b. June 6, 1804	d. March 10, 1888
Leonard	*b. November 2, 1806*	*d. May 14, 1830*
Susan	b. July 27, 1809	d. May 29, 1837

The final deployment for Jacob as a member of the Easton militia occurred on August 4, 1780 when he was once again mustered into service in Captain Josiah Keith's Company. Their orders were to march on Tiverton, Newport, Rhode Island where they would assist their French allies if they were attacked by British forces. After they were there for eight days it appeared the expected attack was not going to occur, so the Easton militia returned home.

In 1781, Jacob, Joanna Dean and their infant child Caleb sailed from the Town of Barnstable in Barnstable County, Massachusetts along the coast to Maine and then up the Kennebec River to Fort Western in Augusta, Kennebec, Maine. From there they went by a small boat, a bateau, further up the Kennebec River to Caratunk Falls, Lincoln, Maine where they settled just above the falls on five acres of land on the west side of the river. (This section of Maine was then known as the Caratunk Settlement). At that time there was just one other family, the Joseph Cook family, living in that area.

Jacob cleared the land, built a cabin and planted crops on what became their home farm in that remote area of Maine. George Wood Clapp wrote in his book "The Life and Work of James Leon Williams" that "Some idea of the isolation may be formed in the fact that the nearest mill at which wheat or corn could be ground into flour or meal was fifty miles away. The grain was carried in sacks on the back of their horse along bridle paths through the forest. The man (Jacob) walked, carried his gun and watched."

By the time the 1790 United States Federal Census for Caratunk Town (spelled "Carrytunck" in that census document) was taken there were twenty-four households listed in addition to that of Jacob, Joanna Dean and their children.

Two of Jacob and Joanna Dean's children died on the home farm in Caratunk Town at young ages. Their eighth child Kezia died on July 15, 1795 at the age of two months and Suky, their eleventh child died March 1, 1801 at the age of twelve days. The causes of their deaths are not known. Both Kezia and Suky were buried in a local cemetery which is now known as the Bingham Village Cemetery in Bingham, Somerset, Maine.

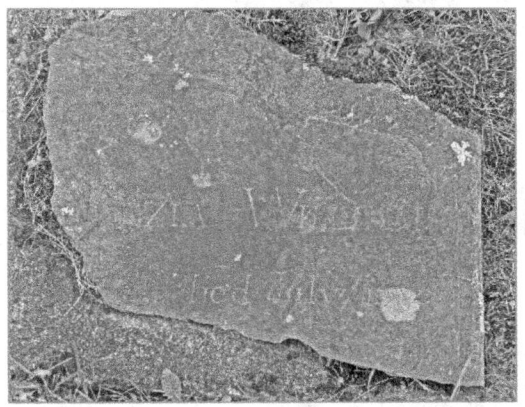

Gravestones for Kezia Williams (top) and Suky Williams (bottom)
(Photographs from the Collection of Jeffrey Nelson Williams and Jacqueline Pon Williams)

Jacob Williams must have been quite the local character. In his book "The Kennebec Valley", published in 1887, Seth Harding Whitney included the following anecdote about Jacob, "The salmon were plenty in the river, and easily obtained; the moose were plenty in forests around him, so plenty that Mr. Williams at one time was eating his dinner, and seeing a moose crossing the interval, he shot him from the window." This bit of lore was repeated again in the book "Embden Town of Yore", written by Ernest George Walker which was first published in 1929.

The 1800 United States Federal Census continued to list Jacob, Joanna and their children as living in Caratunk Settlement.

Jacob was one of the signers of the petition for a new town and town government dated December 12, 1803 which was submitted to the Senate and House of Representatives of the Commonwealth of Massachusetts. The neighborhood which had been locally referred to as "Queenstown" became officially known as "Emden" when it was incorporated on June 22, 1804. At the time it was incorporated Emden was part of Kennebec County, Maine. Sometime later in 1805 the letter 'b" was added to the town name and since then it has been known as "Embden".

From the records of the first town meeting of Embden, on September 6, 1804, it was noted that Jacob, along with three other members of the community, were voted in as a committee to "lay out the road in the Eastern ward from Anson Road to the Million-Acre Line". Additional Embden town records indicate that Jacob frequently served as a town official, including as a "Selectman" in 1805 and 1806 and as the "Town Moderator" in 1807 and 1809.

Not only was Jacob a town official and a well-known moose hunter, he was also one of the wealthiest farmers in the area. Over the years, Jacob had expanded his land holdings in and around Embden and also owned a grain mill on the Kennebec River.

In the 1810 United States Federal Census records Jacob, Joanna Dean and eight of their children were listed as living in the new town of Embden, which as of 1809 was part of the newly formed Somerset County.

On July 12, 1814, just four years after the 1810 Census was taken, Jacob died at the age of fifty-four. The exact place and cause of his death have not been found. He was buried in the Bingham Village Cemetery in Bingham.

At the time of the 1820 United States Federal Census Joanna Dean and some of her children were recorded as still living in Embden.

Leonard, the fourteenth child Jacob and Joanna Dean died on May 14, 1830 at the age of twenty-three. The cause and place of his death have not been found. Additionally, no record has been found to indicate that Leonard had ever married or had any children. As such his documented history will end here. Leonard was also buried in the Bingham Village Cemetery in Bingham.

Gravestone for Leonard Williams
(Photograph from the Collection of Jeffrey Nelson Williams and Jacqueline Pon Williams)

On June 27, 1839 Joanna Dean filed to receive the widow's military pension for Jacob's service during the Revolutionary War. Her pension was granted on July 2, 1839.

Joanna Dean survived Jacob by thirty years and never remarried. She died at age eighty on October 8, 1844. Her place and cause of death have not been found. She too was buried in the family plot at the Bingham Village Cemetery in Bingham with her husband and children.

Gravestone for Jacob Williams (left)
(Photograph Courtesy of Carrie & Kevin)
Gravestone for Joanna Dean Williams (right)
(Photograph Courtesy of Rod Headington)

SOURCES:

Jacob Williams
Birth: (1) "Massachusetts, Town and Vital Records, 1620-1988", [database on-line], Provo, UT, USA: Ancestry.com Operations, Inc., 2011, Record of Births, Marriages and Deaths, Easthampton, Massachusetts, Page 76; (2) "Massachusetts, Town and Vital Records, 1620-1988", [database on-line], Provo, UT, USA: Ancestry.com Operations, Inc., 2011, Record of Births, Marriages and Deaths, Easthampton, Massachusetts, Page 1197.
Death: (1) "Maine Families in 1790, Volume 1", Edited by Ruth Gray, Pages 289 & 290, Maine Genealogical Society, Special Publication No. 2, Picton Press, Camden, Maine, Copyright 1988; (2) Edmund West, comp., "Family Data Collection - Individual Records", [database on-line], Provo, UT, USA: Ancestry.com Operations Inc, 2000; (3) "Maine Old Cemetery Association Special Publication Number 12, Edition No. 1: Series 1, 2 and 3", Page 335, Picton Press, Rockland, Maine, Copyright 2006; (4) "Maine, Nathan Hale Cemetery Collection, ca. 1780-1980," database with images, FamilySearch, (https://familysearch.org/ark: /61903/1:1: QVJ5-SFQ5).
Graveyard: (1) "Bingham Village Cemetery" by Nancy Hamlin Davis and Ruth Hamlin, Record 1997, Old Canada Road Historical Society; (2) "Maine Old Cemetery Association Special Publication Number 12, Edition No. 1: Series 1, 2 and 3", Page 335, Picton Press, Rockland, Maine, Copyright 2006; (3) "Maine, Nathan Hale Cemetery Collection, ca. 1780-1980," database with images, FamilySearch, (https://familysearch.org/ark:/61903 /1:1: QVJ5-SFQ5). (4) Find A Grave, Memorial #27752518.

Joanna Dean Williams
Birth: "Massachusetts, Town and Vital Records, 1620-1988", [database on-line], Provo, UT, USA: Ancestry.com Operations, Inc., 2011, Record of Births, Marriages and Deaths, Easthampton, Massachusetts, Page 162.
Marriage: (1) "Maine Families in 1790, Volume 1", Edited by Ruth Gray, Pages 289 & 290, Maine Genealogical Society, Special Publication No. 2, Picton Press, Camden, Maine, Copyright 1988; (2) "Massachusetts, Town and Vital Records, 1620-1988", [database on-line], Provo, UT, USA: Ancestry.com Operations, Inc., 2011, Record of Births, Marriages and Deaths, Easthampton, Massachusetts, Page 154; (3) "Easton, Massachusetts Marriages; 1720-1802", (Online database: AmericanAncestors.org, New England Historic Genealogical Society, 2003); (4) Original typescript: Marriages at Easton, Massachusetts from Earliest Entry Down to 1802. R. Stanton Avery Special Collections, New England Historic Genealogical Society, Boston, MA.
Death: (1) "Maine Families in 1790, Volume 1", Edited by Ruth Gray, Pages 289 & 290, Maine Genealogical Society, Special Publication No. 2, Picton Press, Camden, Maine, Copyright 1988; (2) "Maine Old Cemetery Association Special Publication Number 12, Edition No. 1: Series 1, 2 and 3", Page 335, Picton Press, Rockland, Maine, Copyright 2006; (3) "Maine, Nathan Hale Cemetery Collection, ca. 1780-1980," database with images, FamilySearch, (https://familysearch.org/ark:/61903/1:1:QVJ5-SFWC); (4) Gravestone.
Graveyard: (1) "Bingham Village Cemetery" by Nancy Hamlin Davis and Ruth Hamlin, Record 1998, Old Canada Road Historical Society; (2) "Maine Old Cemetery Association Special Publication Number 12, Edition No. 1: Series 1, 2 and 3", Page 335, Picton Press, Rockland, Maine, Copyright 2006; (3) "Maine, Nathan Hale Cemetery Collection, ca. 1780-1980," database with images, FamilySearch, (https://familysearch.org/ark:/61903 /1:1: QVJ5-SFWC); (4) Find A Grave, Memorial #32339832.

Kezia Williams
Birth: (1) "Maine Families in 1790, Volume 1", Edited by Ruth Gray, Page 290, Maine Genealogical Society, Special Publication No. 2, Picton Press, Camden, Maine, Copyright 1988; (2) "Embden Town of Yore" by Ernest George Walker, Page 119, Published by Independent-Reporter Company, Skowhegan, Maine, 1929; (3) "The Kennebec Valley" by Seth Harding Whitney, Page 98 Published by Sprague, Burleigh and Flynt, Augusta, Maine, 1887.
Death: (1) "Maine Families in 1790, Volume 1", Edited by Ruth Gray, Page 290, Maine Genealogical Society, Special Publication No. 2, Picton Press, Camden, Maine, Copyright 1988; (2) Gravestone.
Graveyard: Find A Grave, Memorial #129631905.

Suky Williams
Birth: (1) "Maine Families in 1790, Volume 1", Edited by Ruth Gray, Page 290, Maine Genealogical Society, Special Publication No. 2, Picton Press, Camden, Maine, Copyright 1988; (2) "Embden Town of Yore" by Ernest George Walker, Page 119, Published by Independent-Reporter Company, Skowhegan, Maine, 1929; (3) "The Kennebec Valley" by Seth Harding Whitney, Page 98 Published by Sprague, Burleigh and Flynt, Augusta, Maine, 1887.
Death: "Maine Families in 1790, Volume 1", Edited by Ruth Gray, Page 290, Maine Genealogical Society, Special Publication No. 2, Picton Press, Camden, Maine, Copyright 1988.
Graveyard: (1) "Bingham Village Cemetery" by Nancy Hamlin Davis and Ruth Hamlin, Record 2001, Old Canada Road Historical Society; (2) "Maine Old Cemetery Association Special Publication Number 12, Edition No. 1: Series 1, 2 and 3", Page 335, Picton Press, Rockland, Maine, Copyright 2006: (3) "Maine, Nathan Hale Cemetery Collection, ca. 1780-1980," database with images, FamilySearch, (https://familysearch.org/ark:/61903 /1:1: QVJ5-SFQP).

Leonard Williams
Birth: (1) "Maine Families in 1790, Volume 1", Edited by Ruth Gray, Page 290, Maine Genealogical Society, Special Publication No. 2, Picton Press, Camden, Maine, Copyright 1988; (2) "Embden Town of Yore" by Ernest George Walker, Page 119, Published by Independent-Reporter Company, Skowhegan, Maine, 1929; (3) "The Kennebec Valley" by Seth Harding Whitney, Page 98 Published by Sprague, Burleigh and Flynt, Augusta, Maine, 1887.
Death: (1) "Maine Old Cemetery Association Special Publication Number 12, Edition No. 1: Series 1, 2 and 3", Page 335, Picton Press, Rockland, Maine, Copyright 2006; (2) "Maine, Nathan Hale Cemetery Collection, ca. 1780-1980," database with images, FamilySearch (https://familysearch.org/ark:/61903/1:1:QVJ5-SFQP); (3) Gravestone.
Graveyard: (1) "Bingham Village Cemetery" by Nancy Hamlin Davis and Ruth Hamlin, Record 1999, Old Canada Road Historical Society; (2) "Maine Old Cemetery Association Special Publication Number 12, Edition No. 1: Series 1, 2 and 3", Page 335, Picton Press, Rockland, Maine, Copyright 2006; (3) "Maine, Nathan Hale Cemetery Collection, ca. 1780-1980," database with images, FamilySearch, (https://familysearch.org/ark:/61903/1:1: QVJ5-SFQP).

Historical Accounts: (1) 1790 United States Federal Census for Caratunk Town, Lincoln, Maine; (2) 1800 United States Federal Census for Embden, Somerset, Maine; (3) 1810 United States Federal Census for Embden, Somerset, Maine; (4) 1820 United States Federal Census for Embden, Somerset, Maine; (5) "History of the Town of Easton Massachusetts" by William L. Chaffin, Page 219-234, Published by John Wilson and Son, University Press, Cambridge, Massachusetts, 1886; (6) "Massachusetts Soldiers and Sailors of the Revolutionary War" prepared and published by the Secretary of the Commonwealth, Volume 17 Pages 438 & 439, Write & Potter Printing Co., Boston, Massachusetts; (7) "Embden Town of Yore" by Ernest George Walker, Published by Independent-Reporter Company, Skowhegan, Maine, 1929; (8) "The Kennebec Valley" by Seth Harding Whitney, Published by Sprague, Burleigh and Flynt, Augusta, Maine, 1887; (9) Heads of families at the first census of the United States taken in the year 1790: Maine (Washington, D. C., Govt. Print Office, 1908); (10) United States of America, Bureau of the Census; Second Census of the United States, National Archives and Records Administration, 1800. M32. Roll 7; (11) Revolutionary War Service Records, Massachusetts Fourth Regiment; (12) Affidavit from Joseph Maynard, Revolutionary War Pension and Bounty-Land Warrant Application Files, (www.fold3.com).

II

The Second Generation

The Children of Jacob Williams and Joanna Dean Williams

Caleb Williams
(1780 - 1856)

Caleb was the first child of Jacob Williams and Joanna Dean Williams. He was born in Barnstable, Barnstable County, Massachusetts on July 10, 1780.

When he was around one-year old, Caleb traveled with his parents by ship from Barnstable along the coast to Maine and up the Kennebec River to Fort Western in Augusta, Kennebec, Maine. Once there, they took a small boat, a bateau, further up the Kennebec River to Caratunk Falls, Lincoln, Maine where his parents made their new home just above the falls on five acres of land on the west side of the river.

On September 29, 1803, Caleb, age twenty-three, filed his intentions to marry Elizabeth Whitman, age twenty-one, with the Town Clerk of Anson, Kennebec, Maine. (Anson became part of Somerset County, Maine in 1809) They were subsequently married on October 20, 1803 in Anson by Bezer Bryant, Esquire. Elizabeth, born on March 7, 1781 in Bridgewater, Plymouth, Massachusetts, was the daughter of Zechariah Whitman and Abigail Wood.

Caleb and Elizabeth followed in the footsteps of his parents and had a large family with fourteen children.

Charlotte	b. January 7, 1804	d. March 17, 1848
Mary Polly	b. March 31, 1805	d. October 5, 1889
Abigail	*b. June 25, 1806*	*d. July 29, 1809*
Betsey	b. October 31, 1807	d. September 8, 1884
Zachariah	b. June 11, 1809	d. December 20, 1898
Amos	b. February 26, 1811	d. May 8, 1883
Foster	b. November 20, 1812	d. October 25, 1884
Warren	b. July 1, 1814	d. February 15, 1884
Abigail	b. February 2, 1817	d. January 7, 1880
Albert	*b. January 2, 1819*	*d. October 8, 1820*
Sally	*b. August 17, 1820*	*d. September 8, 1820*
Albert	b. March 23, 1822	d. November 10, 1867
Cyrena	b. June 27, 1824	d. January 26, 1898
Marshall W.	*b. December 26, 1826*	*d. April 23, 1844*

On December 12, 1803, like his father Jacob, Caleb was one of the signers of the petition that was submitted to the Senate and House of Representatives of the Commonwealth of Massachusetts to form new town and town government. That new town, Emden, Kennebec, Maine, was incorporated on June 22, 1804.

The third child of Caleb and Elizabeth, Abigail, died on July 29, 1809 when she was three years old. The cause and place of her death is not known. She was buried in the Bingham Village Cemetery in Bingham, Somerset, Maine.

When the 1810 and 1820 United States Federal Census' were taken, Caleb, Elizabeth and their family were listed as living in Embden. (The town's name was now spelled with a "b" and became part of Somerset County in 1809) Caleb, like his father, was a farmer and an occasional town official of Embden, including serving as the town "Collector and Constable" in 1815 and 1822.

Sally, the eleventh child of Caleb and Elizabeth, died on September 8, 1820 when she was just twenty-two days old and Albert, their tenth child, was twenty-one months old when he died thirty days later on October 8,1820. The exact places and causes of their deaths have not been found. Sally and Albert were buried in the Bingham Village Cemetery in Bingham.

Gravestone for Abigail Williams, Albert Williams and Sally Williams
(Photograph from the Collection of Jeffrey Nelson Williams and Jacqueline Pon Williams)

Around 1825, Caleb expanded his holdings along the Kennebec River and purchased 125 acres of land in Somerset County, just south of his father's property, which included the water power for the Caratunk Settlement.

Celeb and his family were still living and farming in the town of Embden when the 1830 and 1840 United States Federal Census' were taken.

The fourteenth child of Caleb and Elizabeth, Marshall W., was seventeen years old when he died April 23, 1844 having never married or had children. The cause and the place of his death are also not known. He was buried in the Pleasantdale Cemetery in Embden.

Gravestone for Marshall W. Williams
(Photograph from the Collection of Jeffrey Nelson Williams and Jacqueline Pon Williams)

After having held town meetings in various houses and schools, in 1845 the town officials of Embden decided to build an official Town House. Caleb, along with a group of other citizens, was asked to "draw a draft for said house and report it to the town". On March 2, 1846, the town voted to build the Town House which still stands today on Cross Town Road and is listed on the National Register of Historic Places.

Embden Town House in September 2018
(Photograph from the Collection of Jeffrey Nelson Williams and Jacqueline Pon Williams)

On March 9, 1856 Caleb died at age seventy-five. His place and cause of death have not been found. Caleb was buried in the Pleasantdale Cemetery in Embden near his son Marshall W.

A little more than three years later, on August 12, 1858, Elizabeth died at the age of seventy-seven. The cause and place of her death are also not known. Elizabeth was also buried alongside her husband in Embden at the Pleasantdale Cemetery.

Gravestones for Caleb Williams (left) and Elizabeth Whitman (right)
(Photographs from the Collection of Jeffrey Nelson Williams and Jacqueline Pon Williams)

SOURCES:

Caleb Williams
Birth: (1) Original Record of Maine Towns & Cities, Town of Embden, Disk 1, Page 58, Picton Press, Rockland Maine, Copyright 2005; (2) "Maine Families in 1790, Volume 1", Edited by Ruth Gray, Page 290, Maine Genealogical Society, Special Publication No. 2, Picton Press, Camden, Maine, Copyright 1988; (3) Edmund West, comp., "Family Data Collection - Individual Records ", [database on-line], Provo, UT, USA: Ancestry.com Operations Inc, 2000; (4) "Embden Town of Yore" by Ernest George Walker, Page 119, Published by Independent-Reporter Company, Skowhegan, Maine, 1929; (4) "The Kennebec Valley" by Seth Harding Whitney, Page 98, Published by Sprague, Burleigh and Flynt, Augusta, Maine, 1887.
Death: (1) Edmund West, comp., "Family Data Collection - Individual Records ", [database on-line], Provo, UT, USA: Ancestry.com Operations Inc, 2000; (2) "Maine, Faylene Hutton Cemetery Collection, ca. 1780-1990," database with images, FamilySearch, (https://familysearch.org/ark:/61903/1.1/QKM1-WKGD) - Accession #5030; (3) Gravestone.
Graveyard: (1) "Pleasant Dale/Murphy/Boothby Cemetery" complied by Nancy Hamlin Davis and Ruth Hamlin, Record 129, Old Canada Road Historical Society; (2) Find A Grave, Memorial #52820267.

Elizabeth Whitman
Birth: "History of the Descendants of John Whitman of Weymouth, Mass." by Charles H. Farnam, A.M., Page 851, Tuttle, Morehouse & Taylor printers, New Haven, 1889.
Marriage: (1) Original Record of Maine Towns & Cities, Town of Anson, Page 28, Picton Press, Rockland Maine, Copyright 2005; (2) Original Record of Maine Towns & Cities, Town of Anson, Page 31, Picton Press, Rockland Maine, Copyright 2005; (3) "Vital Records – Town of Anson Maine, Part 1" compiled by David H. Ela, Pages 23 & 26, 1975; (4) "Maine Families in 1790, Volume 1", Edited by Ruth Gray, Page 290, Maine Genealogical Society, Special Publication No. 2, Picton Press, Camden, Maine, Copyright 1988; (5) "Embden Town of Yore" by Ernest George Walker, Page 696, Published by Independent-Reporter Company, Skowhegan, Maine, 1929; (6) "History of the Descendants of John Whitman of Weymouth, Mass." by Charles H. Farnam, A.M., Page 851, Tuttle, Morehouse & Taylor printers, New Haven, 1889; (7) Edmund West, comp., "Family Data Collection - Individual Records", [database on-line], Provo, UT, USA: Ancestry.com Operations Inc., 2000.
Death: (1) "History of the Descendants of John Whitman of Weymouth, Mass." by Charles H. Farnam, A.M., Page 851, Tuttle, Morehouse & Taylor printers, New Haven, 1889; (2) "Maine, Faylene Hutton Cemetery Collection, ca. 1780-1990," database with images, FamilySearch, (https://familysearch.org/ark:/61903/1.1/QKM1-WKGD) - Accession #5030.
Graveyard: (1) "Pleasant Dale/Murphy/Boothby Cemetery" complied by Nancy Hamlin Davis and Ruth Hamlin, Record 130, Old Canada Road Historical Society; (2) Find A Grave, Memorial #52820332.

Abigail Williams
Birth: "History of the Descendants of John Whitman of Weymouth, Mass." by Charles H. Farnam, A.M., Page 854, Tuttle, Morehouse & Taylor printers, New Haven, 1889.
Death: (1) "History of the Descendants of John Whitman of Weymouth, Mass." by Charles H. Farnam, A.M., Page 854, Tuttle, Morehouse & Taylor printers, New Haven, 1889; (2) Gravestone.
Graveyard: (1) "Bingham Village Cemetery" by Nancy Hamlin Davis and Ruth Hamlin, Record 2002, Old Canada Road Historical Society; (2) "Maine Old Cemetery Association Special Publication Number 12, Edition No. 1: Series 1, 2 and 3", Page 335, Picton Press, Rockland, Maine, Copyright 2006; (3) Find A Grave, Memorial #82115404.

Albert Williams
Birth: "History of the Descendants of John Whitman of Weymouth, Mass." by Charles H. Farnam, A.M., Page 859, Tuttle, Morehouse & Taylor printers, New Haven, 1889.
Death: (1) "History of the Descendants of John Whitman of Weymouth, Mass." by Charles H. Farnam, A.M., Page 859, Tuttle, Morehouse & Taylor printers, New Haven, 1889; (2) Gravestone.
Graveyard: (1) "Bingham Village Cemetery" by Nancy Hamlin Davis and Ruth Hamlin, Record 2003, Old Canada Road Historical Society; (2) "Maine Old Cemetery Association Special Publication Number 12, Edition No. 1: Series 1, 2 and 3", Page 335, Picton Press, Rockland, Maine, Copyright 2006; (3) Find A Grave, Memorial #82115406.

Sally Williams
Birth: "History of the Descendants of John Whitman of Weymouth, Mass." by Charles H. Farnam, A.M., Page 859, Tuttle, Morehouse & Taylor printers, New Haven, 1889.
Death: (1) "History of the Descendants of John Whitman of Weymouth, Mass." by Charles H. Farnam, A.M., Page 859, Tuttle, Morehouse & Taylor printers, New Haven, 1889; (2) Gravestone.
Graveyard: (1) "Bingham Village Cemetery" by Nancy Hamlin Davis and Ruth Hamlin, Record 2004, Old Canada Road Historical Society; (2) "Maine Old Cemetery Association Special Publication Number 12, Edition No. 1: Series 1, 2 and 3", Page 335, Picton Press, Rockland, Maine, Copyright 2006; (3) Find A Grave, Memorial #82115413.

Marshall W. Williams
Birth: "History of the Descendants of John Whitman of Weymouth, Mass." by Charles H. Farnam, A.M., Page 860, Tuttle, Morehouse & Taylor printers, New Haven, 1889.
Death: (1) "History of the Descendants of John Whitman of Weymouth, Mass." by Charles H. Farnam, A.M., Page 860, Tuttle, Morehouse & Taylor printers, New Haven, 1889; (2) "Maine, Faylene Hutton Cemetery Collection, ca. 1780-1990," database with images, FamilySearch (https://familysearch.org/ark:/61903/1.1/QKM1-WKGD) - Accession #5030; (3) Gravestone.
Graveyard: (1) "Pleasant Dale/Murphy/Boothby Cemetery" complied by Nancy Hamlin Davis and Ruth Hamlin, Record 131, Old Canada Road Historical Society; (2) Find A Grave, Memorial #118457853.

Historical Accounts: (1) 1810 United States Federal Census for Embden, Somerset, Maine; (2) 1820 United States Federal Census for Embden, Somerset, Maine; (3) 1830 United States Federal Census for Embden, Somerset, Maine; (4) 1840 United States Federal Census for Embden, Somerset, Maine; (5) 1850 United States Federal Census for Embden, Somerset, Maine; (6) "Embden Town of Yore" by Ernest George Walker, Published by Independent-Reporter Company, Skowhegan, Maine, 1929.

Daniel Williams
(1782 - 1874)

The second child of Jacob Williams and Joanna Dean Williams was Daniel who was born on July 22, 1782. He was the first of Jacob Williams and Joanna Dean's children to be born on the family farm at Caratunk Settlement which was then part of Lincoln County, Maine.

On May 30, 1805, at age twenty-two, Daniel was married to Abigail Maynard, age twenty, in Anson, Kennebec, Maine by Bezer Bryant, Esquire. (Anson was part of Kennebec County until it became part of Somerset County, Maine in 1809) Abigail, the daughter of Joseph Maynard and Abigail Merriam, was born on September 1, 1784 in Concord, Middlesex, Massachusetts.

Daniel and Abigail had nine children together.

Sewall	b. September 24, 1805	d. November 5, 1867
Nelson	b. July 1, 1807	d.
Daniel Prescott	b. February 7, 1809	d. November 19, 1876
Abigail Maynard	b. October 16, 1812	d. September 12, 1882
Rhoda L.	*b. 1814*	*d. June 5, 1837*
Silas M. (a twin)	*b. March 28, 1816*	*d. March 26, 1840*
Simon M. (a twin)	*b. March 28, 1816*	*d. January 11, 1822*
Jotham A.	*b. 1824*	*d. April 1, 1847*
John Quincy Adams	b. April 30, 1828	d. September 9, 1907

Like his father and other members of his family, Daniel served as a town official for Embden, Somerset, Maine in 1815, 1817 and 1819.

The 1820 United States Federal Census recorded Daniel, Abigail and their children as living in Embden.

Simon M., the seventh child of Daniel and Abigail, died of an unknown cause on January 11, 1822 at the age of five years. He was buried in the Pierce Cemetery in Solon, Somerset, Maine.

The fifth child of Daniel and Abigail, Rhoda L., died on June 5, 1837 when she was twenty-three years old. The place and cause of her death are not known. She was buried in Solon at the Pierce Cemetery.

At the time of the 1840 United States Federal Census Daniel, Abigail and their children were recorded as living along the East Kennebec River in Somerset County, Maine.

Silas M., the sixth child of Daniel and Abigail, died when he was twenty-three years old March 26, 1840 and Jotham A., their eighth child, who coincidentally was also twenty-three years old when he died at The Forks, Somerset, Maine on April 1, 1847. Silas M. and Jotham A. had never married or had children. The cause and place of death for Silas M., as well as the cause of death for Jotham A. have not been found. They were buried in the Pierce Cemetery in Solon with their siblings.

Gravestones for Rhoda L. Williams (top left), Silas M. Williams (top right), Simon M. Williams (lower left) and Jotham A. Williams (lower right)
(Photographs from the Collection of Jeffrey Nelson Williams and Jacqueline Pon Williams)

Abigail, at age sixty-four, preceded Daniel in death on December 24, 1848. Her place and cause of death are not known. She was also buried in the family plot in the Pierce Cemetery in Solon.

Daniel, at age sixty-six, married his second wife Elvira J. (Lane) Whitney, age forty-nine and the widow of Silas Whitney, on April 9, 1849. She was born on April 21, 1799 in Brownfield, Oxford, Maine to William Lane and Alice Haines. No record has been found to indicate Daniel and Elvira J. had any children together.

In the 1850, 1860 and 1870 United States Federal Census' Daniel, Elvira J. and their family were recorded as living in Solon with Daniel working as a "farmer".

Daniel died on July 18, 1874 at age ninety-one in Caratunk, Somerset, Maine. The cause of his death has not been found. He was buried in the family plot in the Pierce Cemetery in Solon.

Gravestones for Daniel Williams (left) and Abigail Maynard (right)
(Photographs from the Collection of Jeffrey Nelson Williams and Jacqueline Pon Williams)

At the time the 1880 United States Federal Census was taken Elvira J. had moved to Lowell, Middlesex, Massachusetts where she was recorded as living on Nineteenth Street.

Elvira J. outlived Daniel by more than twenty years dying on April 22, 1896 of "pneumonia" in Lowell, at the age of ninety-six. She was buried in the Evergreen Cemetery in Solon.

SOURCES:

Daniel Williams
Birth: (1) Original Record of Maine Towns & Cities, Town of Embden, Disk 1, Page 58, Picton Press, Rockland Maine, Copyright 2005; (2) Original Record of Maine Towns & Cities, Town of Bingham, Page 26, Copyright 2005, Picton Press, Rockland Maine; (3) "Maine, Births and Christenings, 1739-1900," index, FamilySearch, (https://familysearch.org/pal:/MM9.1.1/F439-TYQ); (4) "Maine Families in 1790, Volume 1", Edited by Ruth Gray, Page 290, Maine Genealogical Society, Special Publication No. 2, Picton Press, Camden, Maine, Copyright 1988; (5) Edmund West, comp., "Family Data Collection - Individual Records", [database on-line]. Provo, UT, USA: Ancestry.com Operations Inc., 2000; (6) "Embden Town of Yore" by Ernest George Walker, Page 119, Published by Independent-Reporter Company, Skowhegan, Maine, 1929; (7) "The Kennebec Valley" by Seth Harding Whitney, Page 98 Published by Sprague, Burleigh and Flynt, Augusta, Maine, 1887.
Death: (1) "Maine Families in 1790, Volume 1", Edited by Ruth Gray, Page 290, Maine Genealogical Society, Special Publication No. 2, Picton Press, Camden, Maine, Copyright 1988; (2) Edmund West, comp., "Family Data Collection - Individual Records", [database on-line]. Provo, UT, USA: Ancestry.com Operations Inc., 2000; (3) "Maine, Faylene Hutton Cemetery Collection, 1780-1980," database with images, FamilySearch, (https://familysearch.org/ark:/61903/1.1/QKM1-WKR9) - Accession #5044; (4) Gravestone.
Graveyard: (1) "Maine Old Cemetery Association Special Publication Number 12, Edition No. 1: Series 1, 2 and 3", Page 2004, Picton Press, Rockland, Maine, Copyright 2006; (2) "Maine, Faylene Hutton Cemetery Collection, 1780-1980," database with images, FamilySearch, (https://familysearch.org/ark:/61903/1.1/QKM1-WKR9) - Accession #5044; (3) Find A Grave, Memorial #52832320.

Abigail Maynard
Birth: Original Record of Maine Towns & Cities, Town of Bingham, Page 26, Picton Press, Rockland Maine, Copyright 2005.
Marriage: (1) "Vital Records – Town of Anson Maine, Part 1" compiled by David H. Ela, Page 27, 1975; (2) Original Record of Maine Towns & Cities, Town of Anson, Page 32, Picton Press, Rockland Maine, Copyright 2005; (3) "Maine, Marriages, 1771-1907," index, FamilySearch, (https://familysearch.org/pal:/MM9.1.1/F4XH-JNG); (4) "Maine Families in 1790, Volume 1", Edited by Ruth Gray, Page 290, Maine Genealogical Society, Special Publication No. 2, Picton Press, Camden, Maine, Copyright 1988; (5) "Embden Town of Yore" by Ernest George Walker, Page 696, Published by Independent-Reporter Company, Skowhegan, Maine, 1929.
Death: (1) "Maine, Faylene Hutton Cemetery Collection, 1780-1980," database with images, FamilySearch, (https://familysearch.org/ark:/61903/1.1/QKM1-WKR9) - Accession #5044; (2) Gravestone.
Graveyard: (1) "Maine Old Cemetery Association Special Publication Number 12, Edition No. 1: Series 1, 2 and 3", Page 2004, Picton Press, Rockland, Maine, Copyright 2006; (2) "Maine, Faylene Hutton Cemetery Collection, 1780-1980," database with images, FamilySearch, (https://familysearch.org/ark:/61903/1.1/QKM1-WKR9) - Accession #5044; (3) Find A Grave, Memorial #52832165.

Rhoda L. Williams
Birth:
Death: (1) "Maine, Faylene Hutton Cemetery Collection, 1780-1980," database with images, FamilySearch, (https://familysearch.org/ark:/61903/1.1/QKM1-WKR9) - Accession #5044; (2) Gravestone.
Graveyard: (1) "Maine Old Cemetery Association Special Publication Number 12, Edition No. 1: Series 1, 2 and 3", Page 2004, Picton Press, Rockland, Maine, Copyright 2006; (2) "Maine, Faylene Hutton Cemetery Collection, 1780-1980," database with images, FamilySearch, (https://familysearch.org/ark:/61903/1.1/QKM1-WKR9) - Accession #5044; (3) Find A Grave, Memorial #82698339.

Silas M. Williams
Birth:
Death: (1) "Maine, Faylene Hutton Cemetery Collection, 1780-1980," database with images, FamilySearch, (https://familysearch.org/ark:/61903/1.1/QKM1-WKR9) - Accession #5044; (2) Gravestone.
Graveyard: (1) "Maine Old Cemetery Association Special Publication Number 12, Edition No. 1: Series 1, 2 and 3", Page 2004, Picton Press, Rockland, Maine, Copyright 2006; (2) Find A Grave, Memorial #82698470.

Simon M. Williams
Birth:
Death: (1) "Maine, Faylene Hutton Cemetery Collection, 1780-1980," database with images, FamilySearch, (https://familysearch.org/ark:/61903/1.1/QKM1-WKR9) - Accession #5044; (2) Gravestone.
Graveyard: (1) "Maine Old Cemetery Association Special Publication Number 12, Edition No. 1: Series 1, 2 and 3", Page 2004, Picton Press, Rockland, Maine, Copyright 2006; (2) "Maine, Faylene Hutton Cemetery Collection, 1780-1980," database with images, FamilySearch, (https://familysearch.org/ark:/61903/1.1/QKM1-WKR9) - Accession #5044; (3) Find A Grave, Memorial #82698520.

Jotham A. Williams
Birth:
Death: (1) "Maine, Faylene Hutton Cemetery Collection, 1780-1980," database with images, FamilySearch, (https://familysearch.org/ark:/61903/1.1/QKM1-WKR9) - Accession #5044; (2) Gravestone.
Graveyard: (1) "Maine Old Cemetery Association Special Publication Number 12, Edition No. 1: Series 1, 2 and 3", Page 2004, Picton Press, Rockland, Maine, Copyright 2006; (2) "Maine, Faylene Hutton Cemetery Collection, 1780-1980," database with images, FamilySearch, (https://familysearch.org/ark:/61903/1.1/QKM1-WKR9) - Accession #5044; (3) Find A Grave, Memorial #82698417.

Elvira J. Lane
Birth: "Maine, Births and Christenings, 1739-1900," index, FamilySearch, (https://familysearch.org/ark:/61903/1.1: F44L-J3T).
Marriage: "Maine, Marriages, 1771-1907" index, FamilySearch, (https://familysearch.org/pal:/MM9.1.1/F4XC-FMX).
Death: (1) "Massachusetts, Town and Vital Records, 1620-1988", [database on-line], Provo, UT, USA: Ancestry.com Operations, Inc., 2011, Deaths in the City of Lowell in the year 1896, Page 159; (2) Record of a Death, Maine Vital Records.
Graveyard: (1) "Maine, Faylene Hutton Cemetery Collection, 1780-1980," database with images, FamilySearch, (https://familysearch.org/ark:/61903/1.1/QKM1-9RWS) - Accession #5593; (2) Find A Grave, Memorial #173301773.

Historical Accounts: (1) 1820 United States Federal Census for Embden, Somerset, Maine; (2) 1840 United States Federal Census for East Kennebec River, Somerset, Maine; (3) 1850 United States Federal Census for Solon, Somerset, Maine; (4) 1860 United States Federal Census for Solon, Somerset, Maine, Page 42; (5) 1870 United States Federal Census for Solon, Somerset, Maine, Page 5; (6) 1880 United States Federal Census for Lowell, Middlesex, Massachusetts, Page 28; (7) "Embden Town of Yore" by Ernest George Walker, Published by Independent-Reporter Company, Skowhegan, Maine, 1929.

John Williams
(1784 - 1867)

John, the third child Jacob Williams and Joanna Dean Williams was born on August 20, 1784 in Caratunk Settlement, Lincoln, Maine.

At age twenty-three, John was married on December 21, 1807 to Sally Maynard, age twenty-one, by Bezer Bryant, Esquire in Anson, Kennebec, Maine. (In 1809 Anson became part of Somerset County, Maine) Sally, born on October 27, 1786 in Concord, Middlesex, Massachusetts, was the daughter of Joseph Maynard and Abigail Meriam and the sister of Abigail Maynard, the wife of John's brother Daniel.

During their marriage John and Sally had four children.

Abigail Meriam	b. March 19, 1809	d. December 7, 1856
John Howard	b. May 16, 1810	d. January 1, 1852
Joanna Dean	b. October 29, 1811	d. 1878
Sarah Whitney	b. October 1, 1813	d. December 2, 1871

John, like many in his family, was a farmer in the Embden, Somerset, Maine area. In his book "Embden Town of Yore", George Walker wrote that "He (John) cleared a farm near the Edward Savage mills. It became known as the Williams homestead located on the road from the Thaddeus Boothby farm to the Solon ferry."

In the 1810, 1820 and 1830 United States Federal Census' John, Sally and their family were listed as living in Embden. In 1816 and 1817 John, like others in his family, served as an Embden town official.

Sally died on September 3, 1832 at the age of forty-six. The cause and place of her death are not known. She was buried in the John Williams family plot at the Pleasantdale Cemetery in Embden.

On October 31, 1833, a little more than a year after his first wife's death, John, at age forty-nine, and Belinda Wells age twenty-two, were married in Embden by Christopher Thompson, a Justice of the Peace. Belinda, the daughter of Robert Wells and Mary Littlefield, was born on February 20, 1811 in Lyman, York, Maine.

John and Belinda had an additional seven children together.

Leonard King	*b. October 31, 1834*	*d. August 23, 1838*
Malissa M.	b. June 13, 1836	d. April 8, 1853
Fanny W.	b. November 19, 1838	d. February 5, 1875
Daniel Kingman	b. November 18, 1840	d. July 18, 1918

Belinda Adelaide	b. January 25, 1844	d. March 28, 1890
Cyrus A.	b. January14, 1847	d. June 12, 1887
Isaac Palmer	b. June 1849	d. August 12, 1874

Leonard King the first child of John and Belinda died of an unknown cause on August 23, 1838, at the age of three years and ten months. He was buried in Embden at the Pleasantdale Cemetery in the John Williams family plot.

Gravestone for Leonard King Williams
(Photograph from the Collection of Jeffrey Nelson Williams and Jacqueline Pon Williams)

The 1840, 1850 and 1860 United States Federal Census' recorded John, Belinda and their family as living in Embden with John's occupation listed as "farming".

On October 8, 1867 at age eighty-three, John passed away in Embden. The cause of his death is not known. He was also buried in his family plot at the Pleasantdale Cemetery in Embden along with his first wife Sally and his son Leonard King.

When the 1870 and 1880 United States Federal Census' were taken Belinda was recorded as living with her daughter Belinda Adelaide (commonly known as Adelaide Belinda) in Fairfield, Somerset, Maine.

Five years after the 1880 census was taken, on March 22, 1885, Belinda, John's his second wife, passed away at age seventy-four. The cause and place of Belinda's death have also not been found. She too was buried in Embden in the John Williams family plot at the Pleasantdale Cemetery.

**Gravestones for John Williams (top), Sally Maynard (lower left)
and Belinda Wells (lower right)**
(Photographs from the Collection of Jeffrey Nelson Williams and Jacqueline Pon Williams)

SOURCES:

John Williams
Birth: (1) Original Record of Maine Towns & Cities, Town of Embden, Disk 1, Page 58, Picton Press, Rockland Maine, Copyright 2005; (2) Original Record of Maine Towns & Cities, Town of Embden, Disk 2, Page 21, Picton Press, Rockland Maine, Copyright 2005; (3) "Maine Families in 1790, Volume 1", Edited by Ruth Gray, Page 290, Maine Genealogical Society, Special Publication No. 2, Picton Press, Camden, Maine, Copyright 1988; (4) "Embden Town of Yore" by Ernest George Walker, Page 119, Published by Independent-Reporter Company, Skowhegan, Maine, 1929; (5) "The Kennebec Valley" by Seth Harding Whitney, Page 98, Published by Sprague, Burleigh and Flynt, Augusta, Maine, 1887.
Death: (1) "Maine Families in 1790, Volume 1", Edited by Ruth Gray, Page 290, Maine Genealogical Society, Special Publication No. 2, Picton Press, Camden, Maine, Copyright 1988; (2) Edmund West, comp., "Family Data Collection - Individual Records", [database on-line]. Provo, UT, USA: Ancestry.com Operations Inc., 2000; (3) Gravestone.
Graveyard: (1) "Pleasant Dale/Murphy/Boothby Cemetery" complied by Nancy Hamlin Davis and Ruth Hamlin, Old Canada Road Historical Society; (2) Find A Grave, Memorial #32341325.

Sally Maynard
Birth: (1) Original Record of Maine Towns & Cities, Town of Embden, Disk 2, Page 21, Picton Press, Rockland Maine, Copyright 2005; (2) "Edmund West, comp., Family Data Collection - Individual Records", [database on-line]. Provo, UT, USA: Ancestry.com Operations Inc., 2000.
Marriage: (1) "Vital Records – Town of Anson Maine, Part 1" compiled by David H. Ela, Page 38, 1975; (2) Original Record of Maine Towns & Cities, Town of Anson, Page 42, Picton Press, Rockland Maine, Copyright 2005; (3) Original Record of Maine Towns & Cities, Town of Embden, Disk 1, Page 149, Picton Press, Rockland Maine, Copyright 2005; (4) "Maine Families in 1790, Volume 1", Edited by Ruth Gray, Page 290, Maine Genealogical Society, Special Publication No. 2, Picton Press, Camden, Maine, Copyright 1988; (5) Edmund West, comp., "Family Data Collection - Individual Records", [database on-line]. Provo, UT, USA: Ancestry.com Operations Inc., 2000; (6) "Embden Town of Yore" by Ernest George Walker, Page 697, Published by Independent-Reporter Company, Skowhegan, Maine, 1929.
Death: (1) Edmund West, comp., "Family Data Collection - Individual Records", [database on-line]. Provo, UT, USA: Ancestry.com Operations Inc., 2000; (2) Gravestone.
Graveyard: (1) "Pleasant Dale/Murphy/Boothby Cemetery" complied by Nancy Hamlin Davis and Ruth Hamlin, Old Canada Road Historical Society; (2) Find A Grave, Memorial #32341365.

Belinda Wells
Birth: "Maine, Births and Christenings, 1739-1900," index, FamilySearch, (https://familysearch.org/pal:/MM9.1.1/F4MN-TNL).
Marriage: (1) "Maine Families in 1790, Volume 1", Edited by Ruth Gray, Page 290, Maine Genealogical Society, Special Publication No. 2, Picton Press, Camden, Maine, Copyright 1988; (2) "Embden Town of Yore" by Ernest George Walker, Page 705, Published by Independent-Reporter Company, Skowhegan, Maine, 1929.
Death: (1) "Maine, Faylene Hutton Cemetery Collection, ca. 1780-1990," database with images, FamilySearch, (https:// familysearch.org/ark:/61903/1.1/QKM1-WKLZ) - Accession #5030"; (2) Gravestone.
Graveyard: (1) "Pleasant Dale/Murphy/Boothby Cemetery" complied by Nancy Hamlin Davis and Ruth Hamlin, Old Canada Road Historical Society; (2) Find A Grave, Memorial #52818870.

Leonard King Williams
Birth: Original Record of Maine Towns & Cities, Town of Embden, Disk 2, Page 21, Picton Press, Rockland Maine Copyright 2005.
Death: Gravestone.
Graveyard: (1) "Pleasant Dale/Murphy/Boothby Cemetery" complied by Nancy Hamlin Davis and Ruth Hamlin, Old Canada Road Historical Society; (2) Find A Grave, Memorial #62714703.

Historical Accounts: (1) 1810 United States Federal Census for Embden, Somerset, Maine; (2) 1820 United States Federal Census for Embden, Somerset, Maine; (3) 1830 United States Federal Census for Embden, Somerset, Maine; (4) 1840 United States Federal Census Embden, Somerset, Maine; (5) 1850 United States Federal Census for Embden, Somerset, Maine; (6) 1860 United States Federal Census for Embden, Somerset, Maine, Page 61; (7) 1870 United States Federal Census for Fairfield, Somerset, Maine, Page 41; (8) 1880 United States Federal Census for Fairfield, Somerset, Maine, Page 17; (9) "Embden Town of Yore" by Ernest George Walker, Published by Independent-Reporter Company, Skowhegan, Maine, 1929.

Richard Williams
(1787 - 1876)

The fourth child of Jacob Williams and Joanna Dean Williams, Richard was born in Caratunk Settlement, Lincoln, Maine on February 4, 1787.

In 1810, at age twenty-three Richard was married to Abigail Rowe, age twenty-six. The exact date and place of their marriage has not been found. Abigail was born on February 20, 1784 in Massachusetts. The names of her parents and her town of birth are also not known.

Richard and Abigail had six children together.

Joseph	*b. February 28, 1812*	*d.*
Alvin	b. August 15, 1814	d. March 18, 1842
Luther	b. October 23, 1816	d. April 23, 1870
Mary Ann	b. November 24, 1819	d. July 27, 1888
Elvira	*b. 1820*	*d. September 1, 1823*
Calvin	b. May 25, 1829	d. April 19, 1896

On September 1, 1823, Elvira, the fifth child of Richard and Abigail died at the age of three years. Documentation regarding the cause and place of her death has not been found. Elvira was buried in the Richard Williams family plot at the Pleasantdale Cemetery in Embden, Somerset, Maine.

Joseph, the first child of Richard and Abigail was recorded as living in Concord, Somerset, Maine with his parents in the 1830 United States Federal Census. After that additional information regarding his life and death has not been found. As such his documented history will end here.

In the 1840 and 1850 United States Federal Census' Richard, Abigail and their children were recorded as living in Concord. Richard, like his father and brothers was a farmer. He is said to have built a cabin in the Concord area that "was sheathed with boards sawed at a mill newly erected several miles away" which was considered very unusual at that time.

Richard and Abigail were recorded as living with their son Calvin and his family in Concord when the 1860 United States Federal Census was taken.

Three years later, Abigail died on October 22, 1863 at age seventy-nine. Her place and cause of death are not known. She was also buried in Embden in the Richard Williams family plot at the Pleasantdale Cemetery.

As recorded in the 1870 United States Federal Census for Concord, sometime after the death of his wife Richard went to live with Sarah W. (Foss) Witham, the daughter of his niece Sarah Whitney (Williams) Foss.

Almost thirteen years after his wife Abigail passed, Richard, at age eighty-nine, died in Concord on August 30, 1876. The cause of Richard's death has also not been found. He too was buried in his family plot at the Pleasantdale Cemetery in Embden.

Gravestones for Richard Williams & Abigail Rowe (left)
and Elvira Williams (right)
(Photographs from the Collection of Jeffrey Nelson Williams and Jacqueline Pon Williams)

SOURCES:

Richard Williams
Birth: (1) Original Record of Maine Towns & Cities, Town of Embden, Disk 1, Page 58, Picton Press, Rockland Maine, Copyright 2005; (2) Original Record of Maine Towns & Cities, Town of Concord, Page 83, Picton Press, Rockland Maine, Copyright 2005; (3) "The Kennebec Valley" by Seth Harding Whitney, Page 98, Published by Sprague, Burleigh and Flynt, Augusta, Maine, 1887; (4) "Embden Town of Yore" by Ernest George Walker, Page 119, Published by Independent-Reporter Company, Skowhegan, Maine, 1929.
Death: (1) "Maine Families in 1790, Volume 1", Edited by Ruth Gray, Page 290, Maine Genealogical Society, Special Publication No. 2, Picton Press, Camden, Maine, Copyright 1988; (2) "Maine, Faylene Hutton Cemetery Collection, ca. 1780-1990," database with images, FamilySearch, (https://familysearch.org/ark:/61903/1:1:QKM1-WKGD) - Accession #5030; (3) Gravestone.
Graveyard: (1) "Pleasant Dale/Murphy/Boothby Cemetery" complied by Nancy Hamlin Davis and Ruth Hamlin, Old Canada Road Historical Society; (2) Find A Grave, Memorial #52819872.

Abigail Rowe
Birth: (1) Original Record of Maine Towns & Cities, Town of Concord, Page 83, Picton Press, Rockland Maine, Copyright 2005.
Marriage:
Death: (1) "Maine, Faylene Hutton Cemetery Collection, ca. 1780-1990," database with images, FamilySearch, (https://familysearch.org/ark:/61903/1:1:QKM1-WKGD) - Accession #5030; (2) Gravestone.
Graveyard: (1) "Pleasant Dale/Murphy/Boothby Cemetery" complied by Nancy Hamlin Davis and Ruth Hamlin, Old Canada Road Historical Society; (2) Find A Grave, Memorial #52819937.

Joseph Williams
Birth: (1) Original Record of Maine Towns & Cities, Town of Concord, Page 83, Picton Press, Rockland Maine, Copyright 2005; (2) "Maine Births and Christenings 1739-1900," index, Family Search, (https://familysearch.org /pal: /MM9.1.1 /F4Q4-RQD).
Death:
Graveyard:

Elvira Williams
Birth: Original Record of Maine Towns & Cities, Town of Concord, Page 83, Picton Press, Rockland Maine, Copyright 2005.
Death: (1) "Maine, Faylene Hutton Cemetery Collection, ca. 1780-1990," database with images, FamilySearch, (https:// familysearch.org/ark:/61903/1.1/QKM1-WKJ1) – Accession #5030; (2) Gravestone.
Graveyard: (1) "Pleasant Dale/Murphy/Boothby Cemetery" complied by Nancy Hamlin Davis and Ruth Hamlin, Old Canada Road Historical Society; (2) Find A Grave, Memorial #118443481.

Historical Accounts: (1) 1830 United States Federal Census for Concord, Somerset, Maine; (2) 1840 United States Federal Census for Concord, Somerset, Maine; (3) 1850 United States Federal Census for Concord, Somerset, Maine; (4) 1860 United States Federal Census for Concord, Somerset, Maine, Page 65; (5) 1870 United States Federal Census for Concord, Somerset, Maine, Page 10; (6) "Embden Town of Yore" by Ernest George Walker, Published by Independent-Reporter Company, Skowhegan, Maine, 1929; (7) "The Life and Work of James Leon Williams" by George Wood Clapp, Published by The Dental Digest, New York, USA 1925.

Isaac Otis Williams
(1789 - 1860)

Isaac Otis was the fifth child of Jacob Williams and Joanna Dean Williams. He was born on June 15, 1789 at the Caratunk Settlement in Lincoln County, Maine.

On July 11, 1815, at age twenty-five, Isaac Otis and Rachel S. Heald, age fifteen, published their intentions to be married with the Town Clerk of Bingham, Somerset, Maine. They were subsequently married in Anson, Somerset, Maine on October 3, 1815 by Daniel Steward, Jr. Rachel S. was born on November 30, 1799 in Bingham to Ephraim Heald and Mary Steward.

Isaac Otis and Rachel S., like many of the Williams families, had a large family of eleven children.

Eli	*b. December 8, 1816*	*d.*
Otis Isaac	b. November 6, 1818	d. July 17, 1878
Eli S.	b. April 13, 1821	d. October 26, 1884
Mary Jane	b. February 24, 1824	d. September 26, 1887
Ephraim H.	b. March 19, 1826	d. April 26, 1895
Gilman L.	b. January 5, 1828	d. June 20, 1920
Henry	b. June 26, 1832	d.
Nancy Hale	b. July 19, 1834	d. April 10, 1904
Louisa H. (a twin)	*b. August 20, 1836*	*d. January 10, 1839*
Lorena B. (a twin)	*b. August 20, 1836*	*d. January 5, 1839*
Allen B.	b. January 3, 1839	d. January 29, 1904

Other than the records recording his birth no other information has been found regarding the life and death of Eli, the first child of Isaac Otis and Rachel S. It is presumed that he died at a very young age as Isaac Otis and Rachel S. also named their third child Eli.

In January 1839 two of Isaac Otis and Rachel S.'s children, the twins Louisa H. and Lorena B., died with-in five days of each other at age of two years and five months. The causes and places of their deaths are not known. Both girls were buried in the Bingham Village Cemetery in Bingham.

The 1840 and 1850 United States Federal Census' recorded Isaac Otis, Rachel S. and their children as living in Moscow, Somerset, Maine.

On April 16, 1860, at the age of seventy, Isaac Otis died in Bingham. His cause of death was listed as "lung fever". Isaac Otis was buried in Bingham at the Bingham Village Cemetery along with his twin daughters.

When the 1870 United States Federal Census was taken Rachel S. was recorded as living with her tenth child Allen B. and his family in Skowhegan, Somerset, Maine.

Fifteen years after the death of her husband, Rachel S. died on September 11, 1875 at the age of eighty-six. The exact cause and place of her death have not been found. She too was buried in the Isaac Otis Williams family plot at the Bingham Village Cemetery in Bingham.

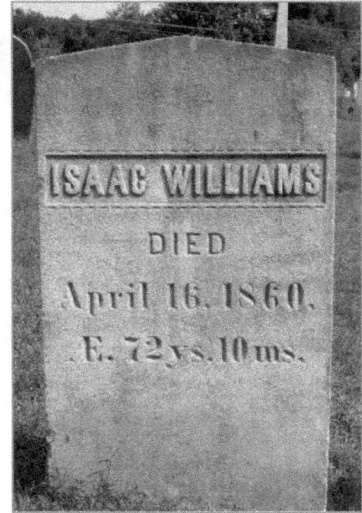 

Gravestones for Louisa Williams and Lorena Williams (top), Isaac Otis Williams (bottom left) and Rachel S. Heald (bottom right)
(Photographs from the Collection of Jeffrey Nelson Williams and Jacqueline Pon Williams)

SOURCES:

Isaac Otis Williams
Birth: (1) Original Record of Maine Towns & Cities, Town of Embden, Disk 1, Page 58, Picton Press, Rockland Maine, Copyright 2005; (2) "Maine Families in 1790, Volume 1", Edited by Ruth Gray, Page 290, Maine Genealogical Society, Special Publication No. 2, Picton Press, Camden, Maine, Copyright 1988; (3) Edmund West, comp., "Family Data Collection - Individual Records", [database on-line]. Provo, UT, USA: Ancestry.com Operations Inc., 2000; (4) "The Kennebec Valley" by Seth Harding Whitney, Page 98, Published by Sprague, Burleigh and Flynt, Augusta, Maine, 1887; (5) "Embden Town of Yore" by Ernest George Walker, Page 119, Published by Independent-Reporter Company, Skowhegan, Maine, 1929.
Death: (1) "Maine Families in 1790, Volume 1", Edited by Ruth Gray, Page 290, Maine Genealogical Society, Special Publication No. 2, Picton Press, Camden, Maine, Copyright 1988; (2) United States Federal Census Mortality Schedules, Somerset, Maine, for the year ending June 30, 1860, Page 1; (3) Edmund West, comp., "Family Data Collection - Individual Records", [database on-line]. Provo, UT, USA: Ancestry.com Operations Inc., 2000; (4) Listing of family births and deaths from the Gilman L. Williams family archives in the collection of Sullyj; (5) Gravestone.
Graveyard: (1) "Maine Old Cemetery Association Special Publication Number 12, Edition No. 1: Series 1, 2 and 3", Page 334, Picton Press, Rockland, Maine, Copyright 2006; (2) "Bingham Village Cemetery" by Nancy Hamlin Davis and Ruth Hamlin, Record 1263, Old Canada Road Historical Society; (3) Find A Grave, Memorial #52840697.

Rachel S. Heald
Birth: (1) Original Record of Maine Towns & Cities, Town of Bingham, Page 12, Picton Press, Rockland Maine, Copyright 2005; (2) Original Record of Maine Towns & Cities, Town of Moscow, Page 49, Picton Press, Rockland Maine, Copyright 2005; (3) Listing of family births and deaths from the Gilman L. Williams family archives in the collection of Sullyj.
Marriage: (1) Original Record of Maine Towns & Cities, Town of Anson, Page 69, Picton Press, Rockland Maine, Copyright 2005; (2) Original Record of Maine Towns & Cities, Town of Bingham, Page 72, Picton Press, Rockland Maine, Copyright 2005; (3) "Vital Records – Town of Anson Maine, Part 1" compiled by David H. Ela, Page 90, 1975; (4) Edmund West, comp., "Family Data Collection - Individual Records", [database on-line]. Provo, UT, USA: Ancestry.com Operations Inc., 2000.
Death: Gravestone.
Graveyard: (1) "Maine Old Cemetery Association Special Publication Number 12, Edition No. 1: Series 1, 2 and 3", Page 334, Picton Press, Rockland, Maine, Copyright 2006; (2) "Bingham Village Cemetery" by Nancy Hamlin Davis and Ruth Hamlin, Record 1264, Old Canada Road Historical Society; (3) Find A Grave, Memorial #52840801.

Eli Williams
Birth: (1) Original Record of Maine Towns & Cities, Town of Bingham, Page 24, Picton Press, Rockland Maine, Copyright 2005; (2) "Maine Births and Christenings, 1739-1900," database, FamilySearch, (https://familysearch.org/ark/61903/1.1:/F439-TL4); (3) Listing of family births and deaths from the Gilman L. Williams family archives in the collection of Sullyj.
Death:
Graveyard:

Louisa Williams
Birth: (1) Original Record of Maine Towns & Cities, Town of Moscow, Page 49, Picton Press, Rockland Maine, Copyright 2005: (2) Listing of family births and deaths from the Gilman L. Williams family archives in the collection of Sullyj.
Death: (1) Original Record of Maine Towns & Cities, Town of Moscow, Page 49, Picton Press, Rockland Maine, Copyright 2005: (2) Listing of family births and deaths from the Gilman L. Williams family archives in the collection of Sullyj.
Graveyard: "Maine Old Cemetery Association Special Publication Number 12, Edition No. 1: Series 1, 2 and 3", Page 334, Picton Press, Rockland, Maine, Copyright 2006; (2) "Bingham Village Cemetery" by Nancy Hamlin Davis and Ruth Hamlin, Record 1265, Old Canada Road Historical Society; (3) Find A Grave, Memorial #110990884.

Lorena Williams
Birth: (1) "Maine, Births and Christenings, 1739-1900," index, FamilySearch, (https://familysearch.org/pal:
/MM9.1.1/F4H9-LZP); (2) Original Record of Maine Towns & Cities, Town of Moscow, Page 49, Picton Press,
Rockland Maine, Copyright 2005; (3) Listing of family births and deaths from the Gilman L. Williams family
archives from the collection of Sullyj.
Death: (1) "Maine, Births and Christenings, 1739-1900," index, FamilySearch (https://familysearch.org/pal:
/MM9.1.1/F47W-W5D); (2) Record of Death, Maine Vital Records; (3) Original Record of Maine Towns &
Cities, Town of Moscow, Page 49, Picton Press, Rockland Maine, Copyright 2005; (4) Listing of family births and
deaths from the Gilman L. Williams family archives in the collection of Sullyj.
Graveyard: (1) "Maine Old Cemetery Association Special Publication Number 12, Edition No. 1: Series 1, 2 and
3", Page 334, Picton Press, Rockland, Maine, Copyright; (2) "Bingham Village Cemetery" by Nancy Hamlin
Davis and Ruth Hamlin, Record 1265, Old Canada Road Historical Society; (3) Find A Grave, Memorial
#82115411.

Historical Accounts: (1) 1840 United States Federal Census for Moscow, Somerset, Maine; (2) 1850 United
States Federal Census for Moscow, Somerset, Maine; (3) 1860 United States Federal Census for Moscow,
Somerset, Maine, Page 54; (4) 1870 United States Federal Census for Skowhegan, Somerset, Maine, Page 59; (5)
"Embden Town of Yore" by Ernest George Walker, Published by Independent-Reporter Company, Skowhegan,
Maine, 1929.

Elsa Williams
(1791 - 1862)

The sixth child of Jacob Williams and Joanna Dean Williams was Elsa who was born in Caratunk Settlement, Lincoln, Maine on August 6, 1791.

On September 12, 1812, at age twenty-one, Elsa married Benjamin Colby Atwood, age twenty-three. The exact place of their marriage has not been found. Benjamin Colby, born in Weare, Hillsborough, New Hampshire on December 31, 1789, was the son of Benjamin Atwood and Mary Colby.

Elsa and Benjamin Colby had eight children together.

Aurilla H.	*b. March 6, 1813*	*d. June 1, 1831*
Benjamin Franklin	b. June 6, 1814	d. May 20, 1904
Mary A.	b. July 14, 1816	d. January 9, 1909
Nancy H.	*b. September 5, 1818*	*d. September 21, 1819*
Jacob Williams	b. March 28, 1821	d. September 22, 1900
Stillman Howard	b. January 28, 1824	d. November 28, 1908
Samuel Colby	*b. May 14, 1828*	*d. April 8, 1831*
William King	b. 1830	d. October 22, 1899

Benjamin Colby was an active member of the Embden, Somerset, Maine community. He served as a town official from 1805, prior to marrying Elsa, through 1829. For the majority of those years he held the position of 1st Selectman and Town Clerk.

In 1816, after his marriage to Elsa, Benjamin Colby owned and operated the Jacob Williams' mill along the Kennebec River which had been established by his father-in-law.

The fourth child of Elsa and Benjamin Colby, Nancy H., died in Embden on September 21, 1819 when she was one year and sixteen days old. The cause of her death has not been found. She was buried in the Benjamin Colby Atwood family plot at the Pleasantdale Cemetery in Embden.

On August 4, 1821, Benjamin Colby sold his mill and fifty-five acres of land to Dr. Edward Savage for $215 and moved his family to Concord, Somerset, Maine. Sometime after that move Benjamin must have become a man of the cloth as he had the title of "Reverend" engraved on his gravestone.

When the 1830 United States Federal Census was taken Elsa, Benjamin Colby and their family were recorded as living in Concord.

Samuel Colby, the seventh child of Elsa and Benjamin Colby, was three years eleven months old when he died in Concord on April 8, 1831. Twenty-three days later on June 1, 1831 Aurilla H. their first child also died in Concord when she was eighteen years old and unmarried. The causes of Samuel Colby and Aurilla's deaths have not been found. Both children were buried in the family plot at the Pleasantdale Cemetery in Embden.

**Gravestones for Nancy Atwood (top left), Aurilla H. Atwood (top right)
and Samuel Colby Atwood (bottom)**
(Photographs from the Collection of Jeffrey Nelson Williams and Jacqueline Pon Williams)

The 1840 and 1850 United States Federal Census' recorded Elsa, Benjamin Colby and their children as living in Concord. Benjamin Colby's occupation was listed as "farmer" in those censuses.

Elsa died in Concord on March 20, 1862 at the age of seventy. Her cause of death is not known. She was buried with her children in Embden at the Pleasantdale Cemetery. (Note: Elsa's name is misspelled as "Elca" on her gravestone)

The 1860 United States Federal Census recorded Benjamin Colby, age seventy, as living with his son Stillman Howard and his family in Embden and working as an "egg collector".

Benjamin survived Elsa by a little over eighteen years. He died on April 23, 1880 of "kidney disease" in Embden at the age of ninety-one. He too was buried in his family plot in the Pleasantdale Cemetery in Embden.

Gravestones for Elsa Williams (left) and Benjamin Colby Atwood (right)
(Photographs from the Collection of Jeffrey Nelson Williams and Jacqueline Pon Williams)

SOURCES:

Elsa Williams
Birth: (1) Original Record of Maine Towns & Cities, Town of Embden, Disk 1, Page 58, Picton Press, Rockland Maine, Copyright 2005; (2) "Maine Families in 1790, Volume 1", Edited by Ruth Gray, Page 290, Maine Genealogical Society, Special Publication No. 2, Picton Press, Camden, Maine, Copyright 1988; (3) "The Kennebec Valley" by Seth Harding Whitney, Page 98, Published by Sprague, Burleigh and Flynt, Augusta, Maine, 1887; (4) "Embden Town of Yore" by Ernest George Walker, Page 119, Published by Independent-Reporter Company, Skowhegan, Maine, 1929; (5) Edmund West, comp., *"Family Data Collection - Individual Records"*, [database on-line], Provo, UT, USA: Ancestry.com Operations Inc, 2000.
Death: (1) "Maine Families in 1790, Volume 1", Edited by Ruth Gray, Page 290, Maine Genealogical Society, Special Publication No. 2, Picton Press, Camden, Maine, Copyright 1988; (2) Edmund West, comp., "Family Data Collection - Individual Records", [database on-line], Provo, UT, USA: Ancestry.com Operations Inc, 2000; (3) Gravestone.
Graveyard: (1) "Pleasant Dale/Murphy/Boothby Cemetery" complied by Nancy Hamlin Davis and Ruth Hamlin, Old Canada Road Historical Society; (2) "Maine Old Cemetery Association Special Publication Number 12, Edition No. 1: Series 1, 2 and 3", Page 556, Picton Press, Rockland, Maine, Copyright 2006; (3) Find A Grave, Memorial #15550286.

Benjamin Colby Atwood
Birth: Original Record of Maine Towns & Cities, Town of Concord, Page 91, Picton Press, Rockland Maine 2005.
Marriage: (1) "Maine, Marriages, 1771-1907," index, FamilySearch, (https://familysearch.org/pal:/MM9.1.1/F462-L59); (2) "Maine Families in 1790, Volume 1", Edited by Ruth Gray, Page 290, Maine Genealogical Society, Special Publication No. 2, Picton Press, Camden, Maine, Copyright 1988; (3) Edmund West, comp., "Family Data Collection - Individual Records", [database on-line], Provo, UT, USA: Ancestry.com Operations Inc, 2000; (4) "Embden Town of Yore" by Ernest George Walker, Page 698, Published by Independent-Reporter Company, Skowhegan, Maine, 1929.
Death: (1) United States Federal Census Mortality Schedules, Somerset, Maine, for the year ending May 31, 1880, Page 1; (2) Gravestone.
Graveyard: (1) "Pleasant Dale/Murphy/Boothby Cemetery" complied by Nancy Hamlin Davis and Ruth Hamlin, Old Canada Road Historical Society; (2) "Maine Old Cemetery Association Special Publication Number 12, Edition No. 1: Series 1, 2 and 3", Page 556, Picton Press, Rockland, Maine, Copyright 2006; (3) Find A Grave, Memorial #15550268.

Aurilla H. Atwood
Birth: (1) Original Record of Maine Towns & Cities, Town of Concord, Page 91, Picton Press, Rockland Maine, Copyright 2005; (2) Edmund West, comp., "Family Data Collection - Individual Records", [database on-line], Provo, UT, USA: Ancestry.com Operations Inc, 2000.
Death: (1) Edmund West, comp., "Family Data Collection - Individual Records", [database on-line], Provo, UT, USA: Ancestry.com Operations Inc, 2000; (2) Gravestone.
Graveyard: (1) "Pleasant Dale/Murphy/Boothby Cemetery" complied by Nancy Hamlin Davis and Ruth Hamlin, Old Canada Road Historical Society; (2) "Maine Old Cemetery Association Special Publication Number 12, Edition No. 1: Series 1, 2 and 3", Page 556, Picton Press, Rockland, Maine, Copyright 2006; (3) Find A Grave, Memorial #118292733.

Nancy W. Atwood
Birth: (1) Original Record of Maine Towns & Cities, Town of Concord, Page 91, Picton Press, Rockland Maine, Copyright 2005; (2) "Maine, Births and Christenings, 1739-1900," index, FamilySearch, (https://familysearch.org/pal:/MM9.1.1/F4Q4-T2Y); (3) Edmund West, comp., "Family Data Collection - Individual Records", [database on-line], Provo, UT, USA: Ancestry.com Operations Inc, 2000.
Death: (1) Edmund West, comp., "Family Data Collection - Individual Records", [database on-line], Provo, UT, USA: Ancestry.com Operations Inc, 2000; (2) Gravestone.
Graveyard: (1) "Pleasant Dale/Murphy/Boothby Cemetery" complied by Nancy Hamlin Davis and Ruth Hamlin, Old Canada Road Historical Society; (2) "Maine Old Cemetery Association Special Publication Number 12, Edition No. 1: Series 1, 2 and 3", Page 556, Picton Press, Rockland, Maine, Copyright 2006; (3) Find A Grave, Memorial #118292831.

Samuel Colby Atwood
Birth: Original Record of Maine Towns & Cities, Town of Concord Maine, Page 91, Picton Press, Rockland Maine, Copyright 2005.
Death: Gravestone.
Graveyard: (1) "Pleasant Dale/Murphy/Boothby Cemetery" complied by Nancy Hamlin Davis and Ruth Hamlin, Old Canada Road Historical Society; (2) "Maine Old Cemetery Association Special Publication Number 12, Edition No. 1: Series 1, 2 and 3", Page 556, Picton Press, Rockland, Maine, Copyright 2006; (3) Find A Grave, Memorial #118292781.

Historical Accounts: (1) 1830 United States Federal Census for Concord, Somerset, Maine; (2) 1840 United States Federal Census for Concord, Somerset, Maine; (3) 1850 United States Federal Census for Concord, Somerset, Maine; (4) 1860 United States Federal Census for Embden, Somerset, Maine, Page 57; (5) "Embden Town of Yore" by Ernest George Walker, Published by Independent-Reporter Company, Skowhegan, Maine, 1929; (6) "South of Lost Nation" by Ernest George Walker, Washington, D.C., July 4, 1939.

Ebenezer Williams
(1793 - 1870)

Ebenezer was the seventh child of Jacob Williams and Joanna Dean Williams. He was born at the Caratunk Settlement, Lincoln, Maine on July 17, 1793.

On March 26, 1816 Ebenezer, age twenty-two, was married in Anson, Somerset, Maine to Mahala Richards, age nineteen, by Daniel Steward, Jr. Mahala was born on July 13, 1794 in Norridgewock, Somerset, Maine. The names of her parents are not known.

Ebenezer and Mahala had eight children together.

Dorcas Brown	b. July 10, 1817	d. May 26, 1862
Truman Allen	b. July 25, 1819	d. November 11, 1894
Willis Richard	b. April 12, 1821	d. May 1, 1897
Alden F.	b. March 18, 1825	d. November 27, 1903
Randell	*b. December 1827*	*d. July 18, 1828*
Moses Henry	b. July 20, 1830	d. September 26, 1895
Sarah Evaline	*b. July 4, 1831*	*d. January 9, 1847*
Mary Ann	*b. March 6, 1834*	*d. September 4, 1836*

In 1816, 1818, 1819 and 1820, as others in his family had, Ebenezer served as a town official of Embden, Somerset, Maine. He, Mahala and his first two children were recorded as living there when the 1820 United States Federal Census was taken.

Sometime after the 1820 census was taken, Ebenezer, Mahala and their children moved to Hodgdon, Washington, Maine where two of their children died at young ages. Randell, their fifth child, died in July 18, 1828 when he was just eight months old and their eighth child Mary Ann was two years old when she died in September 4, 1836. The causes of these two children's deaths have not been found. Randell and Mary Ann were buried in in the Hodgdon Cemetery in Hodgdon.

Ebenezer, Mahala and their children were recorded as still living in Hodgdon, then part of Aroostook County in Maine, when the 1840 United States Federal Census was taken. Hodgdon became part of Aroostook County which was formed from pieces of Penobscot and Washington Counties in 1839.

Mahala died in Hodgdon on December 25, 1840 at the age of forty-three. The exact cause of her death has not been found. She was buried in the Hodgdon Cemetery in Hodgdon alongside her children.

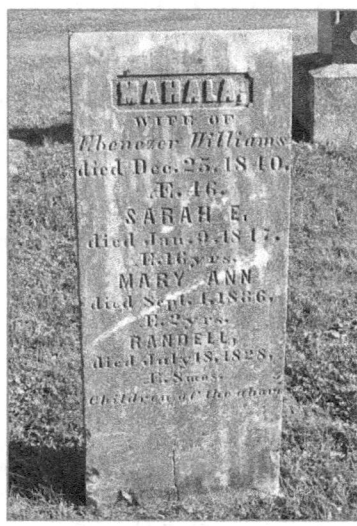

**Gravestone for Mahala Richards, Randell Williams, Sarah Evaline Williams
and Mary Ann Williams**
(Photograph Courtesy of Kate Pyle)

On July 1, 1842 Ebenezer, at age forty-nine, and Martha Ann Cowell, age thirty-five, registered their intentions to marry with the Town Clerk of Hodgdon. On July 19, 1842 they were married in Hodgdon by John Hutchinson, a Justice of the Peace. Martha Ann was born around 1807 in England. The exact date and place of her birth, as well as the names of her parents, have not been found.

Ebenezer had another seven children with his second wife Martha Ann.

Ebenezer W.	*b. September 27, 1842*	*d. November 23, 1862*
Chandler John	b. March 15, 1844	d. June 23, 1908
Charles Jones	b. December 6, 1846	d. December 27, 1928
Cyrus E.	b. September 13, 1850	d.
Mansfield M.	b. December 19, 1852	d. April 19, 1918
James Albert	b. June 2, 1854	d. October 28, 1908
John Randell	*b. November 26, 1856*	*d. September 29, 1858*

The seventh child of Ebenezer and his first wife Mahala, Sarah Evaline, died in Hodgdon on January 9, 1847 when she was fifteen years old. The cause of her death is unknown. She too was buried in Hodgdon at the Hodgdon Cemetery alongside her mother, brother Randell and sister Mary Ann.

In 1849 Ebenezer and Martha Ann moved their family from Hodgdon to Township No. 11, Range 1, Aroostook, Maine and cleared a farm on a lot just east of where Truman Allen, a son from his first marriage, was living.

Ebenezer, Martha Ann and their first three children were recorded as living in Township No. 11, Range 1 when the 1850 and 1860 United States Federal Census' were taken. Ebenezer's occupation in both of those census documents was recorded as "farmer".

John Randell, the seventh child of Ebenezer and his second wife Martha Ann died on September 29, 1858 when he was one year and ten months old. The place and cause of his death, as well as the place of his burial are unknown.

On June 30, 1859 Ebenezer was elected Constable of Cary Plantation, Aroostook, Maine (which included Township No. 11, Range 1). He was reelected to that position on March 31, 1860 and again on March 25, 1861.

The first child of Ebenezer and his second wife Martha Ann, Ebenezer W., died on November 23, 1862 when he was twenty years old. He had never married or had any children. The place and cause of his death, as well as the place of burial are also unknown at this time.

On April 15, 1870, Ebenezer died of "cancer" at age seventy-six in Township No. 11, Range 1. His place of burial has not been found.

Shortly after Ebenezer's death, the 1870 United States Federal Census recorded Martha Ann and her sons, John Chandler, Charles Jones, Cyrus E., Mansfield M., and James Albert, as living on the family farm in Township No. 11, Range 1.

Martha Ann lived a great many years after Ebenezer. She was listed in the 1880 and 1900 United States Federal Census', as still living in Cary Plantation (Township No. 11, Range 1 was renamed Cary Plantation in 1883) with her sons, Cyrus E. and James Albert.

Martha Ann is believed to have died sometime between 1900 and 1910. Her exact date of death and place of burial have not been found.

SOURCES:

Ebenezer Williams
Birth: (1) Original Record of Maine Towns & Cities, Town of Embden, Disk 1, Page 58, Picton Press, Rockland Maine, Copyright 2005; (2) "Maine Families in 1790, Volume 1", Edited by Ruth Gray, Page 290, Maine Genealogical Society, Special Publication No. 2, Picton Press, Camden, Maine, Copyright 1988; (3) Edmund West, comp., "Family Data Collection - Individual Records", [database on-line]. Provo, UT, USA: Ancestry.com Operations Inc., 2000; (4) "The Kennebec Valley" by Seth Harding Whitney, Page 98, Published by Sprague, Burleigh and Flynt, Augusta, Maine, 1887; (5) "Embden Town of Yore" by Ernest George Walker, Page 119, Published by Independent-Reporter Company, Skowhegan, Maine, 1929.
Death: (1) "Maine Families in 1790, Volume 1", Edited by Ruth Gray, Page 290, Maine Genealogical Society, Special Publication No. 2, Picton Press, Camden, Maine, Copyright 1988; (2) United States Federal Census Mortality Schedules, No. 11, Range 1; Aroostook, Maine, for the year ending June 1, 1870, Page 1; (3) Edmund West, comp., "Family Data Collection - Individual Records", [database on-line]. Provo, UT, USA: Ancestry.com Operations Inc., 2000.
Graveyard:

Mahala Richards
Birth:
Marriage: (1) Original Record of Maine Towns & Cities, Town of Anson, Page 69, Picton Press, Rockland Maine, Copyright 2005; (2) "Maine, Marriages, 1771-1907," index, FamilySearch, (https://familysearch.org/ark: /61903/1.1: F462-LYZ); (3) "Vital Records – Town of Anson Maine, Part 1" compiled by David H. Ela, Page 90, 1975; (4) "Maine Families in 1790, Volume 1", Edited by Ruth Gray, Page 290, Maine Genealogical Society, Special Publication No. 2, Picton Press, Camden, Maine, Copyright 1988; (5) "Embden Town of Yore" by Ernest George Walker, Page 699, Published by Independent-Reporter Company, Skowhegan, Maine, 1929.
Death: Gravestone.
Graveyard: Find A Grave, Memorial #116855280.

Randell Williams
Birth:
Death: Gravestone.
Graveyard: Find A Grave, Memorial # 116855366.

Sarah Evaline Williams
Birth:
Death: Gravestone.
Graveyard: Find A Grave, Memorial #116855388.

Mary Ann Williams
Birth:
Death: Gravestone.
Graveyard: Find A Grave, Memorial # 116855320.

Martha Ann Cowell
Birth:
Marriage: (1) Original Record of Maine Towns & Cities, Town of Hodgdon, Page 19, Picton Press, Rockland Maine, Copyright 2005; (2) Original Record of Maine Towns & Cities, Town of Hodgdon, Page 10, Picton Press, Rockland Maine, Copyright 2005; (3) "Maine, Marriages, 1771-1907," index, FamilySearch, (https://familysearch. org/pal:/MM9.1.1/ F4FD-WJQ).
Death:
Graveyard:

Ebenezer W. Williams
Birth
Death:
Graveyard:

John Randell Williams
Birth
Death:
Graveyard:

Historical Accounts: (1) 1820 United States Federal Census, Embden, Somerset, Maine; (2) 1840 United States Federal Census, Hodgdon; Township 5, 3rd Range; Township A, 2nd Range, Aroostook, Maine; (3) 1850 United States Federal Census, Township 11, Range 1, Aroostook, Maine; (4) 1860 United States Federal Census, Township 11, Range 1, Aroostook, Maine, Page 12; (5) 1870 United States Federal Census, Township 11, Range 1, Aroostook, Maine, Page 6; (6) 1880 United States Federal Census Township 11, Range 1, Aroostook, Maine, Page 10; (7) 1900 United States Federal Census, Cary Plantation, Aroostook, Maine, Page 4; (8) Original Record of Maine Towns & Cities, Cary Plantation, Page 9, Picton Press, Rockland Maine, Copyright 2005; (9) Original Record of Maine Towns & Cities, Cary Plantation, Page 10, Picton Press, Rockland Maine, Copyright 2005; (10) Original Record of Maine Towns & Cities, Cary Plantation, Page 24, Picton Press, Rockland Maine, Copyright 2005; (11) "Embden Town of Yore" by Ernest George Walker, Pages 678 & 679, Published by Independent-Reporter Company, Skowhegan, Maine, 1929; (12) "History of Aroostook", Compiled and Written by the Hon. Edward Wiggin, Page 271, Copyright 1922, The Star-Herald Press, Presque Isle, Maine.

Cyrus Williams
(1796 - 1864)

Cyrus was the ninth child of Jacob Williams and Joanna Dean Williams. He was born in Caratunk Settlement, Lincoln, Maine on April 21, 1796.

Cyrus Williams
(Photograph Courtesy of Belgrade Historical Society, McMorrow Collection)

On May 26, 1823, at age twenty-seven, Cyrus and Phydelia C. Perkins, age eighteen, filed their intentions to be married with the Town Clerk of Anson, Somerset, Maine. They were married the next day, May 27, in Anson by Daniel Steward, Jr. Phydelia C. was born on November 2, 1804, in North Anson, Kennebec, Maine. (North Anson became part of became part of Somerset County, Maine when it was formed in 1809) The names of Phydelia C.'s parents have not been found.

Cyrus and Phydelia C. had eleven children together.

Bethia Perkins	b. April 29, 1824	d. February 15, 1913
Emily F.	b. 1826	d. May 19, 1871
Katherine P.	*b. May 30, 1828*	*d. May 31, 1828*
Louisa F.	b. 1831	d. October 19, 1911
Charles E.	b. 1835	d. 1874
Helen	*b. 1836*	*d. November 8, 1837*
Susan H.	b. 1838	d. February 5, 1876
Infant	*b. January 6, 1839*	*d. August 21, 1939*
Maria A.	*b. 1841*	*d. November 17, 1863*
Tiley H.	b. 1843	d. January 21, 1905
Cyrus Henri	b. March 5, 1847	d. February 26, 1905

Cyrus continued the Williams tradition of community service when he was elected as a "Surveyor of the Wood and Bark" at the Town Meeting for Anson held on March 5, 1825.

The third child of Cyrus and Phydelia C., Katherine P., died in Anson on May 31, 1828 when she was just one day old. The cause of her death has not been found. She was buried in the Graveyard Hill Cemetery in North Anson.

When the 1830 United States Federal Census was taken Cyrus, Phydelia C., and their children were recorded as living in Anson.

Cyrus was a "hotel keeper" by profession and owned the Somerset Hotel in Anson from 1830 to 1831. In the Anson Town Records for September 12, 1831 it was noted that "Cyrus Williams got a license to sell all kinds of spirited liquor to be drank in his tavern for the term of one year". After selling the hotel to Henry Stone, Cyrus and his family moved to Waterville, Kennebec, Maine, where according to Ernest George Walker in his book "Embden Town of Yore" Cyrus also "kept a hotel there".

It was in Waterville that Helen, the sixth child of Cyrus and Phydelia C., was born in 1836 and died on November 8, 1837 when she was just one year four months old. The cause of her death is not known. Helen was buried in the Pine Grove Cemetery in Waterville in Lot 175, Grave 7.

On August 21, 1839 the eighth child of Cyrus and Phydelia C., an infant whose gender is not known, died at the age of seven months and fifteen days and was buried in the Graveyard Hill Cemetery in North Anson. The cause and place of that child's death, as well as its place of birth, have not been found.

The 1840 United States Federal Census recorded taken Cyrus, Phydelia C., and their children as living in Waterville.

In the "Illustrated History of Kennebec County Maine" it was documented that at a meeting of the selectmen of Waterville in 1841 it was "resolved that Cyrus Williams having applied for license, this board will grant a license to said Williams to be an Inn holder in said town during the coming year without the right to retail wine, brandy, rum, or any other spirituous, vinous or fermented intoxicating liquors".

The 1850 and 1860 United States Federal Census' for Waterville recorded Cyrus and his family as still living there. In those documents Cyrus' occupation was listed as "Inn holder/Landlord". According to the sign in the photograph from the Belgrade, Kennebec, Maine Historical Society shown below, in 1850 Cyrus had opened a hotel, which also served as the town's stage coach office, located at 1855 Main Street in Waterville.

Cyrus Williams Inn in Waterville
(Photograph Courtesy of Belgrade Historical Society)

Maria A. the ninth child of Cyrus and Phydelia C. was twenty-two years four months old when she died on November 17, 1863. The exact cause and place of her death has not been found. She was buried in Lot 175, Grave 8 at the Pine Grove Cemetery in Waterville. Additionally, no record has been found to indicate that she married or ever gave birth to any children. As such her documented history will end here.

On September 16, 1864, at age sixty-eight, Cyrus died in Waterville. The cause of his death was listed as "dropsy". Cyrus was buried in Lot 175, Grave 1 at the Pine Grove Cemetery in Waterville.

In the 1870 United States Federal Census, Phydelia C. was listed as living in Waterville with her daughter Emily F. Her occupation in that census was recorded as "boarding house keeper" and Emily F.'s was listed as "sewing".

By the time the 1880 United States Federal Census was taken, Phydelia C. was living with her oldest daughter, Tiley H. (Williams) Stover, and her husband in Waterville.

Phydelia C. survived Cyrus by a little more than twenty years. She died at age eighty on November 24, 1884 of an unknown cause. She was buried in Lot 175, Grave 2 at the Pine Grove Cemetery in Waterville alongside her family.

**Cyrus Williams Family Plot Marker, front view (top)
and back view (bottom)**
(Photograph from the Collection of Jeffrey Nelson Williams and Jacqueline Pon Williams)

**Headstones for Helen Williams (top left), Maria A. Williams (top right),
Cyrus Williams (bottom left) and Phydelia C. Perkins (bottom right)**
(Photographs from the Collection of Jeffrey Nelson Williams and Jacqueline Pon Williams)

SOURCES:

Cyrus Williams
Birth: (1) Original Record of Maine Towns & Cities, Town of Embden, Disk 1, Page 58, Picton Press, Rockland Maine, Copyright 2005; (2) "Maine Families in 1790, Volume 1", Edited by Ruth Gray, Page 290, Maine Genealogical Society, Special Publication No. 2, Picton Press, Camden, Maine, Copyright 1988; (3) Edmund West, comp., "Family Data Collection - Individual Records," [database on-line]. Provo, UT, USA: Ancestry.com Operations Inc., 2000; (4) "The Kennebec Valley" by Seth Harding Whitney, Page 98, Published by Sprague, Burleigh and Flynt, Augusta, Maine, 1887; (5) "Embden Town of Yore" by Ernest George Walker, Page 119, Published by Independent-Reporter Company, Skowhegan, Maine, 1929.
Death: (1) City of Waterville, Deaths 1830-1943, Disk 4, Page 1871, Picton Press, Rockland Maine, Copyright 2005; (2) "Maine Families in 1790, Volume 1", Edited by Ruth Gray, Page 290, Maine Genealogical Society, Special Publication No. 2, Picton Press, Camden, Maine, Copyright 1988; (3) Edmund West, comp., "Family Data Collection - Individual Records," [database on-line]. Provo, UT, USA: Ancestry.com Operations Inc., 2000.
Graveyard: (1) Pine Grove Cemetery Records, City of Waterville, Kennebec, Maine; (2) Find A Grave, Memorial #22399049.

Phydelia C. Perkins
Birth:
Marriage: (1) "Vital Records – Town of Anson Maine, Part 1" compiled by David H. Ela, Pages 247 & 249, 1975; (2) "Maine, Marriages, 1771-1907," index, FamilySearch, (https://familysearch.org/pal:/MM9.1.1/F4XH-VL4); (3) Original Record of Maine Towns & Cities, Town of Anson, Disk 2, Page 148, Picton Press, Rockland Maine, Copyright 2005; (4) Original Record of Maine Towns & Cities, Town of Anson, Disk 2, Page 149, Picton Press, Rockland Maine, Copyright 2005; (5) Edmund West, comp., "Family Data Collection - Individual Records," [database on-line]. Provo, UT, USA: Ancestry.com Operations Inc., 2000.
Death:
Graveyard: (1) Pine Grove Cemetery Records, City of Waterville, Kennebec, Maine; (2) Find A Grave, Memorial #22399119.

Katherine P. Williams
Birth: Graveyard Hill Cemetery Records, Anson Historical Society, Anson, Somerset, Maine.
Death: Graveyard Hill Cemetery Records, Anson Historical Society, Anson, Somerset, Maine.
Graveyard: Graveyard Hill Cemetery Records, Anson Historical Society, Anson, Somerset, Maine.

Helen Williams
Birth:
Death:
Graveyard: (1) Pine Grove Cemetery Records, City of Waterville, Kennebec, Maine; (2) Find A Grave, Memorial #22399083.

Infant Williams
Birth: Graveyard Hill Cemetery Records, Anson Historical Society, Anson, Somerset, Maine.
Death: Graveyard Hill Cemetery Records, Anson Historical Society, Anson, Somerset, Maine.
Graveyard: Graveyard Hill Cemetery Records, Anson Historical Society, Anson, Somerset, Maine.

Maria A. Williams
Birth:
Death:
Graveyard: (1) Pine Grove Cemetery Records, City of Waterville, Kennebec, Maine; (2) Find A Grave, Memorial #22399099.

Historical Accounts: (1) 1820 United States Federal Census, Anson, Somerset, Maine; (2) 1840 United States Federal Census, Waterville, Kennebec, Maine; (3) 1850 United States Federal Census for Waterville, Kennebec, Maine; (4) 1860 United States Federal Census for Waterville, Kennebec, Maine; (5) 1870 United States Federal Census for Waterville, Kennebec, Maine, Page 69; (6) 1880 United States Federal Census for Waterville, Kennebec, Maine, Page 48; (7) "Embden Town of Yore" by Ernest George Walker, Page 127, Published by Independent-Reporter Company, Skowhegan, Maine, 1929; (8) Original Record of Maine Towns & Cities, Town of Anson, Disk 2, Page 247, Picton Press, Rockland Maine 2005; (9) "Illustrated History of Kennebec County, Maine, 1625-1799-1892", Editors, Henry D. Kingsbury & Simon L. Deyo, Page 572, Published by H W. Blake & Company, 94 Reade Street, New York, 1892.

Francis Llewellyn Williams
(1798 - 1868)

The tenth child of Jacob Williams and Joanna Dean Williams was Francis Llewellyn. He was born on August 27, 1798 in Caratunk Settlement, Lincoln, Maine.

On his twentieth birthday, August 27, 1818, Francis Llewellyn was married to Nancy D. Hayward, age twenty in Easton, Bristol, Massachusetts by John Poll, a Justice of the Peace. Nancy D., the daughter of Joshua Hayward and Jerusha Filebrown, was born on February 9, 1798 in Easton.

Francis Llewellyn and Nancy D. also carried on the legacy of the Williams' families and had a large family with ten children.

Atwell R.	b. January 1, 1819	d. October 4, 1898
Harriet H.	b. August 27, 1820	d. February 25, 1899
Clarissa Hayward	b. December 15, 1821	d. September 17, 1898
Charles W.	b. October 23, 1823	d. July 17, 1892
Horace S.	b. August 15, 1825	d. 1885
Jason P.	b. June 20, 1828	d. December 13, 1903
Nancy Jane	b. November 13, 1831	d. February 15, 1891
Francis Llewellyn, Jr.	b. October 13, 1834	d. January 5, 1916
Cyrus P.	b. March 20, 1836	d. April 8, 1911
Lewis Kingman	b. June 27, 1838	d. April 28, 1907

The 1820 United States Federal Census recorded Francis Llewellyn, Nancy D. and their first two children as living in Embden, Somerset, Maine. Also, in 1820, like his father and brothers, Francis Llewellyn served as a town official in Embden.

Around 1830 Francis Llewellyn, Nancy D. and their family moved to the Caratunk Settlement area, which since 1809 was part of Somerset County, Maine, where they were recorded as living when the 1830 United States Federal Census was taken.

Francis Llewellyn bought a farm and built a home at Pleasant Pond near the Caratunk Settlement in 1835. He and his family were one of the first to settle and build a home in that area. Additionally, around that time it is believed that Francis Llewellyn built the Pleasant Pond sawmill which he ran until sometime in the 1850's.

In the 1840 and 1850 United States Federal Census' Francis Llewellyn, Nancy D. and their children were recorded as living in No 1, 5th Range, East Kennebec River in Somerset, Maine. The 1850 census listed Francis Llewellyn's occupation as "farmer".

In 1857, 1858 and 1860 Francis Llewellyn served as an "assessor" for Caratunk Plantation (as it was then known) which included the Pleasant Pond area.

Francis Llewellyn was still living with his family and farming in Caratunk Plantation when the 1860 United States Federal Census was taken.

On December 7, 1868 Francis Llewellyn died, at age seventy, of an unknown cause in Caratunk Plantation. He was buried in the Webster Cemetery in Caratunk Plantation.

When the 1870 United States Federal Census was taken, Nancy D. was recorded as living in Caratunk Plantation with her son Horace S. and her daughter Harriett H.

Nancy died two years later on January 21, 1872 at age seventy-three. The cause and place of her death have not been found. She too was buried in the family plot in the Webster Cemetery in Caratunk Plantation.

Gravestones for Francis Llewellyn Williams (left) and Nancy D. Hayward (right)
(Photographs from the Collection of Jeffrey Nelson Williams and Jacqueline Pon Williams)

SOURCES:

Francis Llewellyn Williams
Birth: (1) Original Record of Maine Towns & Cities, Town of Embden, Disk 1, Page 58, Picton Press, Rockland Maine, Copyright 2005; (2) "Maine Families in 1790, Volume 1", Edited by Ruth Gray, Page 290, Maine Genealogical Society, Special Publication No. 2, Picton Press, Camden, Maine, Copyright 1988; (3) Edmund West, comp., "Family Data Collection - Individual Records", [database on-line]. Provo, UT, USA: Ancestry.com Operations Inc., 2000; (4) "The Kennebec Valley" by Seth Harding Whitney, Page 98, Published by Sprague, Burleigh and Flynt, Augusta, Maine, 1887; (5) "Embden Town of Yore" by Ernest George Walker, Page 119, Published by Independent-Reporter Company, Skowhegan, Maine, 1929.
Death: Gravestone.
Graveyard: (1) "Maine Old Cemetery Association Special Publication Number 12, Edition No. 1: Series 1, 2 and 3", Page 526, Picton Press, Rockland, Maine, Copyright 2006; (2) "Caratunk Cemetery, also called Webster Cemetery" by Nancy Hamlin Davis and Ruth Hamlin, Record 113, Old Canada Road Historical Society; (3) Find A Grave, Memorial #49020166.

Nancy D. Hayward
Birth:
Marriage: (1) "Massachusetts, Town and Vital Records, 1620-1988", [database on-line], Provo, UT, USA: Ancestry.com Operations, Inc., 2011, Page 284; (2) Edmund West, comp., "Family Data Collection - Individual Records", [database on-line]. Provo, UT, USA: Ancestry.com Operations Inc., 2000.
Death: Gravestone.
Graveyard: (1) "Maine Old Cemetery Association Special Publication Number 12, Edition No. 1: Series 1, 2 and 3", Page 526, Picton Press, Rockland, Maine, Copyright 2006; (2) "Caratunk Cemetery, also called Webster Cemetery" by Nancy Hamlin Davis and Ruth Hamlin, Record 112, Old Canada Road Historical Society; (3) Find A Grave Index, Memorial #490200321.

Historical Accounts: (1) 1820 United States Federal Census for Embden, Somerset, Maine; (2) 1830 United States Federal Census for No. 1, 5th Range, Somerset, Maine; (3) 1840 United States Federal Census for No. 1, 5th Range, Somerset, Maine; (4) 1850 United States Federal Census for No. 1, 5th Range, Somerset, Maine; (5) 1860 United States Federal Census for No. 1, 5th Range, Somerset, Maine; (6) 1870 United States Federal Census for Caratunk, Somerset, Maine, Page 1; (7) "Embden Town of Yore" by Ernest George Walker, Page 127, Published by Independent-Reporter Company, Skowhegan, Maine, 1929; (8) Original Record of Maine Towns & Cities, Caratunk Plantation, Pages 39, 42 & 47, Picton Press, Rockland Maine, Copyright 2005; (9) "The Sesquicentennial History of Caratunk, Maine" by Donna McAllister, Printed by Carrabassett Printers, North Anson, Maine, Page 66.

Jacob Williams, Jr.
(1802 - 1854)

Jacob, Jr. was the twelfth child of Jacob Williams and Joanna Dean Williams. He was born in Caratunk Settlement, Kennebec, Maine on March 16, 1802. (Kennebec County was set off from Lincoln County in 1799)

On February 20, 1822, at age nineteen, Jacob, Jr. and Parmelia Savage, age seventeen, filed their intentions to be married with the Town Clerk of Embden, Somerset Maine. They granted a certificate of marriage on March 5, 1822 and were subsequently married there by Elisha Coolidge, Justice of the Peace. Parmelia was born on April 2, 1804 in Embden to Dr. Edward Savage, a well-known Free Will Baptist preacher in Somerset County, and Sarah Smith.

Jacob, Jr. and Parmelia had ten children together.

Juliann	*b. 1824*	*d. May 7, 1835*
Sophronia Sawyer	b. April 21, 1826	d. November 19, 1926
Adaline C.	*b. July 1828*	*d. September 9, 1844*
Elbridge S.	b. 1832	d. August 26, 1862
Elsie Atwood	b. March 27, 1835	d. February 19, 1905
Mary	*b. 1837*	*d.*
Leonard H.	b. July 12, 1840	d. September 14, 1914
Randall Benjamin	b. May 20, 1844	d. July 26, 1926
Adelaide Pamelia	b. November 7, 1847	d. December 18, 1932
Israel S.	*b.*	*d. June 5, 1853*

The first child of Jacob, Jr. and Parmelia, Juliann, died on May 7, 1835 when she was eleven years old. The cause and place of her death have not been found. She was buried in the Jacob Williams, Jr. family plot at the Bingham Village Cemetery in Bingham, Somerset, Maine.

When the 1840 United States Federal Census for Concord, Somerset, Maine was taken, Jacob, Jr. and his family were recorded as having moved there.

Adaline C., the third child of Jacob, Jr. and Parmelia, died September 9, 1844 when she was sixteen years old. The place and cause of her death have also not been found. Adaline C. was buried in the family plot at the Bingham Village Cemetery in Bingham.

In the 1850 United States Federal Census, at the age of forty-eight, Jacob, Jr., Parmelia and their children Elbridge S., Elsie Atwood, Mary, Leonard, Benjamin Randell and Adelaide Pamelia were recorded as living in Bingham. In that census Jacob, Jr.'s occupation was listed as "shoemaker".

Additional information regarding the life and death of Jacob, Jr. and Parmelia's sixth child Mary has not been found beyond the date of the taking of the 1850 census. As such her documented history will end here.

On June 5, 1853 the tenth child Israel S. of Jacob, Jr. and Parmelia died of a cause not found. As Israel S. was not listed in the 1850 United States Federal Census, it is presumed that he was born sometime in the early 1850's after the census was taken. Israel S. was also buried in the family plot in Bingham at the Bingham Village Cemetery.

Gravestones for Juliann Williams & Adaline C. Williams (left),
and Israel S. Williams (right)
(Photographs from the Collection of Jeffrey Nelson Williams and Jacqueline Pon Williams)

Jacob, Jr. died, at the age of fifty-one, on January 6, 1854 in Solon, Somerset, Maine. The cause of his death is not known. He was buried at Bingham in his family plot at the Bingham Village Cemetery.

Parmelia remarried at age fifty-six to John Kinsman, age seventy, on August 25, 1858 in Solon. John, the son of Jonathan Kinsman and Hannah Burnham, was born February 21, 1790 in Saco, York, Maine.

When the 1860 United States Federal Census was taken Parmelia and John were recorded in as living in Athens, Somerset, Maine with John's occupation listed as "farmer". John died December 2, 1866 in Athens at the age of seventy-six of a cause not found. He was buried at the Mount Rest Cemetery in Athens.

In the 1870 United States Federal Census, at the age of sixty-six, Parmelia was recorded as living in Solon in the home of her daughter Adelaide Pamelia (Williams) Shattuck and her family.

By the time the 1880 United States Federal Census was taken, Parmelia had moved to Boston, Suffolk, Massachusetts and was still living her daughter Adelaide Pamelia (Williams) Shattuck and her family who had also moved there.

Parmelia died in Barnstable, Barnstable County, Massachusetts on December 25, 1889 at the age of eighty-five. Her cause of death was listed as "heart disease". Her body was returned to Maine where she was buried with Jacob, Jr. and three of her children in the family plot in the Bingham Village Cemetery in Bingham.

Gravestones for Jacob Williams, Jr. (left) and Parmelia H. Savage (right)
(Photographs from the Collection of Jeffrey Nelson Williams and Jacqueline Pon Williams)

SOURCES:

Jacob Williams, Jr.
Birth: (1) Original Record of Maine Towns & Cities, Town of Embden, Disk 1, Page 58, Picton Press, Rockland Maine, Copyright 2005; (2) "Maine Families in 1790, Volume 9", Edited by Joseph Crook Anderson II, CG, FASG, Pages 418 & 419, Maine Genealogical Society, Special Publication No. 48, Picton Press, Rockport, Maine, Copyright December 2005; (3) Edmund West, comp., "Family Data Collection - Individual Records", [database on-line]. Provo, UT, USA: Ancestry.com Operations Inc., 2000; (4) "The Kennebec Valley" by Seth Harding Whitney, Page 98, Published by Sprague, Burleigh and Flynt, Augusta, Maine, 1887; (5) "Embden Town of Yore" by Ernest George Walker, Page 119, Published by Independent-Reporter Company, Skowhegan, Maine, 1929.
Death: (1) "Maine Families in 1790, Volume 1", Edited by Ruth Gray, Page 290, Maine Genealogical Society, Special Publication No. 2, Picton Press, Camden, Maine, Copyright 1988; (2) Edmund West, comp., "Family Data Collection - Individual Records", [database on-line]. Provo, UT, USA: Ancestry.com Operations Inc., 2000; (3) Gravestone.
Graveyard: (1) "Maine Old Cemetery Association Special Publication Number 12, Edition No. 1: Series 1, 2 and 3", Page 335, Picton Press, Rockland, Maine, Copyright 2006; (2) "Bingham Village Cemetery" by Nancy Hamlin Davis and Ruth Hamlin, Record 1499, Old Canada Road Historical Society; (3) "Nathan Hale Cemetery Collection, ca. 1780-1980," database with images, FamilySearch, (https://familysearch.org/ark:/61903/1:1:QVJ5-SFQT); (4) Find A Grave, Memorial #52844644.

Parmelia Savage
Birth: Original Record of Maine Towns & Cities, Town of Embden, Disk 1, Page 132, Picton Press, Rockland Maine, Copyright 2005.
Marriage: (1) Original Record of Maine Towns & Cities, Town of Embden, Disk 2, Page 32, Picton Press, Rockland Maine, Copyright 2005; (2) Original Record of Maine Towns & Cities, Town of Solon, Page 56, Picton Press, Rockland Maine, Copyright 2005; (3) "Maine Families in 1790, Volume 9", Edited by Joseph Crook Anderson II, CG, FASG, Pages 418 & 419, Maine Genealogical Society, Special Publication No. 48, Picton Press, Rockport, Maine, Copyright December 2005; (4) "Embden Town of Yore" by Ernest George Walker, Page 701, Published by Independent-Reporter Company, Skowhegan, Maine, 1929; (5) Edmund West, comp., "Family Data Collection - Individual Records", [database on-line]. Provo, UT, USA: Ancestry.com Operations Inc., 2000.
Death: Gravestone.
Graveyard: (1) "Maine Old Cemetery Association Special Publication Number 12, Edition No. 1: Series 1, 2 and 3", Page 335, Picton Press, Rockland, Maine, Copyright 2006; (2) "Bingham Village Cemetery" by Nancy Hamlin Davis and Ruth Hamlin, Record 1500, Old Canada Road Historical Society; (3) "Nathan Hale Cemetery Collection, ca. 1780-1980," database with images, FamilySearch, (https://familysearch.org/ark:/61903/1:1:QVJ5-SFQT); (4) Find A Grave, Memorial #52844749.

Juliann Williams
Birth:
Death: Gravestone.
Graveyard: (1) "Maine Old Cemetery Association Special Publication Number 12, Edition No. 1: Series 1, 2 and 3", Page 335, Picton Press, Rockland, Maine, Copyright 2006; (2) "Bingham Village Cemetery" by Nancy Hamlin Davis and Ruth Hamlin, Record 1502, Old Canada Road Historical Society; (3) "Nathan Hale Cemetery Collection, ca. 1780-1980," database with images, FamilySearch, (https://familysearch.org/ark:/61903/1:1:QVJ5-SFQT); (4) Find A Grave, Memorial #82115410.

Adaline C. Williams
Birth:
Death: Gravestone.
Graveyard: (1) "Maine Old Cemetery Association Special Publication Number 12, Edition No. 1: Series 1, 2 and 3", Page 335, Picton Press, Rockland, Maine, Copyright 2006; (2) "Bingham Village Cemetery" by Nancy Hamlin Davis and Ruth Hamlin, Record 1501, Old Canada Road Historical Society; (3) "Nathan Hale Cemetery Collection, ca. 1780-1980," database with images, FamilySearch, (https://familysearch.org/ark:/61903/1:1:QVJ5-SFQT); (4) Find A Grave, Memorial #82115405.

Mary Williams
Birth:
Death:
Graveyard:

Israel S. Williams
Birth:
Death: Gravestone.
Graveyard: (1) "Maine Old Cemetery Association Special Publication Number 12, Edition No. 1: Series 1, 2 and 3", Page 335, Picton Press, Rockland, Maine, Copyright 2006; (2) "Bingham Village Cemetery" by Nancy Hamlin Davis and Ruth Hamlin, Record 1503, Old Canada Road Historical Society; (3) "Nathan Hale Cemetery Collection, ca. 1780-1980," database with images, FamilySearch, (https://familysearch.org/ark:/61903/1:1:QVJ5-SFQT); (4) Find A Grave, Memorial #82115409.

John Kinsman
Birth: Edmund West, comp., "Family Data Collection - Individual Records", [database on-line]. Provo, UT, USA: Ancestry.com Operations Inc., 2000
Marriage: "Maine, Marriages, 1771-1907," index, FamilySearch, (https://familysearch.org/pal:/MM9.1.1/F4F1-SQD)
Death:
Graveyard: Find A Grave, Memorial #125276385.

Historical Accounts: (1) 1840 United States Federal Census for Concord, Somerset, Maine; (2) 1850 United States Federal Census for Bingham, Somerset, Maine; (3) 1860 United States Federal Census for Athens, Somerset, Maine, Page 14; (4) 1870 United States Federal Census for Solon, Somerset, Maine, Page 25; (5) 1880 United States Federal Census for Boston, Suffolk, Massachusetts, Page 33; (6) "Maine Families in 1790, Volume 9", Edited by Joseph Crook Anderson II, CG, FASG, Pages 418 & 419, Maine Genealogical Society, Special Publication No. 48, Picton Press, Rockport, Maine, Copyright December 2005.

Chandler Nason Williams
(1804 - 1888)

The thirteenth child of Jacob Williams and Joanna Dean Williams was Chandler Nason who was born on June 6, 1804 in Caratunk Settlement, Kennebec, Maine.

On March 5, 1828, at age twenty-three, Chandler Nason and Rebecca Hunnewell, age twenty-eight, filed their intentions to marry with the Town Clerk of Solon, Somerset, Maine. They were married shortly thereafter, on March 17, 1828, in Solon. Rebecca, the daughter of William Hunnewell and Rebecca Snell, was born in Solon on May 10, 1799.

Chandler Nason and Rebecca had five children together.

Unnamed Infant	*b. March 1829*	*d. March 20, 1829*
Laura	b. February 10, 1830	d. August 11, 1912
Nason Chandler	b. January 20, 1834	d. May 2, 1922
Jacob Omar	*b. December 1835*	*d. August 13, 1837*
Milo Reed	b. February 21, 1838	d. June 13, 1913

Two of Chandler Nason and Rebecca's children died at young ages. Their first child, an unnamed infant, is presumed to have died at, or near, birth on March 20, 1829 and their fourth child Jacob Omar died on August 13, 1837 when he was one year eight months old. The causes and places of their deaths have not been found. Both children were buried in the Pleasantdale Cemetery in Embden, Somerset, Maine.

Gravestone for Unnamed Infant Williams and Jacob Omar Williams
(Photograph from the Collection of Jeffrey Nelson Williams and Jacqueline Pon Williams)

Chandler Nason was a member of the Third Regiment, First Brigade, 8th Division of the Maine Militia in Embden. He rose to the rank of colonel and commanded the Third Regiment from July 27, 1837 to April 15, 1839.

The 1840 United States Federal Census recorded Chandler Nason, Rebecca and their children as living in Embden.

By the time the 1850 United States Federal Census was taken Chandler Nason, Rebecca and their children had moved to Moscow, Somerset, Maine. Chandler Nason's occupation was listed as "farmer" in that census. They were still living and farming in Moscow at the time of the 1860 and 1870 United States Federal Census'.

On June 8, 1875, Rebecca died at age seventy-six, in Moscow. The cause of her death is not known. She was buried with her children in the Pleasantdale Cemetery in Embden.

When the 1880 United States Federal Census was taken, Chandler Nason, age seventy-six, was recorded as living with his daughter, Laura (Williams) Clark her family in Concord, Somerset, Maine.

Sometime after the 1880 Census, Chandler Nason went across the country to Jackson in Amador County, California where his son Nason Chandler lived. Chandler Nason died there on March 10, 1888 at the age of eighty-three. The cause of his death has not been found. His body was returned to Maine where he was buried at Embden in his family plot at the Pleasantdale Cemetery.

Gravestones for Chandler Nason Williams, Jr. (left) and Rebecca Hunnewell (right)
(Photographs from the Collection of Jeffrey Nelson Williams and Jacqueline Pon Williams)

SOURCES:

Chandler Nason Williams
Birth: (1) Original Record of Maine Towns & Cities, Town of Embden, Page 58, Picton Press, Rockland Maine, Copyright 2005; (2) "Maine Families in 1790, Volume 9", Edited by Joseph Crook Anderson II, CG, FASG, Pages 418 & 419, Maine Genealogical Society, Special Publication No. 48, Picton Press, Rockport, Maine, Copyright December 2005; (3) Edmund West, comp., "Family Data Collection - Individual Records", [database on-line], Provo, UT, USA: Ancestry.com Operations Inc., 2000; (4) "The Kennebec Valley" by Seth Harding Whitney, Page 98, Published by Sprague, Burleigh and Flynt, Augusta, Maine, 1887; (5) "Embden Town of Yore" by Ernest George Walker, Page 119, Published by Independent-Reporter Company, Skowhegan, Maine, 1929.
Death: (1) "Maine Families in 1790, Volume 9", Edited by Joseph Crook Anderson II, CG, FASG, Pages 418 & 419, Maine Genealogical Society, Special Publication No. 48, Picton Press, Rockport, Maine, Copyright December 2005; (2) Edmund West, comp., "Family Data Collection - Individual Records", [database on-line], Provo, UT, USA: Ancestry.com Operations Inc., 2000; (3) Gravestone.
Graveyard: (1) "Pleasant Dale/Murphy/Boothby Cemetery" complied by Nancy Hamlin Davis and Ruth Hamlin, Record 90, Old Canada Road Historical Society; (2) Find A Grave, Memorial #52819452.

Rebecca Hunnewell
Birth: Original Record of Maine Towns & Cities, Town of Solon, Page 11, Picton Press, Rockland Maine, Copyright 2005.
Marriage: (1) Original Record of Maine Towns & Cities, Town of Solon, Page 61, Picton Press, Rockland Maine, Copyright 2005; (2) Edmund West, comp., "Family Data Collection - Individual Records", [database on-line], Provo, UT, USA: Ancestry.com Operations Inc., 2000; (3) "Maine, Marriages, 1771-1907," index FamilySearch, (https://familysearch.org/pal:/MM9.1.1/F4FB-YPJ); (4) "Embden Town of Yore" by Ernest George Walker, Page 703, Published by Independent-Reporter Company, Skowhegan, Maine, 1929.
Death: Gravestone.
Graveyard: (1) "Pleasant Dale/Murphy/Boothby Cemetery" complied by Nancy Hamlin Davis and Ruth Hamlin, Record 91, Old Canada Road Historical Society; (2) Find A Grave, Memorial #52819631.

Unnamed Infant Williams
Birth:
Death: Gravestone.
Graveyard: (1) "Pleasant Dale/Murphy/Boothby Cemetery" complied by Nancy Hamlin Davis and Ruth Hamlin, Record 93, Old Canada Road Historical Society; (2) Find A Grave, Memorial #118443000.

Jacob Omar Williams
Birth:
Death: Gravestone.
Graveyard: (1) "Pleasant Dale/Murphy/Boothby Cemetery" complied by Nancy Hamlin Davis and Ruth Hamlin, Record 92, Old Canada Road Historical Society; (2) Find A Grave, Memorial #118442796.

Historical Accounts: (1) 1840 United States Federal Census for Embden, Somerset, Maine; (2) 1850 United States Federal Census for Moscow, Somerset, Maine; (3) 1860 United States Federal Census for Moscow, Somerset, Maine, Page 4; (4) 1870 United States Federal Census for Moscow, Somerset, Maine, Page 3; (5) 1880 United States Federal Census for Concord, Somerset, Maine, Page 8; (6) "Embden Town of Yore" by Ernest George Walker, Page 129, Published by Independent-Reporter Company, Skowhegan, Maine, 1929.

Susan Williams
(1809 - 1837)

Susan was the fifteenth, and last, child of Jacob Williams and Joanna Dean Williams. She was born in in Caratunk Settlement, Somerset, Maine on July 27, 1809. (Caratunk Settlement became part of Somerset County when it was set off from Kennebec County in 1809)

On January 8, 1830, at age twenty, Susan and Theodore Hamblet, age twenty-one, filed their intentions to be married with the Town Clerk of Solon, Somerset, Maine. They were subsequently married in Solon on February 12, 1830 by Theodore's father John Hamblet, a Justice of the Peace. Theodore was born on February 19, 1808, in Solon to John Hamblet and Phebe Hunnewell.

Susan and Theodore had three children together.

Aura	b. August 15, 1831	d. October 28, 1870
Jotham Lowell	b. March 8, 1833	d. February 24, 1913
Susan Jane	b. August 26, 1836	d. December 26, 1895

When the 1830 United States Federal Census was taken, Susan and Theodore were recorded as living in Solon

On May 29, 1837, Susan died at age twenty-seven, in Solon. The cause of her death has not been found. She was buried in the Village Cemetery in Solon.

Theodore, at age thirty, was married to his second wife Maria A. Brown, age twenty-five, on May 20, 1838 in Solon. The exact date and place of Maria's birth, as well as the names of her parents, have not been found. Theodore and Maria A. had two children during their marriage.

In the 1850 United States Federal Census Theodore, Maria A., his children from his marriage to Susan and their children and were recorded as living in Madison, Somerset, Maine. Theodore's occupation was listed as "farmer".

The 1860 United States Federal Census recorded Theodore, Maria A. and their children were living in Solon. Theodore was still listed as working as a "farmer".

On August 10, 1863 Theodore died at the age of fifty-five. The cause and place of his death have not been found. He was buried in the Village Cemetery in Solon beside his first wife Susan.

Maria A. outlived Theodore by almost seventeen years, passing away on April 30, 1880. Her place and cause of death are also not known. She too was buried in the Village Cemetery in Solon.

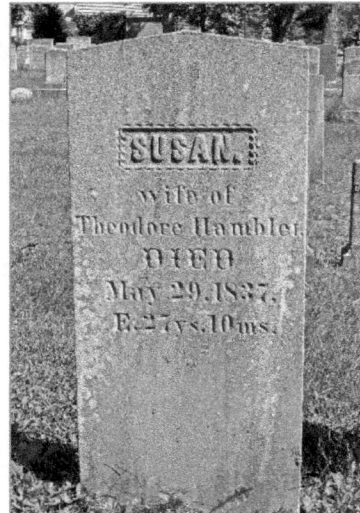

Gravestones for Susan Williams (left) and Theodore Hamblet (right)
(Photographs from the Collection of Jeffrey Nelson Williams and Jacqueline Pon Williams)

SOURCES:

Susan Williams
Birth: (1) Original Record of Maine Towns & Cities, Town of Embden, Disk 1, Page 58, Picton Press, Rockland Maine, Copyright 2005; (2) "Maine Families in 1790, Volume 9", Edited by Joseph Crook Anderson II, CG, FASG, Pages 418 & 419, Maine Genealogical Society, Special Publication No. 48, Picton Press, Rockport, Maine, Copyright December 2005; (3) "The Kennebec Valley" by Seth Harding Whitney, Page 98, Published by Sprague, Burleigh and Flynt, Augusta, Maine, 1887; (4) "Embden Town of Yore" by Ernest George Walker, Page 119, Published by Independent-Reporter Company, Skowhegan, Maine, 1929.
Death: (1) Original Record of Maine Towns & Cities, Town of Solon Maine, Page 16, Picton Press, Rockland Maine, Copyright 2005; (2) "Maine Families in 1790, Volume 9", Edited by Joseph Crook Anderson II, CG, FASG, Pages 418 & 419, Maine Genealogical Society, Special Publication No. 48, Picton Press, Rockport, Maine, Copyright December 2005; (3) Gravestone.
Graveyard: Find A Grave, Memorial #112281684.

Theodore Hamblet
Birth: (1) Original Record of Maine Towns & Cities, Town of Solon, Page 10, Picton Press, Rockland Maine, Copyright 2005; (2) "Maine, Births and Christenings, 1739-1900," index, FamilySearch, (https://familysearch.org /pal: /MM9.1.1/FW1H-HMR).
Marriage: (1) Original Record of Maine Towns & Cities, Town of Solon, Page 62, Picton Press, Rockland Maine, Copyright 2005; (2) Original Record of Maine Towns & Cities, Town of Solon, Page 63, Picton Press, Rockland Maine, Copyright 2005; (3) "Maine, Marriages, 1771-1907," index FamilySearch, (https://familysearch.org/pal: /MM9.1.1/F4FB-YYM).
Death: Gravestone.
Graveyard: Find A Grave, Memorial #112281527.

Maria A. Brown
Birth:
Marriage: Original Record of Maine Towns & Cities, Town of Solon, Page 72, Picton Press, Rockland Maine, Copyright 2005
Death: Gravestone.
Graveyard: Find A Grave, Memorial #112281527.

Historical Accounts: (1) 1830 United States Federal Census for Solon, Somerset, Maine; (2) 1850 United States Federal Census for Madison, Somerset, Maine; (3) 1860 United States Federal Census for Solon, Somerset, Maine, Page 50.

III

The Third Generation

The Grand Children of
Jacob Williams and Joanna Dean Williams

The Children of Caleb Williams

The Children of Daniel Williams

The Children of John Williams

The Children of Chandler Nason Williams

The Children of Susan Williams

Charlotte Williams
(1804 - 1848)

The first child of Caleb Williams and Elizabeth Whitman was Charlotte. She was born on January 7, 1804 in Embden, Kennebec, Maine. (Embden would become part of Somerset County when it was set off from Kennebec County in 1809)

On September 3, 1829 Charlotte, age twenty-five, was married to Jonah Houghton, age twenty-two, in Anson, Somerset, Maine by Jotham Dinsmore, a Justice of the Peace. Jonah, born in Anson on December 14, 1806, was the son of Thomas Houghton and Susannah Crosby.

Charlotte and Jonah had four children during their marriage.

Marshall W.	b. June 7, 1830	d. March 27, 1898
Warren W.	b. January 3, 1832	d. December 10, 1887
Jonah, Jr.	b. May 15, 1839	d. December 23, 1896
Betsey	b. March 26, 1845	d. November 4, 1873

The 1830 and 1840 United States Census' recorded Charlotte, Jonah and their children as living in Anson.

Charlotte died on March 17, 1848 at the age of forty-four. The cause and place of her death have not been found. She was buried in the Gilman-Heald Cemetery in Anson.

On August 28, 1848, at age forty-one, Jonah and Emeline (Hooper) Clapp, age thirty-one, filed their intentions to be married with the Town Clerk of Anson. They were married thirteen days later, on September 10, 1848, in Anson by Howard Winslow, a Minister of the Gospel. Emeline, the daughter of Isaac Story Hooper and Eunice Lincoln, was born in Ripley, Somerset, Maine on July 16, 1817. No record has been found to indicate that Jonah and Emeline ever had any children together, although Emeline did have a son, Nathanial F. Clapp, from her first marriage.

In the 1850, 1860, 1870 and 1880 United States Census' Jonah, Emeline and their children from both their first marriages were recorded as living in Anson with Jonah working as a "farmer".

At age seventy-nine Jonah died in Anson on October 16, 1866 of a cause not known. Jonah was buried in the Gilman-Heald Cemetery in Anson in the same plot as his first wife Charlotte.

Additional information regarding the life and death of Emeline has not been found.

Gravestones for Charlotte Williams (left) and Jonah Houghton (right)
(Photographs Courtesy of Gail Kelly)

SOURCES:

Charlotte Williams
Birth: (1) Original Record of Maine Towns & Cities, Town of Embden, Disk 1, Page 119, Picton Press, Rockland Maine, Copyright 2005; (2) Original Record of Maine Towns & Cities, Town of Anson, Page 247, Picton Press, Rockland Maine, Copyright 2005; (3) "Vital Records – Town of Anson Maine, Part 1" compiled by David H. Ela, Page 442, 1975; (4) "History of the Descendants of John Whitman of Weymouth, Mass" by Charles H. Farnam, A.M., Page 851, Tuttle, Morehouse & Taylor printers, New Haven, 1889.
Death: (1) "History of the Descendants of John Whitman of Weymouth, Mass" by Charles H. Farnam, A.M., Page 851, Tuttle, Morehouse & Taylor printers, New Haven, 1889; (2) "Maine, Nathan Hale Cemetery Collection, ca. 1780-1980," database with images, FamilySearch, (https://familysearch.org/ark:/61903/1:1:QVJ5-4NNJ); (3) Gravestone.
Graveyard: (1) "Maine Old Cemetery Association Special Publication Number 12, Edition No. 1: Series 1, 2 and 3", Page 25, Picton Press, Rockland, Maine, Copyright 2006; (2) "Maine, Nathan Hale Cemetery Collection, ca. 1780-1980," database with images, FamilySearch, (https://familysearch.org/ark:/61903/1:1:QVJ5-4NNJ).

Jonah Houghton
Birth: (1) Original Record of Maine Towns & Cities, Town of Anson, Disk 2, Page 525, Picton Press, Rockland Maine, Copyright 2005; (2) "Maine, Births and Christenings, 1739-1900," index, FamilySearch, (https://familysearch.org/pal:/MM9.1.1/F4SF-L87); (3) "History of the Descendants of John Whitman of Weymouth, Mass" by Charles H. Farnam, A.M., Page 851, Tuttle, Morehouse & Taylor printers, New Haven, 1889; (4) "Vital Records – Town of Anson Maine, Part 1" compiled by David H. Ela, Page 442, 1975.
Marriage: (1) "Vital Records – Town of Anson Maine, Part 1" compiled by David H. Ela, Page 396, 1975; (2) Original Record of Maine Towns & Cities, Town of Anson, Page 223, Picton Press, Rockland Maine, Copyright 2005; (3) "Embden Town of Yore" by Ernest George Walker, Page 703, Published by Independent-Reporter Company, Skowhegan, Maine, 1929; (4) "History of the Descendants of John Whitman of Weymouth, Mass" by Charles H. Farnam, A.M., Page 851, Tuttle, Morehouse & Taylor printers, New Haven, 1889.
Death: (1) "Maine, Nathan Hale Cemetery Collection, ca. 1780-1980," database with images, FamilySearch, (https://familysearch.org/ark:/61903/1:1:QVJ5-4NNJ); (2) Gravestone.
Graveyard: (1) "Maine Old Cemetery Association Special Publication Number 12, Edition No. 1: Series 1, 2 and 3", Page 25, Picton Press, Rockland, Maine, Copyright 2006; (2) "Maine, Nathan Hale Cemetery Collection, ca. 1780-1980," database with images, FamilySearch, (https://familysearch.org/ark:/61903/1:1:QVJ5-4NNJ).

Emeline Hooper
Birth: "Maine Births and Christenings, 1739-1900," database, FamilySearch (https://familysearch.org/ark/61903/
1.1:/FW17-G6X).
Marriage: (1) Original Record of Maine Towns & Cities, Town of Anson, Disk 1, Page 47, Picton Press,
Rockland Maine, Copyright 2005; (2) Maine Marriage Returns, Somerset County 1834-1890, Disk 1, Page 162,
Copyright 2005, Picton Press, Rockland Maine; (3) "Maine, Marriages, 1771-1907," index, FamilySearch
(https://familysearch.org/pal:/MM9.1.1/F4XH-FQM).
Death:
Graveyard:

Historical Accounts: (1) 1830 United States Federal Census for Anson, Somerset, Maine; (2) 1840 United States
Federal Census for Anson, Somerset, Maine; (3) 1850 United States Federal Census for Anson, Somerset, Maine;
(4) 1860 United States Federal Census for Anson, Somerset, Maine, Page 39; (5) 1870 United States Federal
Census for Anson, Somerset, Maine, Page 29; (6) 1880 United States Federal Census for Anson, Somerset, Maine,
Page 51.

Mary Polly Williams
(1805 - 1889)

Mary Polly, the second child of Caleb Williams and Elizabeth Whitman was born on March 31, 1805 in Embden, Kennebec County, Maine.

On August 6, 1826, age twenty-one, Mary Polly and Jonathan D. Eames, also age twenty-one, filed their intentions to be married with the Town Clerk of Embden, Somerset, Maine. (Embden had become part of Somerset County when it was set off from Kennebec County in 1809) They were subsequently married on September 10, 1826, although the exact location is not known. Jonathan D., the son of Jonathan Eames and Thankful Olive Young, was born on July 18, 1805 in Madison, Somerset, Maine.

Mary Polly Williams and Jonathan D. Eames
(Photographs from "Embden Town of Yore" by Ernest George Walker, 1929)

Mary Polly and Jonathan D. had eleven children together.

Caleb (a twin)	*b. May 24, 1827*	*d. June 17, 1827*
Phineas (a twin)	b. May 24, 1827	d. February 12, 1905
Jonathan Whitman	b. December 23, 1828	d. November 10, 1897
Austin	b. February 16, 1831	d. November 11, 1893
Almond	b. December 4, 1833	d. May 27, 1924
George L.	b. November 30, 1835	d. November 13, 1898
Cyrena	b. February 16, 1838	d. February 20, 1876
Martin	*b. November 24, 1840*	*d. October 15, 1842*
Martin V.	b. November 20, 1843	d. March 9, 1864
Adeline W.	b. February 6, 1846	d. May 29, 1906
Owen	*b. April 15, 1848*	*d. September 13, 1850*

Caleb, the first child of Mary Polly and Jonathan D., died when he was just twenty-four days old on June 17,1827. Their eighth child and first boy who they named Martin died on October 15, 1842. And Owen, their eleventh child died on September 13, 1850 when he was just two years old. The places and causes of deaths for all three children have not been found. Caleb, Martin and Owen were buried in the Jonathan Eames family plot at the Sunset Cemetery in North Anson, Somerset, Maine.

Gravestones for Caleb Eames (top), Martin Eames (lower left) and Owen Eames (lower right)
(Photographs from the Collection of Jeffrey Nelson Williams and Jacqueline Pon Williams)

When the 1850 United States Federal Census was taken Mary Polly, Jonathan D. and their children were recorded as living and farming in Embden.

Mary Polly and Jonathan D. were still living and farming in Embden at the time the 1860 and 1870 United States Federal Census' were taken.

Jonathan D., at age seventy, preceded Mary Polly in death on August 13, 1875. The place and cause of his death are not known. He was buried with his children in his family plot in North Anson at the Sunset Cemetery.

In the 1880 United States Federal Census Mary Polly was listed as living with her son Phineas and his family in Embden.

Mary Polly died of an unknown cause on October 5, 1889 at the age of eighty-four. She too was buried in the family plot at the Sunset Cemetery in North Anson.

Gravestones for Mary Polly Williams (left) and Jonathan D. Eames (right)
(Photographs from the Collection of Jeffrey Nelson Williams and Jacqueline Pon Williams)

SOURCES:

Mary Polly Williams
Birth: (1) Original Record of Maine Towns & Cities, Town of Embden, Disk 1, Page 119, Picton Press, Rockland Maine, Copyright 2005; (2) "History of the Descendants of John Whitman of Weymouth, Mass" by Charles H. Farnam, A.M., Page 852, Tuttle, Morehouse & Taylor printers, New Haven, 1889.
Death: (1) "Maine, Faylene Hutton Cemetery Collection, ca. 1780-1990," database with images, FamilySearch, (https://familysearch.org/ark:/61903/1:1:QKM1-WKGD) - Accession #4107; (2) Gravestone.
Graveyard: (1) Burial Records, Sunset Cemetery, North Anson, Maine; (2) "Maine Old Cemetery Association Special Publication Number 12, Edition No. 1: Series 1, 2 and 3", Page 89, Picton Press, Rockland, Maine, Copyright 2006; (3) Find A Grave, Memorial #152200396.

Jonathan D. Eames

Births: (1) "History of the Descendants of John Whitman of Weymouth, Mass" by Charles H. Farnam, A.M., Page 852, Tuttle, Morehouse & Taylor printers, New Haven, 1889; (2) "Eames-Ames Genealogy, Descendants of Robert of Woburn and Thomas of Framingham, Massachusetts, 1634-1931", Written and Compiled by Wilmot Spofford Ames, Page 38, Gardiner, Maine, 1931.

Marriage: (1) "Embden Town of Yore" by Ernest George Walker, Page 702, Published by Independent-Reporter Company, Skowhegan, Maine, 1929; (2) Original Record of Maine Towns & Cities, Town of Embden, Disk 1, Page 36, Picton Press, Rockland Maine, Copyright 2005; (3) "History of the Descendants of John Whitman of Weymouth, Mass" by Charles H. Farnam, A.M., Page 852, Tuttle, Morehouse & Taylor printers, New Haven, 1889.

Death: (1) "History of the Descendants of John Whitman of Weymouth, Mass" by Charles H. Farnam, A.M., Page 852, Tuttle, Morehouse & Taylor printers, New Haven, 1889; (2) Gravestone.

Graveyard: (1) Burial Records, Sunset Cemetery, North Anson, Maine; (2) "Maine Old Cemetery Association Special Publication Number 12, Edition No. 1: Series 1, 2 and 3", Page 89, Picton Press, Rockland, Maine, Copyright 2006; (3) "Maine, Faylene Hutton Cemetery Collection, ca. 1780-1990," database with images, FamilySearch, (https://familysearch.org/ark:/61903/1:1:QKM1-WKGD) - Accession #4107; (4) Find A Grave, Memorial #91659095.

Caleb Eames

Birth: (1) "History of the Descendants of John Whitman of Weymouth, Mass" by Charles H. Farnam, A.M., Page 852, Tuttle, Morehouse & Taylor printers, New Haven, 1889; (2) "Eames-Ames Genealogy, Descendants of Robert of Woburn and Thomas of Framingham, Massachusetts, 1634-1931", Written and Compiled by Wilmot Spofford Ames, Page 38, Gardiner, Maine, 1931.

Death: (1) "Maine, Faylene Hutton Cemetery Collection, ca. 1780-1990," database with images, FamilySearch, (https://familysearch.org/ark:/61903/1:1:QKM1-WKGD) - Accession #4107; (2) Gravestone.

Graveyard: (1) Burial Records, Sunset Cemetery, North Anson, Maine; (2) "Maine Old Cemetery Association Special Publication Number 12, Edition No. 1: Series 1, 2 and 3", Page 89, Picton Press, Rockland, Maine, Copyright 2006; (3) "Maine, Faylene Hutton Cemetery Collection, ca. 1780-1990," database with images, FamilySearch, (https://familysearch.org/ark:/61903/1:1:QKM1-WKGD) - Accession #4107; (4) Find A Grave, Memorial #91659144.

Martin Eames

Birth: "History of the Descendants of John Whitman of Weymouth, Mass" by Charles H. Farnam, A.M., Page 852, Tuttle, Morehouse & Taylor printers, New Haven, 1889.

Death: (1) "Maine, Faylene Hutton Cemetery Collection, ca. 1780-1990," database with images, FamilySearch, (https://familysearch.org/ark:/61903/1:1:QKM1-WKGD) - Accession #4107; (2) Gravestone.

Graveyard: (1) Burial Records, Sunset Cemetery, North Anson, Maine; (2) "Maine Old Cemetery Association Special Publication Number 12, Edition No. 1: Series 1, 2 and 3", Page 89, Picton Press, Rockland, Maine, Copyright 2006; (3) "Maine, Faylene Hutton Cemetery Collection, ca. 1780-1990," database with images, FamilySearch, (https://familysearch.org/ark:/61903/1:1:QKM1-WKGD) - Accession #4107; (4) Find A Grave, Memorial #91659167.

Owen Eames

Birth: "History of the Descendants of John Whitman of Weymouth, Mass" by Charles H. Farnam, A.M., Page 854, Tuttle, Morehouse & Taylor printers, New Haven, 1889.

Death: (1) "Maine, Faylene Hutton Cemetery Collection, ca. 1780-1990," database with images, FamilySearch, (https://familysearch.org/ark:/61903/1:1:QKM1-WKGD) - Accession #4107; (2) Gravestone.

Graveyard: (1) Burial Records, Sunset Cemetery, North Anson, Maine; (2) "Maine Old Cemetery Association Special Publication Number 12, Edition No. 1: Series 1, 2 and 3", Page 89, Picton Press, Rockland, Maine, Copyright 2006; (3) "Maine, Faylene Hutton Cemetery Collection, ca. 1780-1990," database with images, FamilySearch, (https://familysearch.org/ark:/61903/1:1:QKM1-WKGD) - Accession #4107; (4) Find A Grave, Memorial #91659127.

Historical Accounts: (1) 1850 United States Federal Census for Embden, Somerset, Maine; (2) 1860 United States Federal Census for Embden, Somerset, Maine, Page 54; (3) 1870 United States Federal Census for Embden, Somerset, Maine Page 4; (4) 1880 United States Federal Census for Embden, Somerset, Maine, Page 6.

Betsey Williams
(1807 - 1884)

The fourth child of Caleb Williams and Elizabeth Whitman was Betsey. She was born in Embden, Kennebec, Maine on October 31, 1807.

On July 6, 1828 Betsey, age twenty, and Joshua Gray, Jr., age twenty-four, filed their intentions to be married with the Town Clerk of Embden. They were subsequently married by Benjamin C. Atwood, a Justice of the Peace in Embden, on July 31, 1828. Joshua, Jr. was born on November 22, 1803 in Embden to Joshua Gray and Hannah McFadden.

Betsey and Joshua, Jr. had eight children together.

Enos	b. February 4, 1829	d. June 21, 1917
Adeline	*b. July 25, 1830*	*d. November 13, 1833*
Joseph Eugene	b. March 9, 1832	d. November 29, 1885
Franklin N.	b. October 28, 1833	d. October 27, 1865
Joshua Omar	b. November 29, 1835	d. November 7, 1870
Helen	b. December 17, 1837	d. December 2, 1910
Elizabeth M.	b. November 17, 1840	d. July 29, 1929
Jonas Marshall	b. October 29, 1846	d. August 23, 1880

The second child of Betsey and Joshua, Jr., Adeline, died at age three on November 13, 1833. Her cause and place of death are not known. She was buried in the Gray Cemetery in Embden.

Gravestone for Adeline Gray
(Photograph Courtesy of Marydenise Daggett)

In the 1830 and 1840 United States Federal Census' Betsey, Joshua, Jr. and their children were recorded as living in Embden

Betsey, Joshua, Jr. and their family were still living in Embden when the 1850 and 1860 United States Federal Census' were taken. In those census documents Joshua Jr.'s occupation was recorded as "farmer".

Joshua, Jr., at age seventy-two, preceded Betsey in death on August 27, 1876. The cause and place of his death are not known. He was buried in Embden at the Gray Cemetery. During his adult life Joshua Jr. served as a town officer of Embden where in 1833, 1834 and 1836 he was a town Selectman. He also held the position of town Constable in 1839 and 1857. And in 1846, 1863 and 1864 he served as the town Treasurer. Additionally, Joshua, Jr. also served as a Captain in the Embden Militia.

The 1880 United States Federal Census recorded Betsey as living with her eighth child, Jonas Marshall., and his family in Embden.

Betsey died in Embden of an unknown cause on September 8, 1884 at the age of seventy-six and was buried in the Sunset Cemetery in North Anson, Somerset, Maine. In her Will, which was written on October 22, 1881, Betsey first left the family farm in Embden to her son Joseph Eugene, second her hardwood secretary to her son Enos, and third all of her remaining property to be divided equally by her son Joseph Eugene and her two daughters Helen (Gray) Hilton and Elizabeth M. (Gray) Miller.

Gravestone for Betsey Williams
(Photograph from the Collection of Jeffrey Nelson Williams and Jacqueline Pon Williams)

SOURCES:

Betsey Williams
Birth: (1) Original Record of Maine Towns & Cities, Town of Embden, Disk 1, Page 119, Picton Press, Rockland Maine, Copyright 2005; (2) "History of the Descendants of John Whitman of Weymouth, Mass" by Charles H. Farnam, A.M., Page 854. Tuttle, Morehouse & Taylor printers, New Haven, 1889.
Death: "History of the Descendants of John Whitman of Weymouth, Mass" by Charles H. Farnam, A.M., Page 854. Tuttle, Morehouse & Taylor printers, New Haven, 1889.
Graveyard: (1) Burial Records, Sunset Cemetery, North Anson, Maine; (2) "Maine Old Cemetery Association Special Publication Number 12, Edition No. 1: Series 1, 2 and 3", Page 99, Picton Press, Rockland, Maine, Copyright 2006; (3) Find A Grave, Memorial #86207306.

Joshua Gray, Jr.
Birth: "History of the Descendants of John Whitman of Weymouth, Mass" by Charles H. Farnam, A.M., Page 854. Tuttle, Morehouse & Taylor printers, New Haven, 1889.
Marriage: (1) "Maine, Marriages, 1771-1907," index, FamilySearch, (https://familysearch.org/pal:/MM9.1.1 /F462-2TB); (2) "Embden Town of Yore" by Ernest George Walker, Page 703, Published by Independent-Reporter Company, Skowhegan, Maine, 1929; (3) Original Record of Maine Towns & Cities, Town of Embden, Disk 2, Page 38, Picton Press, Rockland Maine, Copyright 2005; (4) "History of the Descendants of John Whitman of Weymouth, Mass" by Charles H. Farnam, A.M., Page 854. Tuttle, Morehouse & Taylor printers, New Haven, 1889.
Death: (1) "History of the Descendants of John Whitman of Weymouth, Mass" by Charles H. Farnam, A.M., Page 854. Tuttle, Morehouse & Taylor printers, New Haven, 1889; (2) "Maine, Faylene Hutton Cemetery Collection, ca. 1780-1990," database with images, FamilySearch, (https://familysearch.org/ark:/61903/1:1:QKM1-S3RD).
Graveyard: "Maine, Faylene Hutton Cemetery Collection, ca. 1780-1990," database with images, FamilySearch, (https://familysearch.org/ark:/61903/1:1:QKM1-S3RD).

Adeline Gray
Birth: (1) Original Record of Maine Towns & Cities, Town of Embden, Disk 1, Page 100, Picton Press, Rockland Maine, Copyright 2005; (2) Original Record of Maine Towns & Cities, Town of Embden, Disk 2, Page 8, Picton Press, Rockland Maine, Copyright 2005; (3)) "History of the Descendants of John Whitman of Weymouth, Mass" by Charles H. Farnam, A.M., Page 854. Tuttle, Morehouse & Taylor printers, New Haven, 1889.
Death: (1) Original Record of Maine Towns & Cities, Town of Embden, Disk 1, Page 100, Picton Press, Rockland Maine, Copyright 2005; (2) Original Record of Maine Towns & Cities, Town of Embden, Disk 2, Page 8, Picton Press, Rockland Maine, Copyright 2005; (3) "History of the Descendants of John Whitman of Weymouth, Mass" by Charles H. Farnam, A.M., Page 854. Tuttle, Morehouse & Taylor printers, New Haven, 1889; (4) "Maine, Faylene Hutton Cemetery Collection, ca. 1780-1990," database with images, FamilySearch, (https://familysearch. org/ark: /61903/1:1: QKM1-S3RD).
Graveyard: (1) "Maine, Faylene Hutton Cemetery Collection, ca. 1780-1990," database with images, FamilySearch, (https://familysearch.org/ark:/61903/1:1:QKM1-S3RD); (2) Find A Grave, Memorial #70902605.

Historical Accounts: (1) 1830 United States Federal Census for Embden, Somerset, Maine; (2) 1840 United States Federal Census for Embden, Somerset, Maine; (3) 1850 United States Federal Census for Embden, Somerset, Maine; (4) 1860 United States Federal Census for Embden, Somerset, Maine, Page 55; (5) 1880 United States Federal Census for Embden, Somerset, Maine, Page 4; (6) "Embden Town of Yore" by Ernest George Walker, Published by Independent-Reporter Company, Skowhegan, Maine, 1929; (7) "Maine, Wills and Probate Records, 1584-1999 ", [database on-line]. Provo, UT, USA: Ancestry.com Operations Inc, 2015, Somerset County Probate Records, Volume 54, 1878-1884, Pages 590 & 591.

Zachariah Williams
(1809 - 1898)

Zachariah was the fifth child of Caleb Williams and Elizabeth Whitman. He was born in Embden, Somerset, Maine on June 11, 1809. (Somerset County was set off from Kennebec County in 1809)

On October 14, 1830 Zachariah, age twenty-one, was married to Sarah Ann McFaden, age twenty, in Embden by Christopher Thompson, a Justice of the Peace. Sarah Ann, the daughter of John McFaden and Lucy Dunlap, was born on January 21, 1810 in Starks, Somerset, Maine.

During their marriage Zachariah and Sarah Ann had six children together.

Arminda	*b. April 20, 1831*	*d. May 18, 1831*
Cornelia	b. December 13, 1832	d. December 6, 1860
Llewellyn	*b. May 2, 1835*	*d. February 17, 1842*
Lucy Ellen	b. July 10, 1837	d. April 27, 1902
Elizabeth	b. May 13, 1839	d. April 15, 1932
Tilson	*b. July 27, 1841*	*d. December 16, 1846*

Arminda, the first child of Zachariah and Sarah Ann, died on May 18, 1831 when she was just twenty-eight days old. The cause and place of her death are not known. She was buried in the Pleasantdale Cemetery in Embden.

Between the years of 1837 and 1843, Zachariah served as a Lieutenant in Company D of the East Embden Militia.

In the 1840 United States Census Zachariah, Sarah Ann and their children were listed as living in Embden.

On February 17, 1842 Llewellyn, the third child of Zachariah and Sarah Ann, died when he was six years and eight months old. The cause and place of his death are also not known. He was buried with his sister Arminda in Embden at the Pleasantdale Cemetery.

Two months later, on April 13, 1842, Sarah Ann died at age thirty-two. The place and cause of her death have also not been found. She was buried in the family plot at the Pleasantdale Cemetery in Embden alongside her children Arminda and Llewellyn.

Gravestones for Arminda & Llewellyn Williams (left)
and Sarah Ann McFaden (right)
(Photographs Courtesy of Rick Rollins)

On March 21, 1843, not quite a year after his first wife's death, Zachariah, then age thirty-two, married Nancy (Berry) Wells, age twenty-seven, the widow of Horace Wells. Nancy, born on February 16, 1816 in Concord, Somerset, Maine, was the daughter of Samuel Berry and Mary Howard.

Zachariah had six more children with his second wife Nancy.

Matilda	b. September 26, 1843	d. August 1879
Sarah	b. April 30, 1845	d. 1937
Harriet T.	b. June 28, 1847	d. November 24, 1877
Joel	*b. April 7, 1849*	*d. March 12, 1866*
Marietta	b. October 22, 1852	d. March 29, 1912
Webster	b. March 29, 1856	d. 1934

The sixth child of Zachariah and his first wife Sarah Ann, Tilson, was five years and five months old when he died on December 16, 1846. Like his mother and two siblings the cause and place of his death are not known. He too was buried in the family plot at the Pleasantdale Cemetery in Embden.

When the 1850 United States Federal Census was taken, Zachariah and Nancy were listed as living in Embden where he was a "farmer". However, in the 1860 United States Federal Census they were listed as living and farming in Concord (This from all indications is the same location with a different town name used for the census).

In 1856, like others in his family, Zachariah served as a Selectman for the Town of Embden.

Joel, the fourth child of Zachariah and his second wife Nancy died on March 12, 1866 when he was sixteen years old. The place and cause of his death have also not been found. He too was buried in Embden at the Pleasantdale Cemetery.

Gravestones for Tilson Williams (left) and Joel Williams (right)
(Photographs Courtesy of Rick Rollins)

The 1870 United States Federal Census recorded Zachariah and Nancy and their family as still living and farming in Embden.

By the time the 1880 United States Federal Census was taken, Zachariah and Nancy had moved and were recorded as living with their son Webster and his wife in North Anson, Somerset, Maine.

On December 20, 1898 at the age of eighty-nine Zachariah died of "senility" in Anson, Somerset, Maine. He was buried in the Sunset Cemetery in North Anson.

When the 1900 United States Federal Census was taken on June 9, 1900, Nancy was recorded as still living with her son Webster and his wife in North Anson. She died in Anson fifteen days later, on June 24th, of "heart disease" at the age of eighty-four. Nancy was buried alongside her husband Zachariah in the Sunset Cemetery in North Anson.

Gravestone for Zachariah Williams and Nancy Berry
(Photograph from the Collection of Jeffrey Nelson Williams and Jacqueline Pon Williams)

SOURCES:

Zachariah Williams
Birth: (1) Original Record of Maine Towns & Cities, Town of Embden, Disk 1, Page 119, Picton Press, Rockland Maine, Copyright 2005; (2) "History of the Descendants of John Whitman of Weymouth, Mass" by Charles H. Farnam, A.M., Page 855, Tuttle, Morehouse & Taylor printers, New Haven, 1889; (3) "Maine, Births and Christenings, 1739-1900," index, FamilySearch, (https://familysearch.org/pal:/MM9.1.1/F4Q4-YT1).
Death: (1) Record of Death, Maine Vital Records; (2) Gravestone.
Graveyard: (1) Burial Records, Sunset Cemetery, North Anson, Maine; (2) "Maine Old Cemetery Association Special Publication Number 12, Edition No. 1: Series 1, 2 and 3", Page 169, Picton Press, Rockland, Maine, Copyright 2006; (3) Find A Grave, Memorial #130465326.

Sarah Ann McFaden
Birth: (1) Original Record of Maine Towns & Cities, Town of Embden, Disk 1, Page 115, Picton Press, Rockland Maine, Copyright 2005; (2) "History of the Descendants of John Whitman of Weymouth, Mass" by Charles H. Farnam, A.M., Page 855, Tuttle, Morehouse & Taylor printers, New Haven, 1889.
Marriage: (1) "Maine, Marriages, 1771-1907," index, FamilySearch, (https://familysearch.org/pal:/MM9.1.1 /F462-2HM); (2) "Embden Town of Yore" by Ernest George Walker, Page 704, Published by Independent-Reporter Company, Skowhegan, Maine, 1929; (3) Original Record of Maine Towns & Cities, Town of Embden, Disk 2, Page 31, Picton Press, Rockland Maine, Copyright 2005; (4) "History of the Descendants of John Whitman of Weymouth, Mass" by Charles H. Farnam, A.M., Page 855, Tuttle, Morehouse & Taylor printers, New Haven, 1889.
Death: (1) "History of the Descendants of John Whitman of Weymouth, Mass" by Charles H. Farnam, A.M., Page 855, Tuttle, Morehouse & Taylor printers, New Haven, 1889; (2) Gravestone.
Graveyard: (1) "Pleasant Dale/Murphy/Boothby Cemetery" complied by Nancy Hamlin Davis and Ruth Hamlin, Record 119, Old Canada Road Historical Society; (2) Find A Grave, Memorial #118447262.

Arminda Williams
Birth: (1) Original Record of Maine Towns & Cities, Town of Embden, Disk 1, Page 98, Picton Press, Rockland Maine, Copyright 2005; (2) "History of the Descendants of John Whitman of Weymouth, Mass" by Charles H. Farnam, A.M., Page 855, Tuttle, Morehouse & Taylor printers, New Haven, 1889.
Death: (1) Original Record of Maine Towns & Cities, Town of Embden, Disk 1, Page 98, Picton Press, Rockland Maine Copyright 2005; (2) "History of the Descendants of John Whitman of Weymouth, Mass" by Charles H. Farnam, A.M., Page 855, Tuttle, Morehouse & Taylor printers, New Haven, 1889; (3) Gravestone.
Graveyard: (1) "Pleasant Dale/Murphy/Boothby Cemetery" complied by Nancy Hamlin Davis and Ruth Hamlin, Record 120, Old Canada Road Historical Society; (2) Find A Grave, Memorial #118447331.

Llewellyn Williams
Birth: (1) Original Record of Maine Towns & Cities, Town of Embden, Disk 1, Page 98, Picton Press, Rockland Maine, Copyright 2005; (2) "History of the Descendants of John Whitman of Weymouth, Mass" by Charles H. Farnam, A.M., Page 855, Tuttle, Morehouse & Taylor printers, New Haven, 1889.
Death: (1) "History of the Descendants of John Whitman of Weymouth, Mass" by Charles H. Farnam, A.M., Page 855, Tuttle, Morehouse & Taylor printers, New Haven, 1889; (2) Gravestone.
Graveyard: (1) "Pleasant Dale/Murphy/Boothby Cemetery" complied by Nancy Hamlin Davis and Ruth Hamlin, Record 121, Old Canada Road Historical Society; (2) Find A Grave, Memorial #118447377.

Tilson Williams
Birth: (1) Original Record of Maine Towns & Cities, Town of Embden, Disk 1, Page 98, Picton Press, Rockland Maine, Copyright 2005; (2) "History of the Descendants of John Whitman of Weymouth, Mass" by Charles H. Farnam, A.M., Page 856, Tuttle, Morehouse & Taylor printers, New Haven, 1889.
Death: (1) "History of the Descendants of John Whitman of Weymouth, Mass" by Charles H. Farnam, A.M., Page 856, Tuttle, Morehouse & Taylor printers, New Haven, 1889; (2) Gravestone.
Graveyard: (1) "Pleasant Dale/Murphy/Boothby Cemetery" complied by Nancy Hamlin Davis and Ruth Hamlin, Record 122, Old Canada Road Historical Society; (2) Find A Grave, Memorial #118447441.

Nancy Berry
Birth: (1) Original Record of Maine Towns & Cities, Town of Concord, Page 98, Picton Press, Rockland Maine, Copyright 2005; (2) "History of the Descendants of John Whitman of Weymouth, Mass" by Charles H. Farnam, A.M., Page 855, Tuttle, Morehouse & Taylor printers, New Haven, 1889.
Marriage: (1) "Embden Town of Yore" by Ernest George Walker, Page 708, Published by Independent-Reporter Company, Skowhegan, Maine, 1929; (2) "South of Lost Nation" by Ernest George Walker, Page 21, Washington D.C., July 4, 1939, Retyped in 1994-1995 by Dean Lyons for the Embden Historical Society.
Death: (1) Record of Death, Maine Vital Records; (2) Gravestone.
Graveyard: (1) Burial Records, Sunset Cemetery, North Anson, Maine; (2) "Maine Old Cemetery Association Special Publication Number 12, Edition No. 1: Series 1, 2 and 3", Page 169, Picton Press, Rockland, Maine, Copyright 2006; (3) Find A Grave, Memorial #130465363.

Joel Williams
Birth: "History of the Descendants of John Whitman of Weymouth, Mass" by Charles H. Farnam, A.M., Page 856, Tuttle, Morehouse & Taylor printers, New Haven, 1889.
Death: (1) "History of the Descendants of John Whitman of Weymouth, Mass" by Charles H. Farnam, A.M., Page 856, Tuttle, Morehouse & Taylor printers, New Haven, 1889; (2) Gravestone.
Graveyard: (1) "Pleasant Dale/Murphy/Boothby Cemetery" complied by Nancy Hamlin Davis and Ruth Hamlin, Record 123, Old Canada Road Historical Society; (2) Find A Grave, Memorial #118447474.

Historical Accounts: (1) 1840 United States Federal Census for Embden, Somerset, Maine; (2) 1850 United States Federal Census for Embden, Somerset, Maine; (3) 1860 United States Federal Census for Concord, Somerset, Maine, Page 65; (4) 1870 United States Federal Census for Embden, Somerset, Maine, Page 8; (5) 1880 United States Federal Census for North Anson, Somerset, Maine, Page 6; (6) 1900 United States Federal Census for Anson, Somerset, Maine, Page 9; (7) "Embden Town of Yore" by Ernest George Walker, Pages 120 & 606, Published by Independent-Reporter Company, Skowhegan, Maine, 1929.

Amos Williams
(1811 - 1883)

The sixth child of Caleb Williams and Elizabeth Whitman was Amos, who was born on February 26, 1811 in Embden, Somerset, Maine.

In the 1840 United States Census Amos was recorded as living in Embden in his own household.

Shortly after the 1840 census was taken, on February 1, 1841, Amos, age thirty, and Albina Rowe, age twenty-one, filed their intentions to be married with the Town Clerks of Embden and Concord, Somerset, Maine. They were subsequently granted a marriage certificate in Embden on February 14th. Albina, born in Concord on July 19, 1820, was the daughter of Paul Rowe and Mary Stevens.

Amos Williams and Albina Rowe
(Photographs from "Embden Town of Yore" by Ernest George Walker, 1929)

Amos and Albina had nine children together who were all born in Embden.

Celestia	b. December 29, 1841	d. October 29, 1906
Sumner	*b. July 28, 1843*	*d. August 7, 1843*
Marshall L.	b. January 30, 1845	d. August 10, 1923
Esther	b. December 28, 1846	d. January 16, 1892
Effie A.	b. January 18, 1850	d. November 15, 1933
Freeman R.	b. October 27, 1852	d. 1929
Frederick Amos	b. August 20, 1856	d. December 17, 1894
Mary S.	b. August 2, 1858	d.
Flora S.	b. September 18, 1860	d. 1934

The second child of Amos and Albina, Sumner, died on August 7, 1843 when he was 10 days old. His cause and place of death have not been found. He was buried at the Pleasantdale Cemetery in Embden.

Gravestone for Sumner Williams
(Photograph from the Collection of Jeffrey Nelson Williams and Jacqueline Pon Williams)

Amos, like many of the Williams family, had significant farm holdings in the Embden area. The size and value of his holdings were reflected in the 1850 and 1860 United States Census' for Embden where Amos, Albina and their children were recorded as living on their family farm.

Albina died of on April 2, 1862 at the age of thirty-two. The cause and place of her death have not been found. She was buried at Embden in the Pleasantdale Cemetery.

When the 1870 and 1880 United States Census' were taken, Amos and some of his children were recorded as still living on the family farm in Embden.

Amos outlived his wife by twenty-one years. He died of an unknown cause and unknown place on May 8, 1883, at age seventy-two. He was buried in Embden at the Pleasantdale Cemetery in the same plot as his wife Albina and son Sumner.

Gravestones for Amos Williams (left) and Albina Rowe (right)
(Photographs from the Collection of Jeffrey Nelson Williams and Jacqueline Pon Williams)

SOURCES:

Amos Williams
Birth: (1) Original Record of Maine Towns & Cities, Town of Embden, Disk 1, Page 119, Picton Press, Rockland Maine, Copyright 2005; (2) Original Record of Maine Towns & Cities, Town of Embden, Disk 1, Page 98, Picton Press, Rockland Maine, Copyright 2005; (3) "History of the Descendants of John Whitman of Weymouth, Mass" by Charles H. Farnam, A.M., Page 856, Tuttle, Morehouse & Taylor printers, New Haven, 1889.
Death: (1) "History of the Descendants of John Whitman of Weymouth, Mass" by Charles H. Farnam, A.M., Page 856, Tuttle, Morehouse & Taylor printers, New Haven, 1889; (2) "Maine, Faylene Hutton Cemetery Collection, ca. 1780-1990," database with images, FamilySearch, (https://familysearch.org/ark:/61903/1:1:QKM1-WKKX) - Accession #5030; (3) Gravestone.
Graveyard: (1) "Pleasant Dale/Murphy/Boothby Cemetery" complied by Nancy Hamlin Davis and Ruth Hamlin, Record 60, Old Canada Road Historical Society; (2) "Maine Old Cemetery Association Special Publication Number 12, Edition No. 1: Series 1, 2 and 3", Page 558, Picton Press, Rockland, Maine, Copyright 2006; (3) Find A Grave, Memorial #118293297.

Albina Rowe
Birth: (1) Original Record of Maine Towns & Cities, Town of Concord, Page 79, Picton Press, Rockland Maine, Copyright 2005; (2) Original Record of Maine Towns & Cities, Town of Embden, Disk 1, Page 98, Picton Press, Rockland Maine, Copyright 2005; (3) "Maine, Births and Christenings, 1739-1900," FamilySearch, https://familysearch.org/pal: /MM9.1.1 /F4Q4-P2B.
Marriage: (1) "Maine, Marriages, 1771-1907," index, FamilySearch, (https://familysearch.org/pal:/MM9.1.1 /F462-2TB); (2) "Embden Town of Yore" by Ernest George Walker, Page 703, Published by Independent-Reporter Company, Skowhegan, Maine, 1929; (3) Original Record of Maine Towns & Cities, Town of Concord, Page 137, Picton Press, Rockland Maine, Copyright 2005; Original Record of Maine Towns & Cities, Town of Embden, Disk 1, Page 363, Picton Press, Rockland Maine, Copyright 2005.
Death: (1) "History of the Descendants of John Whitman of Weymouth, Mass" by Charles H. Farnam, A.M., Page 856, Tuttle, Morehouse & Taylor printers, New Haven, 1889; (2) "Maine, Faylene Hutton Cemetery Collection, ca. 1780-1990," database with images, FamilySearch, (https://familysearch.org/ark:/61903/1:1:QKM1-WKKX) - Accession #5030; (3) Gravestone.
Graveyard: (1) "Pleasant Dale/Murphy/Boothby Cemetery" complied by Nancy Hamlin Davis and Ruth Hamlin, Record 61, Old Canada Road Historical Society; (2). "Maine Old Cemetery Association Special Publication Number 12, Edition No. 1: Series 1, 2 and 3", Page 558, Picton Press, Rockland, Maine, Copyright 2006; (3) Find A Grave, Memorial #118293429.

Sumner Williams
Birth: (1) "History of the Descendants of John Whitman of Weymouth, Mass" by Charles H. Farnam, A.M., Page 857, Tuttle, Morehouse & Taylor printers, New Haven, 1889; (2) Gravestone.
Death: (1) "History of the Descendants of John Whitman of Weymouth, Mass" by Charles H. Farnam, A.M., Page 857, Tuttle, Morehouse & Taylor printers, New Haven, 1889; (2) "Maine, Faylene Hutton Cemetery Collection, ca. 1780-1990," database with images, FamilySearch, (https://familysearch.org/ark:/61903/1:1:QKM1-WKKX) - Accession #5030; (3) Gravestone.
Graveyard: (1) "Pleasant Dale/Murphy/Boothby Cemetery" complied by Nancy Hamlin Davis and Ruth Hamlin, Record 62, Old Canada Road Historical Society; (2). "Maine Old Cemetery Association Special Publication Number 12, Edition No. 1: Series 1, 2 and 3", Page 558, Picton Press, Rockland, Maine, Copyright 2006; (3) Find A Grave, Memorial #118293462.

Historical Accounts: (1) 1840 United States Federal Census for Embden, Somerset, Maine; (2) 1850 United States Federal Census for Embden, Somerset, Maine; (3) 1860 United States Federal Census for Embden, Somerset, Maine, Page 56; (4) 1870 United States Federal Census for Embden, Somerset, Maine, Page 6; (5) 1880 United States Federal Census for Embden, Somerset, Maine, Page 7; (6) "Embden Town of Yore" by Ernest George Walker, Pages 23 & 120, Published by Independent-Reporter Company, Skowhegan, Maine, 1929.

Foster Williams
(1812 - 1884)

Foster was the seventh child of Caleb Williams and Elizabeth Whitman. He was born in Embden, Somerset, Maine on November 20, 1812.

On October 17, 1834 Foster, age twenty-one, and eighteen-year-old Elsa Ayer filed their banns of matrimony with the Town Clerk of Embden. They were subsequently married, at a location not known, on November 3, 1834. Elsa (commonly known as Elsie), the daughter of Stephen Ayer and Zilphia Eames, was born on May 16, 1816 in Solon, Somerset, Maine.

Foster and Elsa had eight children together.

Adeline G. (a twin)	b. February 28, 1835	d. March 12, 1911
Ai Cotman (a twin)	b. February 28, 1835	d. January 10, 1887
Betsey W.	*b. February 23, 1837*	*d. January 23, 1859*
Paulinus Foster	b. February 11, 1839	d. January 15, 1914
Priscilla A.	b. June 13, 1841	d. 1929
Delora Arvilla	b. June 29, 1845	d. February 11, 1919
Isora D.	b. March 20, 1847	d. September 20, 1899
Angela	b. December 25, 1856	d. February 22, 1934

The 1840 United States Federal Census recorded Foster, Elsa and their first four children as living in Embden,

When the 1850 United States Federal Census was taken Foster, Elsa and their family had moved to Jackman, Somerset, Maine. In that census Foster's occupation was listed as "inn holder".

The third child of Foster and Elsa, Betsey W., died at the age of twenty-one on January 23, 1859. The cause and place of her death have not been found. Additionally, there is no record of her marrying or having had children. Betsey W. was buried in the Village Cemetery in Solon.

At the time of the 1860 United States Federal Census Foster, Elsa and their children had moved to Solon. Foster's occupation in that census document was listed as a "dealer in farm produce".

Elsa died in Solon on January 11, 1869 at the age of fifty-two. The cause of her death is also not known. She was buried in the family plot in the Village Cemetery in Solon alongside her daughter Betsey W.

After Elsa's death, when the 1870 United States Federal Census was taken, Foster was working as a "stage driver" and living in Solon with his two youngest daughters.

On August 14, 1871, at age fifty-six, Foster and Rosilla Ann (Smith) Jewett, age forty-seven, filed their intentions to be married with the Town Clerk of Solon. They were married in Solon five days later, on August 19th, by Henry Crockett, a Clergyman. Born on December 7, 1823 in Solon, Rosilla Ann was the daughter of Benjamin Smith and Betsey Parkman. She had previously been married to William Jewett from whom she was divorced in 1869. Foster and his second wife Rosilla Ann did not have any children together.

Foster and Rosilla Ann were recorded as living in Solon at the time of the 1880 United States Federal Census in which he was listed as working as a "laborer".

Four years later Foster died in Solon on October 25, 1884 at age seventy-one. The cause of his death has not been found. He was also buried in the Village Cemetery in Solon.

Rosilla Ann outlived her husband by eleven years dying on December 18, 1895 at the age of seventy-two. The place and cause of her death have not been found. She was buried in the Jewett cemetery in Madison, Somerset, Maine with her first husband.

Gravestone for Betsey W. Williams
(Photograph from the Collection of Jeffrey Nelson Williams and Jacqueline Pon Williams)

**Gravestones for Foster Williams (top left), Elsa Ayer (top right)
and Rosilla Ann Smith (bottom)**
(Photographs from the Collection of Jeffrey Nelson Williams and Jacqueline Pon Williams)

SOURCES:

Foster Williams
Birth: (1) Original Record of Maine Towns & Cities, Town of Embden, Disk 1, Page 119, Picton Press, Rockland Maine, Copyright 2005; (2) "History of the Descendants of John Whitman of Weymouth Mass." by Charles H. Farnam, A. M., Page 857, Printed by Tuttle, Morehouse and Taylor Printers, 1889.
Death: (1) "History of the Descendants of John Whitman of Weymouth Mass." by Charles H. Farnam, A. M., Page 857, Printed by Tuttle, Morehouse and Taylor Printers, 1889; (2) Gravestone.
Graveyard: Find A Grave, Memorial #85615498.

Elsa Ayer
Birth: (1) Original Record of Maine Towns & Cities, Town of Solon, Page 18, Picton Press, Rockland Maine, Copyright 2005; (2) Original Record of Maine Towns & Cities, Town of Embden, Disk 1, Page 122, Picton Press, Rockland Maine, Copyright 2005; (3) "History of the Descendants of John Whitman of Weymouth Mass." by Charles H. Farnam, A. M., Page 857, Printed by Tuttle, Morehouse and Taylor Printers, 1889.
Marriage: (1) Original Record of Maine Towns & Cities, Town of Embden, Disk 1, Page 367, Picton Press, Rockland Maine, Copyright 2005; (2) "Maine, Marriages, 1771-1907," index, FamilySearch, (https://familysearch.org/pal:/MM9.1.1/F462-KYS); (3) "History of the Descendants of John Whitman of Weymouth Mass." by Charles H. Farnam, A. M., Page 857, Printed by Tuttle, Morehouse and Taylor Printers, 1889; (4) "Embden Town of Yore" by Ernest George Walker, Page 706, Published by Independent-Reporter Company, Skowhegan, Maine, 1929.
Death: (1) "History of the Descendants of John Whitman of Weymouth Mass." by Charles H. Farnam, A. M., Page 857, Printed by Tuttle, Morehouse and Taylor Printers, 1889; (2) Gravestone.
Graveyard: Find A Grave, Memorial #85615561.

Betsey W. Williams
Birth: (1) Original Record of Maine Towns & Cities, Town of Embden, Disk 2 Page 18, Picton Press, Rockland Maine, Copyright 2005; (2) "History of the Descendants of John Whitman of Weymouth Mass." by Charles H. Farnam, A. M., Page 857, Printed by Tuttle, Morehouse and Taylor Printers, 1889.
Death: (1) "History of the Descendants of John Whitman of Weymouth Mass." by Charles H. Farnam, A. M., Page 857, Printed by Tuttle, Morehouse and Taylor Printers, 1889; (2) Gravestone.
Graveyard: Find A Grave, Memorial #85615654.

Rosilla Ann Smith
Birth:
Marriage: (1) Original Record of Maine Towns & Cities, Town of Solon, Page 150, Picton Press, Rockland Maine, Copyright 2005; (2) "Maine, Marriages, 1771-1907," database, FamilySearch, (https://familysearch.org/ark: /61903/1:1: F4F1-M6P); (3) "History of the Descendants of John Whitman of Weymouth Mass." by Charles H. Farnam, A. M., Page 857, Printed by Tuttle, Morehouse and Taylor Printers, 1889.
Death: Gravestone.
Graveyard: (1) "Jewett Cemetery", updated by Dassie Jackson and Lena Arno in 2002 and 2003, page 7, Madison Historical Society; (2) Find A Grave, Memorial #53040922.

Historical Accounts: (1) 1840 United States Federal Census for Embden, Somerset, Maine; (2) 1850 United States Federal Census for Jackman, Somerset, Maine; (3) 1860 United States Federal Census for Solon, Somerset, Maine, Page 46; (4) 1870 United States Federal Census for Solon, Somerset, Maine, Page 30; (5) 1880 United States Federal Census for Solon, Somerset, Maine, Page 9; (6) "History of Moose River Valley", Page 37, Reprinted in 1994 by The Jackman Moose River Valley Historical Society.

Warren Williams
(1814 - 1884)

The eighth child of Caleb Williams and Elizabeth Whitman was Warren. He was born in Embden, Somerset, Maine on July 1, 1814.

In the 1840 United States Census Warren was recorded as living in Embden in his own household.

Warren, age thirty-three, was married to Sarah Ann Lewis, age twenty, in Industry, Franklin, Maine on March 3, 1848 by Asaph Boyden, a Justice of the Peace. Sarah Ann was born in Industry on March 11, 1828. The names of her parents have not been found.

Warren and Sarah Ann had eleven children together.

Rose Ella	*b. February 12, 1849*	*d. August 14, 1870*
Hattie M.	*b. August 12, 1850*	*d. August 28, 1870*
David Lewis	b. September 24, 1854	d. February 23, 1934
Joseph G.	b. May 29, 1856	d. July 23, 1936
Sarah Lizzie	*b. March 21, 1859*	*d. October 28, 1876*
Lewis Warren	b. August 23, 1861	d. May 5, 1947
Ellen C.	b. August 14, 1863	d. June 7, 1894
Eugene M.	b. April 17, 1865	d. November 10, 1893
Bert C.	b. February 13, 1868	d. December 8, 1951
Arthur M. (a twin)	*b. April 27, 1870*	*d.*
Mary M. (a twin)	*b. April 27, 1870*	*d.*

At the time of the 1850 United States Census Warren, Sarah Ann and their first child Rose Ella were recorded as living in Waterville, Kennebec, Maine where Warren was working as a "stable hand".

By the time the 1860 United States Federal Census was taken Warren, Sarah Ann and their children had moved back to Embden. They were still living there at the time of the 1870 United States Federal Census. Like many of the Williams of Somerset County Maine, Warren's occupation was listed as a "farmer" in those censuses.

Three of Warren and Sarah Ann's children died in the 1870's. Their first child, Rose Ella, died on August 14, 1870 when she was twenty-one years old, their second child, Hattie M., died on August 28, 1870 when she was twenty and their fifth child, Sarah Lizzie, was seventeen when she died on October 23, 1876. The causes and locations of their deaths have not been found. All three of these children had not yet married and were buried in the Warren Williams family plot at the Pleasantdale Cemetery in Embden.

**Gravestone for Rose Ella Williams, Hattie M. Williams
and Sarah Lizzie Williams**
(Photograph from the Collection of Jeffrey Nelson Williams and Jacqueline Pon Williams)

Additional information regarding the lives and deaths of the tenth and eleventh children of Warren and Sarah Ann, the twins Arthur M. and Mary M., beyond their listing in the 1870 census has not been found. It is presumed that they died in infancy and as such their documented history will end here.

Sarah Ann died on June 26, 1876 at the age of forty-eight. The cause and location of her death are not known. She was buried in the family plot in the Pleasantdale Cemetery in Embden.

In the 1880 United States Census Warren was recorded as living in Anson, Somerset, Maine with his late sister Charlotte's husband, Jonah Houghton and Jonah's second wife. Warren's occupation was recorded as "works on farm".

Warren survived his wife Sarah Ann by eight years. On February 14, 1884, Warren died at age sixty-nine and was buried in the Pleasantdale Cemetery in Embden. The cause and location of his death have not been found.

Gravestone for Warren Williams and Sarah Ann Lewis
(Photograph from the Collection of Jeffrey Nelson Williams and Jacqueline Pon Williams)

SOURCES:

Warren Williams
Birth: (1) Original Record of Maine Towns & Cities, Town of Embden, Disk 1, Page 119, Picton Press, Rockland Maine, Copyright 2005; (2) "History of the Descendants of John Whitman of Weymouth Mass." by Charles H. Farnam, A. M., Page 858, Printed by Tuttle, Morehouse and Taylor Printers, 1889.
Death: (1) "History of the Descendants of John Whitman of Weymouth Mass." by Charles H. Farnam, A. M., Page 858, Printed by Tuttle, Morehouse and Taylor Printers, 1889; (2) "Maine, Faylene Hutton Cemetery Collection, ca. 1780-1990," database with images, FamilySearch, (https://familysearch.org/ark:/61903/1:1:QKM1-W2JP) - Accession #5030; (3) Gravestone.
Graveyard: (1) "Pleasant Dale/Murphy/Boothby Cemetery" complied by Nancy Hamlin Davis and Ruth Hamlin, Record 9, Old Canada Road Historical Society; (2) "Maine Old Cemetery Association Special Publication Number 12, Edition No. 1: Series 1, 2 and 3", Page 558, Picton Press, Rockland, Maine, Copyright 2006; (3) Find A Grave, Memorial #118232606.

Sarah Ann Lewis
Birth: "History of the Descendants of John Whitman of Weymouth Mass." by Charles H. Farnam, A. M., Page 858, Printed by Tuttle, Morehouse and Taylor Printers, 1889.
Marriage: (1) Record of Marriage, Maine Vital Records; (2) "History of the Descendants of John Whitman of Weymouth Mass." by Charles H. Farnam, A. M., Page 858, Printed by Tuttle, Morehouse and Taylor Printers, 1889; (3) "Maine, Marriages, 1771-1907," index, FamilySearch, (https://familysearch.org/pal:/MM9.1.1/F4FD-TXY); (4) "Embden Town of Yore" by Ernest George Walker, Page 712, Published by Independent-Reporter Company, Skowhegan, Maine, 1929.
Death: (1) "History of the Descendants of John Whitman of Weymouth Mass." by Charles H. Farnam, A. M., Page 858, Printed by Tuttle, Morehouse and Taylor Printers, 1889; (2) "Maine, Faylene Hutton Cemetery Collection, ca. 1780-1990," database with images, FamilySearch, (https://familysearch.org/ark:/61903/1:1:QKM1-W2JP) - Accession #5030; (3) Gravestone.
Graveyard: (1) "Pleasant Dale/Murphy/Boothby Cemetery" complied by Nancy Hamlin Davis and Ruth Hamlin, Record 10, Old Canada Road Historical Society; (2) "Maine Old Cemetery Association Special Publication Number 12, Edition No. 1: Series 1, 2 and 3", Page 558, Picton Press, Rockland, Maine, Copyright 2006; (3) Find A Grave, Memorial #118232662.

Rose Ella Williams
Birth: "History of the Descendants of John Whitman of Weymouth Mass." by Charles H. Farnam, A. M., Page 858, Printed by Tuttle, Morehouse and Taylor Printers, 1889.
Death: "History of the Descendants of John Whitman of Weymouth Mass." by Charles H. Farnam, A. M., Page 858, Printed by Tuttle, Morehouse and Taylor Printers, 1889.
Graveyard: (1) "Pleasant Dale/Murphy/Boothby Cemetery" complied by Nancy Hamlin Davis and Ruth Hamlin, Record 11, Old Canada Road Historical Society; (2) Find A Grave, Memorial #118232712.

Hattie M. Williams
Birth: "History of the Descendants of John Whitman of Weymouth Mass." by Charles H. Farnam, A. M., Page 858, Printed by Tuttle, Morehouse and Taylor Printers, 1889.
Death: "History of the Descendants of John Whitman of Weymouth Mass." by Charles H. Farnam, A. M., Page 858, Printed by Tuttle, Morehouse and Taylor Printers, 1889.
Graveyard: (1) "Pleasant Dale/Murphy/Boothby Cemetery" complied by Nancy Hamlin Davis and Ruth Hamlin, Record 12, Old Canada Road Historical Society; (2) Find A Grave, Memorial #118232790.

Sarah Lizzie Williams
Birth: "History of the Descendants of John Whitman of Weymouth Mass." by Charles H. Farnam, A. M., Page 858, Printed by Tuttle, Morehouse and Taylor Printers, 1889.
Death: "History of the Descendants of John Whitman of Weymouth Mass." by Charles H. Farnam, A. M., Page 858, Printed by Tuttle, Morehouse and Taylor Printers, 1889.
Graveyard: (1) "Pleasant Dale/Murphy/Boothby Cemetery" complied by Nancy Hamlin Davis and Ruth Hamlin, Record 13, Old Canada Road Historical Society; (2) Find A Grave, Memorial #118232830.

Arthur M. Williams
Birth: "History of the Descendants of John Whitman of Weymouth Mass." by Charles H. Farnam, A. M., Page 859, Printed by Tuttle, Morehouse and Taylor Printers, 1889.
Death:
Graveyard:

Mary M. Williams
Birth:
Death:
Graveyard:

Historical Accounts: (1) 1840 United States Federal Census for Embden, Somerset, Maine; (2) 1850 United States Federal Census for Waterville, Kennebec, Maine; (3) 1860 United States Federal Census for Embden, Somerset, Maine, Page 56; (4) 1870 United States Federal Census for Embden, Somerset, Maine, Page 130; (5) 1880 United States Federal Census for Anson, Somerset, Maine, Page 51.

Abigail Williams
(1817 - 1880)

Abigail, the ninth child of Caleb Williams and Elizabeth Whitman, was born in Embden, Somerset, Maine on February 2, 1817. She was the second child Caleb Williams and Elizabeth Whitman named Abigail (their first daughter named Abigail died at three years old in 1809).

At age twenty-nine Abigail and William Harrison Stevens, age thirty-one, filed their intentions to be married with the Town Clerk of Embden and were granted a marriage certificate in Embden on April 21, 1846. William Harrison, born on December 4, 1814 in Embden, was the son of Jonathan Stevens and Sarah Young.

During their marriage Abigail and William Harrison had two children together.

Corris A.	*b. 1851*	*d. March 2, 1867*
Milford Harrison	b. February 24, 1855	d. December 9, 1920

In the 1850 United States Federal Census Abigail and William Harrison were recorded as living in Embden. William Harrison's occupation was listed as "ferryman". That census document also listed a Caroline V. Stevens, age eleven, as living with Abigail and William Harrison. As she was born several years prior to Abigail and William Harrison's marriage and her birth records have not been found, it is not known who Caroline V.'s parents were.

When the 1860 United States Federal Census was taken, Abigail and William Harrison were recorded as still living in Embden, but William Harrison's occupation was now listed as "farmer".

The first child of Abigail and William Harrison, Corris A., died at age sixteen on March 2, 1867. The cause and place of her death are not known. She was buried in the Pleasantdale Cemetery in Embden.

Preceding his wife Abigail in death, William Harrison died on May 6, 1877 at the age of sixty-two. His cause and place of his death are also not known. He too was buried in Embden at the Pleasantdale Cemetery.

Abigail survived her husband William Harrison by three years, dying on January 7, 1880 of an unknown cause in Fairfield, Somerset, Maine at the age of sixty-two. She was also buried in Embden with her husband at the Pleasantdale Cemetery.

**Gravestones for Abigail Williams & William Harrison Stevens (left)
and Corris A. Stevens (right)**
(Photographs from the Collection of Jeffrey Nelson Williams and Jacqueline Pon Williams)

SOURCES:

Abigail Williams
Birth: (1) Original Record of Maine Towns & Cities, Town of Embden, Disk 1, Page 119, Picton Press, Rockland Maine, Copyright 2005; (2) "History of the Descendants of John Whitman of Weymouth Mass." by Charles H. Farnam, A. M., Page 858, Printed by Tuttle, Morehouse and Taylor Printers, 1889.
Death: (1) United States Federal Mortality Schedules 1850-1885 for Fairfield, Somerset, Maine, Page 1; (2) "History of the Descendants of John Whitman of Weymouth Mass." by Charles H. Farnam, A. M., Page 857, Printed by Tuttle, Morehouse and Taylor Printers, 1889; (3) "Maine, Faylene Hutton Cemetery Collection, ca. 1780-1990," database with images, FamilySearch, (https://familysearch.org/ark:/61903/1:1:QKM1-WLXL) - Accession #5030' (4) Gravestone.
Graveyard: (1) "Pleasant Dale/Murphy/Boothby Cemetery" complied by Nancy Hamlin Davis and Ruth Hamlin, Record 126, Old Canada Road Historical Society; (2) Find A Grave, Memorial #118447683.

William Harrison Stevens
Birth: Original Record of Maine Towns & Cities, Town of Embden, Disk 1, Page 112, Picton Press, Rockland Maine, Copyright 2005.
Marriage: (1) "Maine, Marriages, 1771-1907," index, FamilySearch, (https://familysearch.org/pal:/MM9.1.1 /F462-LZ3); (2) Original Record of Maine Towns & Cities, Town of Embden, Disk 2, Page 53, Picton Press, Rockland Maine, Copyright 2005; (3) "Embden Town of Yore" by Ernest George Walker, Page 711, Published by Independent-Reporter Company, Skowhegan, Maine, 1929.
Death: (1) "Maine, Faylene Hutton Cemetery Collection, ca. 1780-1990," database with images, FamilySearch, (https://familysearch.org/ark:/61903/1:1:QKM1-WLXL) - Accession #5030: (2) Gravestone.
Graveyard: (1) "Pleasant Dale/Murphy/Boothby Cemetery" complied by Nancy Hamlin Davis and Ruth Hamlin, Record 127, Old Canada Road Historical Society; (2) Find A Grave, Memorial #118447623.

Corris A. Stevens
Birth:
Death: (1) "Maine, Faylene Hutton Cemetery Collection, ca. 1780-1990," database with images, FamilySearch, (https://familysearch.org/ark:/61903/1:1:QKM1-WLXL) - Accession #5030; (2) Gravestone.
Graveyard: (1) "Pleasant Dale/Murphy/Boothby Cemetery" complied by Nancy Hamlin Davis and Ruth Hamlin, Record 128, Old Canada Road Historical Society; (2) Find A Grave, Memorial #118447726.

Historical Accounts: (1) 1850 United States Federal Census for Embden, Somerset, Maine; (2) 1860 United States Federal Census for Embden, Somerset, Maine, Page 55; (3) "History of the Descendants of John Whitman of Weymouth Mass." by Charles H. Farnam, A. M., Page 859, Printed by Tuttle, Morehouse and Taylor Printers, 1889.

Albert Williams
(1822 - 1867)

The twelfth child of Caleb Williams and Elizabeth Whitman was Albert. He was born on March 23, 1823 in Embden, Somerset, Maine and was the second child that Caleb Williams and Elizabeth Whitman named Albert (the first child they named Albert died at age twenty-one months old in 1820).

In the 1850 United States Federal Census Albert was listed as living with his father and mother in Embden and was working as a "farmer".

On June 30, 1852, at age twenty-nine, Albert and Ellen Atkinson, age sixteen, were issued a Certificate of Marriage by the Town Clerk of Embden. The exact date and place of their marriage has not been found. Ellen, born on August 4, 1835 in New Vineyard, Franklin, Maine, was the daughter of Christopher Atkinson and Betsey Johnson.

Albert and Ellen had five children during their marriage.

George Atkinson	b. February 16, 1855	d. February 2, 1877
Addie Frances	b. April 10, 1857	d. August 3, 1925
Albert Henry	b. May 9, 1859	d. January 8, 1940
Elizabeth Atkinson	b. May 28, 1861	d. February 1, 1918
Caroline E.	b. April 16, 1865	d. June 25, 1948

After they married Albert and Ellen lived on farm #43 in the Embden area, as recorded in the 1860 United States Federal Census. In 1865, after the birth of their fifth child, Caroline E., Albert and Ellen relocated their family to Baraboo, Sauk, Wisconsin.

Shortly after their arrival in Baraboo, on November 10, 1867, Albert died at age forty-five. The cause of his death has not been found. He was buried in the South Division of the Walnut Hill Cemetery in Baraboo.

After the death of Albert, Ellen, then age thirty-five, married Walworth Delavan Porter, age thirty, in Baraboo on April 7, 1870. Walworth Delavan, the son of Samuel Lyman Porter and Permelia Clark, was born in La Grange, Walworth, Wisconsin on June 1, 1839. Ellen and Walworth Delavan continued to live in Baraboo and had two children during their marriage.

Walworth Delavan, the second husband of Ellen, died on October 30, 1924 at St. Mary's-Ringling Hospital in Baraboo of a "critical illness". He was also buried in the South Division of the Walnut Hill Cemetery in Baraboo.

Ellen, who outlived two husbands, died at her home at 220 Eighth Street in Baraboo on July 22, 1929 at the age of ninety-three. Her obituary indicated that she had been in failing health for several years. Funeral services for Ellen were held at 2:00 P.M. on Thursday July 25th at Trinity Episcopal Church in Baraboo. She too was buried in Baraboo at the South Division of the Walnut Hill Cemetery along with her two husbands.

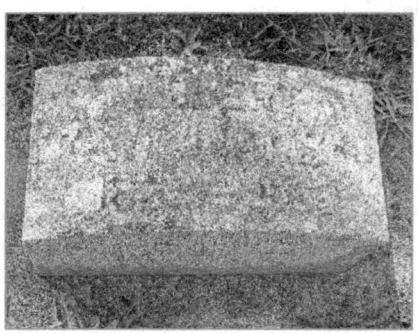

Headstones for Albert Williams (top), Ellen Atkinson (bottom left) and Walworth Delavan Porter (bottom right)
(Photographs Courtesy of Joan Kaul)

SOURCES:

Albert Williams
Birth: (1) Original Record of Maine Towns & Cities, Town of Embden, Disk 1, Page 119, Picton Press, Rockland Maine, Copyright 2005; (2) "History of the Descendants of John Whitman of Weymouth Mass." by Charles H. Farnam, A. M., Page 859, Printed by Tuttle, Morehouse and Taylor Printers, 1889.
Death "History of the Descendants of John Whitman of Weymouth Mass." by Charles H. Farnam, A. M., Page 859, Printed by Tuttle, Morehouse and Taylor Printers, 1889.
Graveyard: (1) Walnut Hill Cemetery Records, Interment.net; (2) Find A Grave, Memorial #70424057.

Ellen Atkinson
Birth: (1) Original Record of Maine Towns & Cities, Town of Embden, Disk 1, Page 105, Picton Press, Rockland Maine, Copyright 2005; (2) "History of the Descendants of John Whitman of Weymouth Mass." by Charles H. Farnam, A. M., Page 859, Printed by Tuttle, Morehouse and Taylor Printers, 1889.
Marriage: "Embden Town of Yore" by Ernest George Walker, Page 714, Published by Independent-Reporter Company, Skowhegan, Maine, 1929.
Death: Obituary, Madison Wisconsin State Journal, Madison, Wisconsin, Wednesday, July 24, 1929, Page 4.
Graveyard: (1) Walnut Hill Cemetery Records, Interment.net; (2) Find A Grave, Memorial #150837614.

Walworth Delavan Porter
Birth: (1) "A Standard History of Sauk County Wisconsin", Volume II, Page 570, The Lewis Publishing Company, Chicago and New York, 1918; (2) Obituary, The Wisconsin State Journal, Madison, Wisconsin, Thursday, October 30, 1924, Page 12.
Marriage: Marriage Index Record, Wisconsin Historical Society.
Death: Obituary, The Wisconsin State Journal, Madison, Wisconsin, Thursday, October 30, 1924, Page 12.
Graveyard: (1) Walnut Hill Cemetery Records, Interment.net; (2) Find A Grave, Memorial #150837434.

Historical Accounts: (1) 1850 United States Federal Census for Embden, Somerset, Maine; (2) 1860 United States Federal Census for Embden, Somerset, Maine, Page 54; (3) 1870 United States Federal Census for Baraboo, Sauk, Wisconsin, Page 36; (4) 1880 United States Federal Census for Baraboo, Sauk, Wisconsin, Page 44; (5) 1900 United States Federal Census for Baraboo, Sauk, Wisconsin, Page 8; (6) 1910 United States Federal Census for Baraboo, Sauk, Wisconsin, Page 8A; (7) 1920 United States Federal Census for Baraboo, Sauk, Wisconsin, Page 5A; (8) "A Standard History of Sauk County Wisconsin", Volume II, Pages 570, 571 & 572, The Lewis Publishing Company, Chicago and New York, 1918.

Cyrena Williams
(1824 - 1898)

Cyrena was the thirteenth child of Caleb Williams and Elizabeth Whitman. She was born in Embden, Somerset, Maine on June 27, 1824.

In the 1850 United States Federal Census Cyrena, then age twenty-five, was listed as living with her parents in Embden.

On March 27, 1852 at the age of twenty-seven, Cyrena and Jotham G. Witham of Embden, age thirty-three and the widower of the late Mercy Angeline Clark, were issued a Certificate of Marriage after filing their intentions to be married with the Town Clerk of Embden. Documentation of the date and place of their marriage has not been found. Jotham G., known locally as "Jote" and the son of Lemuel Witham and Abigail Savage, was born on November 26, 1818 in Embden. With her marriage to Jotham G., Cyrena became a stepmother to the two children that Jotham G. had with his first wife.

Jotham G. Witham
(Photograph from "Embden Town of Yore" by Ernest George Walker, 1929)

Cyrena and Jotham G. had eight children of their own together.

Eugene	*b. February 21, 1853*	*d. April 2, 1854*
Parker	b. March 27, 1855	d. October 21, 1929
Allen	*b. November 7, 1856*	*d. August 28, 1858*
Emma	*b. March 1, 1858*	*d. February 17, 1878*
Dassie	b. December 4, 1859	d. May 10, 1943
Grant	b. December 13, 1861	d. September 24, 1947
Lura	b. February 24, 1864	d. December 10, 1936
Ada Edith	b. December 31, 1865	d. November 28, 1938

Two of Cyrena and Jotham G.'s children died at young ages. Eugene, their first child, died on April 2, 1854 at age thirteen months and Allen, their third child, was one year and ten months when he died on August 28, 1858. The causes and places of death of both children are unknown. They were both buried in the Pleasantdale Cemetery in Embden.

Gravestones for Eugene Witham (left) and Allen Witham (right)
(Photographs from the Collection of Jeffrey Nelson Williams and Jacqueline Pon Williams)

In the 1860 United States Federal Census Cyrena and Jotham G. were listed as living in Embden. Cyrena was listed as "keeping house" and Jotham's occupation was listed as "farmer".

During the 1860's and 1870's Jotham G. served as a Captain in one of the local Embden militias, as a local Justice of the Peace, and in 1862, 1872 and 1874 as a Selectman for the town of Embden.

Emma, the fourth child of Cyrena and Jotham G., died on February 17, 1878 when she was nineteen years old and having never married. The cause and place of her death have not been found. She was also buried in Embden at the Pleasantdale Cemetery.

When the 1880 United States Federal Census was taken Cyrena, Jotham G. and their children were recorded as still living and farming in Embden.

On January 26, 1898 Cyrena, age seventy-three, died of "bronchitis" in Embden. She was buried in the Pleasantdale Cemetery in Embden with her children.

When the 1900 United States Federal Census was taken, Jotham G. was listed as living in Embden with his sixth child, Grant, and his family.

Jotham G. survived Cyrena by over six years dying at the age of eighty-five of "tuberculosis of the bowels" at the home of his son Grant in Embden on July 12, 1904. He was buried in the Pleasantdale Cemetery in Embden alongside his wife and children.

**Gravestones for Emma Witham (top), Cyrena Williams (bottom left)
and Jotham G. Witham (bottom right)**
(Photographs from the Collection of Jeffrey Nelson Williams and Jacqueline Pon Williams)

SOURCES:

Cyrena Williams
Birth: (1) Original Record of Maine Towns & Cities, Town of Embden, Disk 1, Page 119, Picton Press, Rockland Maine, Copyright 2005; (2) "History of the Descendants of John Whitman of Weymouth Mass." by Charles H. Farnam, A. M., Page 859, Printed by Tuttle, Morehouse and Taylor Printers, 1889.
Death: (1) Record of Death, Maine Vital Records; (2) "History of the Descendants of John Whitman of Weymouth Mass." by Charles H. Farnam, A. M., Page 859, Printed by Tuttle, Morehouse and Taylor Printers, 1889; (3) "Maine, Faylene Hutton Cemetery Collection, ca. 1780-1990," database with images, FamilySearch, (https://familysearch.org/ark:/61903/1:1:QKM1-7XMD) - Accession #5030; (4) Gravestone.
Graveyard: (1) "Pleasant Dale/Murphy/Boothby Cemetery" complied by Nancy Hamlin Davis and Ruth Hamlin, Record 158, Old Canada Road Historical Society; (2) Find A Grave, Memorial #118489327.

Jotham Witham
Birth: "History of the Descendants of John Whitman of Weymouth Mass." by Charles H. Farnam, A. M., Page 859, Printed by Tuttle, Morehouse and Taylor Printers, 1889.
Marriage: (1) Original Record of Maine Towns & Cities, Town of Embden, Disk 2, Page 65, Picton Press, Rockland Maine, Copyright 2005; (2) "Maine, Marriages, 1771-1907," index, FamilySearch, (https://familysearch. org/pal:/MM9.1.1 /F462-GW5); (3) "History of the Descendants of John Whitman of Weymouth Mass." by Charles H. Farnam, A. M., Page 859, Printed by Tuttle, Morehouse and Taylor Printers, 1889; (4) "Embden Town of Yore" by Ernest George Walker, Page 714, Published by Independent-Reporter Company, Skowhegan, Maine, 1929.
Death: (1) Record of Death, Maine Vital Records; (2) "Maine Vital Records, 1670-1907," index and images, FamilySearch, (https://familysearch.org/pal:/MM9.1.1/KC67-WHM); (3) Death Notice, The Somerset Reporter, Skowhegan, Maine, Thursday, July 21, 1904, Page 4; (4) "Maine, Faylene Hutton Cemetery Collection, ca. 1780-1990," database with images, FamilySearch, (https://familysearch.org/ark:/61903/1:1:QKM1-7XMD) - Accession #5030; (5) Gravestone.
Graveyard: (1) "Pleasant Dale/Murphy/Boothby Cemetery" complied by Nancy Hamlin Davis and Ruth Hamlin, Record 156, Old Canada Road Historical Society; (2) Find A Grave, Memorial #118489251.

Eugene Witham
Birth: (1) Original Record of Maine Towns & Cities, Town of Embden, Disk 1, Page 143, Picton Press, Rockland Maine, Copyright 2005; (2) "History of the Descendants of John Whitman of Weymouth Mass." by Charles H. Farnam, A. M., Page 859, Printed by Tuttle, Morehouse and Taylor Printers, 1889.
Death: (1) Original Record of Maine Towns & Cities, Town of Embden, Disk 1, Page 143, Picton Press, Rockland Maine, Copyright 2005; (2) "History of the Descendants of John Whitman of Weymouth Mass." by Charles H. Farnam, A. M., Page 859, Printed by Tuttle, Morehouse and Taylor Printers, 1889; (3) Gravestone.
Graveyard: (1) "Pleasant Dale/Murphy/Boothby Cemetery" complied by Nancy Hamlin Davis and Ruth Hamlin, Record 160, Old Canada Road Historical Society; (2) Find A Grave, Memorial #118489507.

Allen Witham
Birth: (1) Original Record of Maine Towns & Cities, Town of Embden, Disk 1, Page 143, Picton Press, Rockland Maine, Copyright 2005; (2) "History of the Descendants of John Whitman of Weymouth Mass." by Charles H. Farnam, A. M., Page 859, Printed by Tuttle, Morehouse and Taylor Printers, 1889.
Death: (1) Original Record of Maine Towns & Cities, Town of Embden, Disk 1, Page 143, Picton Press, Rockland Maine, Copyright 2005; (2) "History of the Descendants of John Whitman of Weymouth Mass." by Charles H. Farnam, A. M., Page 859, Printed by Tuttle, Morehouse and Taylor Printers, 1889; (3) "Maine, Faylene Hutton Cemetery Collection, ca. 1780-1990," database with images, FamilySearch, (https://familysearch.org/ark:/61903 /1:1: QKM1-7XMD) - Accession #5030; (4) Gravestone.
Graveyard: (1) "Pleasant Dale/Murphy/Boothby Cemetery" complied by Nancy Hamlin Davis and Ruth Hamlin, Record 161, Old Canada Road Historical Society; (2) Find A Grave, Memorial #118489569.

Emma Witham
Birth: (1) Original Record of Maine Towns & Cities, Town of Embden, Disk 1, Page 143, Picton Press, Rockland Maine, Copyright 2005; (2) "History of the Descendants of John Whitman of Weymouth Mass." by Charles H. Farnam, A. M., Page 859, Printed by Tuttle, Morehouse and Taylor Printers, 1889.
Death: (1) Original Record of Maine Towns & Cities, Town of Embden, Disk 1, Page 143, Picton Press, Rockland Maine, Copyright 2005; (2) "History of the Descendants of John Whitman of Weymouth Mass." by Charles H. Farnam, A. M., Page 859, Printed by Tuttle, Morehouse and Taylor Printers, 1889; (3) "Maine, Faylene Hutton Cemetery Collection, ca. 1780-1990," database with images, FamilySearch, (https://familysearch.org/ark:/61903 /1:1: QKM1-7XMD) - Accession #5030; (4) Gravestone.
Graveyard: (1) "Pleasant Dale/Murphy/Boothby Cemetery" complied by Nancy Hamlin Davis and Ruth Hamlin, Record 159, Old Canada Road Historical Society; (2) Find A Grave, Memorial #118489458.

Historical Accounts: (1) 1850 United States Federal Census for Embden, Somerset, Maine; (2) 1860 United States Federal Census for Embden, Somerset, Maine; (3) 1880 United States Federal Census for Embden, Somerset, Maine, Page 7; (4) 1900 United States Federal Census for Embden, Somerset, Maine; Page 1; (5) "Embden Town of Yore" by Ernest George Walker, Published by Independent-Reporter Company, Skowhegan, Maine, 1929.

Sewall Williams
(1805 - 1867)

The first child of Daniel Williams and Abigail Maynard was Sewall. He was born on September 24, 1805 in Bingham, Somerset, Maine.

On February 24, 1829 at age twenty-three, Sewall was married to Joanna Savage, age eighteen, in Embden, Somerset, Maine by Benjamin C. Atwood, a Justice of the Peace and Sewell's uncle by marriage. Joanna was born in Embden on September 30, 1810 to Dr. Edward Savage and Sally Sarah Smith.

Sewall and Joanna had four children together.

Martha S.	b. November 20, 1829	d. May 31, 1902
Lucy C.	b. November 7, 1831	d. March 2, 1882
Olive A.	b. April 13, 1836	d. March 16, 1920
Celinda S.	b. March 21, 1839	d. April 20, 1915

When the 1830 United States Federal Census was taken Sewall, Joanna and their first child Martha S. were recorded as living in Embden.

By the time the 1840 United States Federal Census was taken, Sewall, Joanna and their children had moved to Orrington, Penobscot, Maine.

In the 1850 and 1860 United States Federal Census' Sewall, Joanna and their family were still listed as living in Orrington with Sewall working in 1850 as a "carpenter" and then as a "millwright" in 1860.

Sewall died of a cause not found on November 5, 1867 at age sixty-two. The exact location of his death has not been found. He was buried in the Marston Cemetery in Orrington.

Joanna, then age fifty-eight, was married to her second husband John Patten Hinkley, also age fifty-eight, on July 10, 1869 in Old Town, Piscataquis, Maine. John Patten, born on March 11, 1811 in Sangerville, Piscataquis, Maine, was the son of William Hinkley and Rachel Patten. Joanna and John Patten did not have any children together.

The 1870 United States Federal Census recorded Joanna and John Patten as living in Bangor, Penobscot, Maine where John Patten was working as a "ship carpenter". Joanna's daughter Olive A. (Williams) Fling and her son Elmer were recorded as living with them in that census.

Joanna and John Patten had moved to Guilford, Piscataquis, Maine by the time the 1880 United States Federal Census was taken. John Patten was still working as a "ship carpenter".

On March 11, 1890, Joanna died at age seventy-nine. The location and cause of her death are not known. She was also buried in the Marston Cemetery in Orrington alongside her first husband Sewell Williams.

Gravestones for Sewall Williams and Joanna Savage
(Photographs Courtesy of Dale & Patti Mower)

In 1896 John Patten died of "old age" in Guilford at the age of eighty-six. The exact date of his death and the place of his burial have not been found.

SOURCES:

Sewall Williams
Birth: Original Record of Maine Towns & Cities, Town of Bingham, Page 26, Picton Press, Rockland Maine, Copyright 2005.
Death: Gravestone.
Graveyard: Find A Grave, Memorial #139720204.

Joanna Savage
Birth: Original Record of Maine Towns & Cities, Town of Embden, Page 132, Picton Press, Rockland Maine, Copyright 2005.
Marriage: (1) "Maine, Marriages, 1771-1907," index, FamilySearch, (https://familysearch.org/pal:/MM9.1.1/F462-2YH); (2) Original Record of Maine Towns & Cities, Town of Embden, Disk 2, Page 39, Picton Press, Rockland Maine, Copyright 2005; (3) "Embden Town of Yore" by Ernest George Walker, Page 703, Published by Independent-Reporter Company, Skowhegan.
Death: Gravestone.
Graveyard: Find A Grave, Memorial #139720260.

John Patten Hinkley
Birth: (1) "Sprague's Journal of Maine History, Volume 2", Page 165, July 1914; (2) "Maine Births and Christenings, 1739-1900," FamilySearch, (https://familysearch.org/ark:/61903/1:1:F4MR-QJ4).
Marriage: "Maine, Marriages, 1771-1907," index, FamilySearch, (https://familysearch.org/pal:/MM9.1.1/F46M-XSW).
Death: Record of Death, Maine Vital Records.
Graveyard:

Historical Accounts: (1) 1830 United States Federal Census for Embden, Somerset, Maine; (2) 1840 United States Federal Census for Orrington, Penobscot, Maine; (3) 1850 United States Federal Census for Orrington, Penobscot, Maine; (4) 1860 United States Federal Census for Orrington, Penobscot, Maine, Page 47; (5) 1870 United States Federal Census for Bangor, Penobscot, Maine, Page 56; (6) 1880 United States Federal Census for Guilford, Piscataquis, Maine, Page 6.

Nelson Williams
(1807 -)

Nelson, the second child of Daniel Williams and Abigail Maynard, was born in Bingham, Somerset, Maine, USA on July 1, 1807.

Sometime after it was published in 1828, Nelson passed on a bible he once owned to his sister Abigail Maynard. This is believed to have occurred sometime between 1828 and 1838, the year his sister was married. Below is a copy of Nelson's signature from the front cover sheet of that bible.

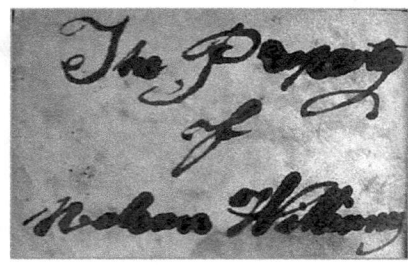

Nelson Williams' signature from the Williams/Briggs Family Bible
(From the Collection of Jeffrey Nelson Williams and Jacqueline Pon Williams)

When the 1830 United States Federal Census was taken Nelson was recorded as living with his parents in Township No. 1, 4th Range, East Kennebec River, Somerset, Maine.

At age thirty-two, on June 6, 1839, Nelson was married to Elizabeth Dunham, age twenty-one, in Lancaster, Saint John, New Brunswick, Canada by Reverend Wilson of the Church of Scotland. Elizabeth, born in 1812, was the daughter of David Alston Dunham and Mary Ann Cathline of Lancaster. The exact date and place of her birth has not been found.

It should be noted that in the Marriage Register for Saint John County, New Brunswick the transcriber listed Nelson's name as "William N. Williams". This is the only official document that has been found that lists his name that way and is believed to be a transposition error.

After their marriage Nelson and Elizabeth traveled back to Maine and made Somerset County their home. They were listed as living in Township No. 1, 4th Range, East Kennebec River when the 1840 United States Federal Census was taken. In that census Nelson was recorded as "employed in agriculture".

During their marriage Nelson and Elizabeth had six children.

John Nelson   b. October 19, 1842   d. March 22, 1924

David D.	*b. April 16, 1844*	*d. January 28, 1845*
Silas M.	b. July 15, 1847	d. December 24, 1918
Eliza Ann	b. 1849	d. August 9, 1882
Phoebe Elizabeth	b. September 24, 1852	d. December 1, 1915
Benjamin Franklin	b. August 24, 1855	d. December 5, 1938

The second child of Nelson and Elizabeth, David D., died on January 28, 1845 at the young age of nine months and twelve days old. The cause and place of his death have not been found. He was buried in the Moscow Union Cemetery in Moscow, Somerset, Maine.

Gravestone for David D. Williams
(Photograph from the Collection of Jeffrey Nelson Williams and Jacqueline Pon Williams)

Sometime in-between the birth of their daughters Eliza Ann in 1849 and Phoebe Elizabeth in 1852, Nelson and Elizabeth moved their family to Saint John County, New Brunswick, Canada where Elizabeth was born. This was the start of the extensive Williams family line in the New Brunswick area.

The 1863-1864 Hutchinson's Saint John Directory listed Nelson as living in Portland, Saint John, New Brunswick at Straight Shore opposite Ruddock's Yard and working as a "millman".

In the 1871 Census of Canada Nelson, Elizabeth and their family were recorded as living in Lancaster. At the time of that census Nelson was working as a "millwright" at the Ritchie and Snowball Mill. The 1871 Lovell's Province of New Brunswick Directory also listed Nelson as employed as a "millwright" and living in Lancaster.

Elizabeth died tragically at age sixty on August 21, 1872. Following her daughter Phoebe Elizabeth, she was rushing to cross the train tracks to reach the platform at the Lancaster Station in South Bay, Saint John, New Brunswick, when she was hit by a PicNic Train as it was backing up into the station. Elizabeth was knocked 12 to 15 feet under the station platform suffering a fractured skull, from which she died soon after being hit. At the time of her death her husband Nelson was working at one of the Ritchie and Snowball mills in Miramichi, Northumberland, New Brunswick. He had just sent some money along with a letter to his wife which she was returning from picking up when her death occurred. A coroner's inquest was held two days later, on August 23, 1872, which concluded that her death was the result of a tragic accident. The exact location of Elizabeth's grave is not known at this time, but her death notice published on August 24, 1872 indicated she was to be interred in Carlton, Saint John, New Brunswick.

On January 6, 1873 Nelson, then age sixty-five, was married to his second wife Annie Sutherland, age twenty-seven, in Newcastle, Northumberland, New Brunswick by W. A. Coleman, a Baptist minister. Annie, who was living with her parents, James and Jane Sutherland in Richibucto, Kent, New Brunswick at that time, was born in Nova Scotia around 1846. The exact date and place of her birth have not been found.

When the McAlpine's Saint John Directory was prepared for 1874-1875, Nelson was listed as living in Fairville, Saint John, New Brunswick and still working as a "millwright".

It is believed that Nelson died sometime between the publishing of McAlpine's Saint John Directory in 1874 and his daughter Eliza Ann's death on September 21, 1882, when he was listed as deceased in her death notice. The exact date and cause of his death, as well as the location of his grave are unknown at this time.

Additional information regarding the life and death of Nelson's second wife Annie has also not been found.

SOURCES:

Nelson Williams
Birth: (1) Original Record of Maine Towns & Cities, Town of Bingham, Maine, Page 26, Picton Press, Rockland Maine, Copyright 2005; (2) "Maine, Births and Christenings, 1739-1900 index, FamilySearch, (https:// familysearch .org/pal:/MM9.1.1/F4H9-WVZ).
Death:
Graveyard:

Elizabeth Dunham
Birth:
Marriage: (1) Saint John, New Brunswick, Marriage Registers, Book B, Page 535, Provincial Archives of New Brunswick; (2) Marriage Notice, "New Brunswick Vital Statistics from Newspapers", by Daniel F. Johnson, Volume 8 1839-1840, Number 320, Provincial Archives of New Brunswick.
Death: (1) Newspaper article, Saint John Daily Telegraph, August 22, 1872; (2) Death Notice, "New Brunswick Vital Statistics from Newspapers", by Daniel F. Johnson, Volume 32, Number 1006, Provincial Archives of New Brunswick.
Graveyard:

David D. Williams
Birth: Record of a Death, Maine Vital Records.
Death: (1) Record of a Death, Maine Vital Records; (2) Gravestone.
Graveyard: (1) "Moscow Union Cemetery" by Nancy Hamlin Davis and Ruth Hamlin, Record 593, Old Canada Road Historical Society; (2) Find A Grave Memorial # 8214990.

Annie Sutherland
Birth:
Marriage: (1) Northumberland, New Brunswick Marriage Registers, 1864-1887, Page 206; (2) Marriage Notice, "New Brunswick Vital Statistics from Newspapers", by Daniel F. Johnson, Volume 33, Number 1701, Provincial Archives of New Brunswick.
Death:
Graveyard:

Historical Accounts: (1) Williams/Briggs Family Bible, from the collection of Jeffrey N. Williams and Jacqueline Pon Williams; (2) 1830 United States Federal Census for Township No. 1, 4th Range, East Kennebec River, Somerset, Maine; (3) 1840 United States Federal Census for Township No. 1, 4th Range, East Kennebec River, Somerset, Maine, Page 94; (4) 1871 Census of Canada for Lancaster, Saint John, New Brunswick, Page 33; (5) 1871 Census of Canada for Richibucto, Kent, New Brunswick, Page 26; (6) Hutchinson's Saint John Directory 1863-1864, Page 258; (7) Lovell's Province of New Brunswick Directory for 1871, Page 230; (8) McAlpine's Saint John Directory 1874-1875, Page 361; (9) Death Notice for Mrs. Peter Cusack (Eliza Ann Williams), "New Brunswick Vital Statistics from Newspapers", by Daniel F. Johnson, Volume 58, Number 288, Provincial Archives of New Brunswick.

Daniel Prescott Williams
(1809 - 1876)

The third child of Daniel Williams and Abigail Maynard was Daniel Prescott (commonly known as "Prescott") who was born on February 7, 1809 in Bingham, Somerset, Maine.

In July 1833 the Town Clerk of Moscow, Somerset, Maine published the intentions to marry for Daniel Prescott, age twenty-four, and Esther M. Holway, age twenty. On July 11th of that same year they were married in Caratunk, Somerset, Maine by Joseph Spaulding, a Justice of the Peace. Esther M. was born in 1813 in Fairfield, Somerset, Maine, to Samuel Holway and Anna Killey. The exact date of her birth has not been found.

Daniel Prescott and Esther M. had nine children together.

Miranda Amaryllis	b. December 1835	d. September 20, 1854
Esther M.	b. December 9, 1838	d. February 2, 1908
Daniel Harrison	b. February 2, 1840	d. April 21, 1922
Charles A.	b. December 11, 1842	d. November 27, 1915
Seth Baker	b. 1846	d. January 28, 1896
Jotham A.	b. June 1847	d.
Cynthia R.	b. February 1849	d. July 19, 1870
Abbie B.	*b. February 1851*	*d. November 20, 1864*
Jonah S.	b. September 18, 1854	d. August 14, 1924

In the 1840 United States Federal Census Daniel Prescott, Esther M. and their family were recorded as living in No. 1, 4th Range, East Kennebec River, Somerset, Maine.

The 1850 and 1860 United States Federal Census' recorded Daniel Prescott, Esther M. and their children as living in The Forks, Somerset, Maine. In both census documents Daniel Prescott's occupation was listed as "farmer".

Abbie B., the eighth child of Daniel Prescott and Esther M., died on November 20, 1864 at the age of thirteen years nine months old. The exact cause and place of her death have not been found. She was buried in the Bean Cemetery at The Forks.

When the 1870 United States Federal Census was taken Daniel Prescott and Esther M. were recorded as still living in The Forks where Daniel Prescott was had continued farming.

On November 19, 1876 Daniel Prescott died in The Forks of an unknown cause at the age of sixty-seven. He was also buried in the family plot at the

Bean Cemetery in The Forks.

A little over three years later, Esther M., also at age sixty-seven, died on February 8, 1880. Her cause and place of death have also not been found. She too was buried at The Forks in the Bean Cemetery with her husband Daniel Prescott and her daughter Abbie B.

**Gravestones for Abbie B. Williams (top) and Daniel Prescott Williams
& Esther M. Holway (bottom)**
(Photographs courtesy Kathy Manning (top) and Wayne Hoar (bottom))

SOURCES:

Daniel Prescott Williams
Birth: (1) Original Record of Maine Towns & Cities, Town of Bingham, Page 26, Picton Press, Rockland Maine, Copyright 2005; (2) "Maine, Births and Christenings, 1739-1900," index, FamilySearch, (https://familysearch.org/pal:/MM9.1.1/F439-TY8).
Death: Gravestone.
Graveyard: (1) "Bean Cemetery (Mountain Road)", From data collected by Leona Sterling and Mildred Smith 1938, Record 12, Old Canada Road Historical Society; (2) Find A Grave, Memorial #77204204.

Esther M. Holway
Birth:
Marriage: (1) Original Record of Maine Towns & Cities, Town of Moscow, Page 71, Picton Press, Rockland Maine, Copyright 2005; (2) Original Record of Maine Towns & Cities, Town of Moscow, Page 83, Picton Press, Rockland Maine, Copyright 2005; (3) "Maine, Marriages, 1771-1907," index, FamilySearch, (https://familysearch.org/pal:/MM9.1.1 /F4FK-NY4).
Death: Gravestone.
Graveyard: (1) "Bean Cemetery (Mountain Road)", From data collected by Leona Sterling and Mildred Smith 1938, Record 12, Old Canada Road Historical Society; (2) Find A Grave, Memorial #77204269.

Abbie B. Williams
Birth:
Death: Gravestone.
Graveyard: (1) "Bean Cemetery (Mountain Road)", From data collected by Leona Sterling and Mildred Smith 1938, Record 12, Old Canada Road Historical Society; (2) Find A Grave, Memorial #85722100.

Historical Accounts: (1) 1840 United States Federal Census for No. 1, 4th Range, East Kennebec River, Somerset, Maine; (2) 1850 United States Federal Census for The Forks, Somerset, Maine; (3) 1860 United States Federal Census for The Forks, Somerset, Maine, Page 66; (4) 1870 United States Federal Census for West Forks, Somerset, Maine, Page 1.

Abigail Maynard Williams
(1812 - 1882)

Abigail Maynard (named after her mother) was the fourth child of Daniel Williams and Abigail Maynard. She was born in Bingham, Somerset, Maine on October 16, 1812.

On February 5, 1838 Abigail Maynard, age twenty-five, and George Briggs, age thirty-one, filed their intentions to be married with the Town Clerk of Moscow, Somerset, Maine. They were subsequently married on March 15, 1838 in Caratunk, Somerset, Maine by Zebinah Houghton, a Justice of the Peace. George was born on May 8, 1807 to Samuel Briggs and Rachel Rowe in Concord, Somerset, Maine.

Abigail Maynard and George had four children together.

Lucy Ann	*b. December 16, 1838*	*d. September 16, 1847*
Cyrus Tilson H.	b. January 9, 1843	d. October 4, 1908
Martha Jane Young	*b. August 6, 1845*	*d. September 23, 1847*
Charles S.	b. February 13, 1852	d. October 26, 1915

When the 1840 United States Federal Census was taken Abigail Maynard, George and their first child Lucy Ann were recorded as living in No. 1, 3rd Range, East Kennebec River in Somerset, Maine.

Abigail Maynard and George's two daughters both died in 1847 at young ages. Lucy Ann died on September 16, 1847 at eight years nine months old and Martha Jane Young died at two years one month old on September 23, 1847. The causes and places of their deaths have not been found. Both Lucy Ann and Martha Jane Young were buried in the Moscow Union Cemetery in Moscow.

Abigail Maynard, George and their two sons were still living in No. 1, 3rd Range, East Kennebec River at the time of the 1850 United States Federal Census. George's occupation was listed as "farming" in that census.

The 1860 and 1870 United States Federal Census' recorded that Abigail Maynard, George and their family as then living in Caratunk where George was "farming".

In the 1880 United States Federal Census Abigail Maynard and George were recorded as living in Carrying Place, Somerset, Maine with their son Cyrus Tilson H. (No. 1, 3rd Range, East Kennebec River had been renamed Carrying Place by that time.) George and their son Cyrus Tilson H.'s occupations were listed as "farmers".

On September 12, 1882 Abigail Maynard died in Carrying Place, at the age of sixty-nine. The exact cause of her death has not been found. She was buried in the Moscow Union Cemetery in Moscow along with her daughters.

George lived to be seventy-eight, passing away in Carrying Place on September 25, 1885. The cause of his death is also not known. He too was buried in the family plot in the Moscow Union Cemetery in Moscow.

 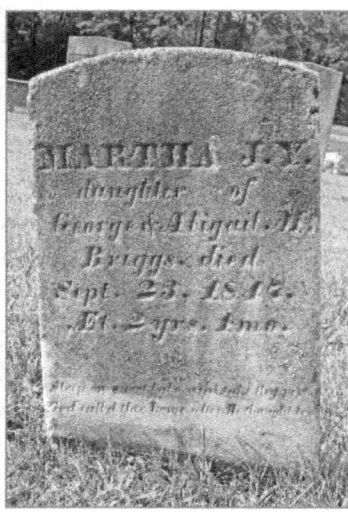

Gravestones for Lucy Ann Briggs (top left), Martha Jane Young Briggs (top right)
and Abigail Maynard Williams & George Briggs (bottom)
(Photographs from the Collection of Jeffrey Nelson Williams and Jacqueline Pon Williams)

SOURCES:

Abigail Maynard Williams
Birth: (1) Williams/Briggs Family Bible, from the Collection of Jeffrey Nelson Williams and Jacqueline Pon Williams; (2) Original Record of Maine Towns & Cities, Town of Bingham, Page 26, Picton Press, Rockland Maine, Copyright 2005; (3) "Maine, Births and Christenings, 1739-1900," index, FamilySearch, (https://familysearch.org/ ark:/61903/1:1: F439-TTP).
Death: Record of a Death, Maine Vital Records.
Graveyard: (1) "Moscow Union Cemetery" by Nancy Hamlin Davis and Ruth Hamlin, Record 590, Old Canada Road Historical Society; (2) Find A Grave Memorial #82149810.

George Briggs
Birth: (1) Williams/Briggs Family Bible, from the Collection of Jeffrey Nelson Williams and Jacqueline Pon Williams; (2) "Maine, Births and Christenings, 1739-1900," index, FamilySearch, (https://familysearch.org/ ark:/61903/1:1: F4Q4-5R6); (3) Original Record of Maine Towns & Cities, Town of Concord, Page 82, Picton Press, Rockland Maine, Copyright 2005.
Marriage: (1) Williams/Briggs Family Bible, from the Collection of Jeffrey Nelson Williams and Jacqueline Pon Williams; (2) Original Record of Maine Towns & Cities, Town of Moscow, Page 78, Picton Press, Rockland Maine, Copyright 2005; (3) Original Record of Maine Towns & Cities, Town of Moscow, Page 87, Picton Press, Rockland Maine, Copyright 2005.
Death: Record of a Death, Maine Vital Records.
Graveyard: (1) "Moscow Union Cemetery" by Nancy Hamlin Davis and Ruth Hamlin, Record 589, Old Canada Road Historical Society; (2) Find A Grave Memorial #82149812.

Lucy Ann Briggs
Birth: Williams/Briggs Family Bible, from the Collection of Jeffrey Nelson Williams and Jacqueline Pon Williams.
Death: (1) Williams/Briggs Family Bible, from the Collection of Jeffrey Nelson Williams and Jacqueline Pon Williams; (2) Record of a Death, Maine Vital Records.
Graveyard: (1) "Moscow Union Cemetery" by Nancy Hamlin Davis and Ruth Hamlin, Record 591, Old Canada Road Historical Society; (2) Find A Grave Memorial #82149815.

Martha Jane Young Briggs
Birth: Williams/Briggs Family Bible, from the Collection of Jeffrey Nelson Williams and Jacqueline Pon Williams.
Death: (1) Williams/Briggs Family Bible, from the Collection of Jeffrey Nelson Williams and Jacqueline Pon Williams; (2) Record of a Death, Maine Vital Records.
Graveyard: (1) "Moscow Union Cemetery" by Nancy Hamlin Davis and Ruth Hamlin, Record 592, Old Canada Road Historical Society; (2) Find A Grave Memorial #821498.

Historical Accounts: (1) 1840 United States Federal Census for No. 1, 3rd Range, East Kennebec River, Somerset, Maine; (2) 1850 United States Federal Census for No. 1, 3rd Range, East Kennebec River, Somerset, Maine; (3) 1860 United States Federal Census for Caratunk, Somerset, Maine, Page 64; (4) 1870 United States Federal Census for Caratunk, Somerset, Maine, Page 4; (5) 1880 United States Federal Census for Carrying Place, Somerset, Maine, Page 8.

John Quincy Adams Williams
(1828 - 1907)

The ninth child of Daniel Williams and Abigail Maynard, John Quincy Adams, was born in Solon, Somerset, Maine on April 30, 1828.

When the 1850 United States Federal Census was taken John Quincy Adams, then age twenty-two, was recorded as living with his father and step-mother in Solon.

On November 8, 1854 John Quincy Adams, age twenty-six, was married to Clarinda Blackwell Moore, age twenty-four, by Reverend Sydney Turner in Bingham, Somerset, Maine. Clarinda Blackwell, born on December 29, 1829 in Moose River, Somerset, Maine, was the daughter of Joseph Moore and Louisa V. Langley.

During their marriage John Quincy Adams and Clarinda Blackwell had only one child together.

Abigail B. M.   b. June 1857   d.

In the 1860 United States Federal Census John Quincy Adams, Clarinda Blackwell and their daughter Abigail B. M. were listed as living in Moscow, Somerset, Maine, with John Quincy Adams's occupation listed as a "farmer".

Sometime after the 1860 United States Federal Census was taken John Quincy Adams and Clarinda Blackwell moved to Caratunk, Somerset, Maine where they were noted as living with their daughter Abigail B. M. in the 1870 United States Federal Census.

The 1880 United States Federal Census recorded John Quincy Adams and Clarinda Blackwell as living in Carrying Place, Somerset, Maine. That census also noted that their daughter Abigail B. M., her husband Elwin Robinson and their son, Harley Cecil Robinson, were living with them. John Quincy Adams's occupation was listed as "farmer" and in 1880 Elwin Robinson's occupation was listed as "works on farm" in that census document.

Clarinda Blackwell died in 1888 at the age of fifty-eight. The exact date, cause and place of her death have not been found. She was buried in the John Quincy Adams Williams family plot in Bingham at the Bingham Village Cemetery. In her Will, Clarinda Blackwell left the sum of $5 from her personal property to their daughter Abigail B. M. (Williams) Robinson, with the remainder of her Estate bequeathed to her husband John Quincy Adams.

Gravestone for Clairinda Blackwell Moore
(Photograph from the Collection of Jeffrey Nelson Williams and Jacqueline Pon Williams)

In 1891, about three years after his first wife passed away, John Quincy Adams, then age sixty-three, was married to his second wife Roxcinda (Holt) Adams, age fifty. Roxcinda was the widow of Seth N. Adams and the daughter of James Holt and Thias Flynt. She was born on March 9, 1841 in Maine. The location of her birth has not been found. During their marriage John Quincy Adams and Roxcinda did not have any children together.

John Quincy Adams and Roxcinda were recorded as still living in Carrying Place when the 1900 United States Federal Census was taken. In that census John Quincy Adams was again listed as working as a "farmer".

On September 9, 1907, at age seventy-nine, John Quincy Adams died of "vascular disease of the heart" in Moscow. He was buried next to his first wife in his family plot in the Bingham Village Cemetery in Bingham. In his Will, John Quincy Adams left the sum of $1 to his daughter Abigail B. M. (Williams) DeSilva and the entire remainder of his Estate to his second wife Roxcinda.

Roxcinda survived her husband John Quincy Adams by a little more than a year, passing away at age sixty-seven on December 12, 1908. The cause and place of her death has not been found. She was buried in the Bingham Village Cemetery in Bingham in the same plot as John Quincy Adams and Clarinda Blackwell.

Gravestones for John Quincy Adams Williams (left) and Roxcinda Holt (right)
(Photographs from the Collection of Jeffrey Nelson Williams and Jacqueline Pon Williams)

SOURCES:

John Quincy Adams Williams
Birth: Record of Death, Maine Vital Records.
Death: Record of Death, Maine Vital Records.
Graveyard: (1) "Maine Old Cemetery Association Special Publication Number 12, Edition No. 1: Series 1, 2 and 3", Page 334, Picton Press, Rockland, Maine, Copyright 2006; (2) "Bingham Village Cemetery" by Nancy Hamlin Davis and Ruth Hamlin, Record 614, Old Canada Road Historical Society; (3) Find A Grave, Memorial #82030175.

Clarinda Blackwell Moore
Birth: "Maine, Birth and Christenings, 739-1900," index, FamilySearch, (https://family search.org/pal:/MM9.1.1 /F4QC-SJ9).
Marriage: (1) Original Record of Maine Towns & Cities, Town of Bingham, Page 168, Picton Press, Rockland Maine, Copyright 2005; (2) "Maine, Marriages, 1771-1907," index, FamilySearch, (https://family search.org/pal:/ MM9.1.1/F4XF-N4R).
Death:
Graveyard: (1) "Maine Old Cemetery Association Special Publication Number 12, Edition No. 1: Series 1, 2 and 3", Page 334, Picton Press, Rockland, Maine, Copyright 2006; (2) "Bingham Village Cemetery" by Nancy Hamlin Davis and Ruth Hamlin, Record 613, Old Canada Road Historical Society; (3) Find A Grave, Memorial #82030192.

Roxcinda Holt
Birth: "Maine, Nathan Hale Cemetery Collection, ca. 1780-1980," database with images, FamilySearch, (https://familysearch.org/ark:/61903/1:1:QVJ5-SFVL).
Marriage:
Death: (1) Death Notice, The Somerset Reporter, Skowhegan, Maine, Thursday, December 17, 1908; (2) Maine, Nathan Hale Cemetery Collection, ca. 1780-1980," database with images, FamilySearch, (https://familysearch.org/ark:/61903/1:1: QVJ5-SFVL); (3) Gravestone.
Graveyard: (1) "Maine Old Cemetery Association Special Publication Number 12, Edition No. 1: Series 1, 2 and 3", Page 334, Picton Press, Rockland, Maine, Copyright 2006; (2) "Bingham Village Cemetery" by Nancy Hamlin Davis and Ruth Hamlin, Record 613, Old Canada Road Historical Society; (3) Find A Grave, Memorial #82030228.

Historical Accounts: (1) 1850 United States Federal Census for Solon, Somerset, Maine; (2) 1850 United States Federal Census for Long Pond Plantation, Somerset, Maine; (3) 1860 United States Federal Census for Moscow, Somerset, Maine, Page 10; (4) 1860 United States Federal Census for Bingham, Somerset, Maine, Page 3; (5) 1870 United States Federal Census for Caratunk, Somerset, Maine, Page 4; (6) 1880 United States Federal Census for Carrying Place, Somerset, Maine, Page 8; (7) 1900 United States Federal Census for Carrying Place, Somerset, Maine, Page 4; (8) Will of Clarinda B. Williams– "Maine, Wills and Probate Records, 1584-1999," [database on-line]. Provo, UT, USA: Ancestry.com Operations, Inc., 2015; (9) Will of John Q. A. Williams– "Maine, Wills and Probate Records, 1584-1999," [database on-line]. Provo, UT, USA: Ancestry.com Operations, Inc., 2015.

Abigail Meriam Williams
(1809 - 1856)

The first child of John Williams and his first wife Sally Maynard was Abigail Meriam. She was born on March 19, 1809 in Anson, Somerset, Maine.

At age twenty-four, on March 28, 1833, Abigail Meriam was married to the widower Nathanial Berry Moulton, age thirty-six, in Embden, Somerset, Maine by Benjamin C. Atwood, a Justice of the Peace. Nathanial Berry, the son of Jonathan Fifield Moulton and Lydia Tuttle Copp, was born on September 15, 1796 in Moultonborough, Strafford, New Hampshire.

With her marriage to Nathanial Berry, Abigail Meriam became a stepmother to his six children that he had with his first wife Betsey Williamson.

Abigail Meriam and Nathanial Berry had an additional eight children together.

Abigail E.	b. December 25, 1833	d. January 1, 1925
William Weston	b. July 2, 1835	d. November 20 1898
Lorenzo H.	b. May 27, 1837	d. July 7, 1920
Esther Tuttle	b. May 10, 1839	d. May 8, 1913
Philander M.	b. May 2, 1841	d. March 28, 1918
Octavia W.	b. May 22, 1843	d. December 18, 1916
Nathaniel Berry, Jr.	b. April 13, 1845	d. January 2, 1896
Wilford F.	b. September 20, 1849	d.

In his book "Embden Town of Yore" Ernest George Walker described Nathanial Berry as "a conspicuous man in Embden and Concord. He was of giant frame, tall and commanding in stature, of stern appearance, with deep set eyes and shaggy brows." On July 4, 1831, Nathanial Berry was commissioned as Captain of H Company in the Embden Militia. At that time H Company was responsible for the protection of the town west of Embden Pond.

The 1840 and 1850 United States Federal Census' recorded Abigail Meriam and Nathanial Berry as living in Concord, Somerset, Maine with Nathanial Berry's occupation being listed as a "farmer".

On December 7, 1856, Abigail Meriam died at the age of forty-seven. Her cause and location of death have not been found. She was buried in the North New Portland Cemetery in New Portland, Somerset, Maine.

Nathaniel Berry, then age sixty-two, was married to his third wife, Philena Mullen, age fourteen, on March 6, 1859 in New Portland by William Bartlett, a Justice of the Peace. Philena (sometimes spelled "Filena"), his niece, was the daughter of Nathaniel Berry's sister Abigail P. Moulton and her husband Daniel

Lee Mullen. She was born in 1848 in Concord, Somerset, Maine. The exact date of her birth is not known. This marriage was fiercely opposed by both families because of the great difference in their ages. No record has been found to indicate that Nathan Berry and Philena had any children together.

The 1860 United States Federal Census recorded Nathan Berry and Philena living in Lexington, Somerset, Maine. By the time the 1870 United States Federal Census was taken Nathan Berry and Philena had moved and were living in Township 1, Franklin, Maine. In both census documents Nathaniel Berry was working as a "farmer".

In the 1880 United States Federal Census, taken in June of that year, Nathanial Berry, then age eighty-three, was listed as living with his son William Weston and his family in Concord. Nathanial Berry's third wife Philena was not listed as living at that residence. Later that year, on December 28, 1880 Nathanial Berry died at the age of eighty-four. The cause and place of his death have not been found. Nathanial Berry was buried at New Portland in the North New Portland Cemetery along with his first two wives.

Gravestone for Abigail Meriam Williams and Nathanial Berry Moulton
(Photograph from the Collection of Jeffrey Nelson Williams and Jacqueline Pon Williams)

Additional information regarding the life and death of Nathaniel Berry's third wife Philena has not been found. As such her documented history will end here.

SOURCES:

Abigail Meriam Williams
Birth: (1) Original Record of Maine Towns & Cities, Town of Embden, Disk 2 Page 21, Picton Press, Rockland Maine, Copyright 2005; (2) Original Record of Maine Towns & Cities, Concord, Page 98, Picton Press, Rockland Maine, Copyright 2005.
Death: (1) Original Record of Maine Towns & Cities, Concord, Page 98, Picton Press, Rockland Maine, Copyright 2005; (2) Gravestone.
Graveyard: (1) Burial Records, North New Portland Cemetery, New Portland, Maine; (2) Find A Grave, Memorial #32340141.

Nathanial Berry Moulton
Birth: (1) Original Record of Maine Towns & Cities, Concord, Page 98, Picton Press, Rockland Maine, Copyright 2005; (2) Original Record of Maine Towns & Cities, Concord, Page 100, Picton Press, Rockland Maine, Copyright 2005.
Marriage: (1) Original Record of Maine Towns & Cities Town Records of Embden, Disk 1 Page 365, Picton Press, Rockland Maine, Copyright 2005; (2) "Maine, Marriages, 1771-1907," index, FamilySearch, (https://familysearch.org/ pal:/MM9.1.1/F462-KPD).
Death: Gravestone.
Graveyard: (1) Burial Records, North New Portland Cemetery, New Portland, Maine; (2) Find A Grave, Memorial #32340141.

Philena Mullen
Birth:
Marriage: (1) Original Record of Maine Towns & Cities, Town of New Portland, Page 158, Picton Press, Rockland Maine, Copyright 2005; (2) "Maine, Marriages, 1771-1907," index, FamilySearch, (https://familysearch.org/pal:/MM9.1.1 /F4XC-W5N).
Death:
Graveyard:

Historical Accounts: (1) 1840 United States Federal Census for Concord, Somerset, Maine; (2) 1850 United States Federal Census for Concord, Somerset, Maine; (3) 1860 United States Federal Census for Lexington, Somerset, Maine, page 40; (4) 1870 United States Federal Census for Township 1, Franklin, Maine, Page 1; (5) 1880 United States Federal Census for Concord, Somerset, Maine, Page 9; (6) "Embden Town of Yore" by Ernest George Walker, Pages 439 and 711, Published by Independent-Reporter Company, Skowhegan, Maine, 1929; (7) "South of Lost Nation" by Ernest George Walker, Washington D. C., July 4, 1939, Retyped in 1994-1995 by Dean Lyons for the Embden Historical Society.

John Howard Williams
(1810 - 1852)

John Howard was the second child of John Williams and his first wife Sally Maynard. He was born in Embden, Somerset, Maine on May 16, 1810.

On December 30, 1837, John Howard, age twenty-seven, was married in Embden to Roxanna Felker, age twenty-five, by his uncle Caleb Williams, a Justice of the Peace. Roxanna was born on November 16, 1812 in Concord, Somerset, Maine to Sarah Felker. The name of her father is not known.

John Howard and Roxanna had three children together.

Sally R.	*b. July 29, 1839*	*d. February 18, 1854*
Mary Ann B.	b. June 9, 1841	d. February 1, 1920
Baby Girl	*b. 1848*	*d. August 6, 1848*

The third child of John Howard and Roxanna, an unnamed baby girl, died on August 6, 1848 at an unknown age, but presumed to be days old. She was buried in the Sunset Cemetery in North Anson, Somerset, Maine.

In the 1850 United States Federal Census John Howard, Roxanna and their children were recorded as living in Embden, with John Howard's occupation listed as a "farmer".

On January 1, 1852, about sixteen months after the 1850 United States Federal Census was taken, John Howard died at the age of forty-one. His cause and place of death are unknown. He was buried in his family plot in the Sunset Cemetery in North Anson.

John Howard and Roxanna's first child, Sally R., died at fourteen years eight months old on February 18, 1854. Her cause and place of death are also not known. She too was buried in the family plot in the Sunset Cemetery in North Anson.

Roxanna was listed in the 1870, 1880 and 1900 United States Federal Census' as living with her daughter, Mary Ann B. (Williams) Burns and her husband Francis on their farm in Embden. Her occupation in 1870 and 1880 was listed as "housekeeper".

Outliving her husband by more than forty-nine years, Roxanna, having never remarried, died in Embden at the age of eight-eight on June 19, 1901. Her cause of death was listed as "shingles". She was buried alongside her family in North Anson at the Sunset Cemetery.

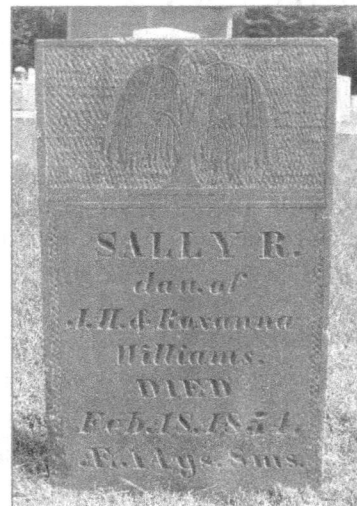

Gravestones for Sally R. Williams (top left), Baby Girl Williams (top right) and John Howard Williams & Roxanna Felker (bottom)
(Photographs from the Collection of Jeffrey Nelson Williams and Jacqueline Pon Williams)

SOURCES:

John Howard Williams
Birth: (1) Original Record of Maine Towns & Cities Town Records of Embden, Disk 2 Page 21, Picton Press, Rockland, Maine Copyright 2005; (2) Original Record of Maine Towns & Cities Town Records of Embden, Disk 1 Page 103, Picton Press, Rockland Maine Copyright 2005; (3) Edmund West, comp., *"Family Data Collection - Individual Records"*, [database on-line], Provo, UT, USA: Ancestry.com Operations Inc, 2000.
Death: Gravestone.
Graveyard: (1) Burial Records, Sunset Cemetery, North Anson, Maine; (2) "Maine Old Cemetery Association Special Publication Number 12, Edition No. 1: Series 1, 2 and 3", Page 168, Picton Press, Rockland, Maine, Copyright 2006; (3) Find A Grave, Memorial #91659814.

Roxanna Felker
Birth: (1) Original Record of Maine Towns & Cities, Concord, Page 90, Picton Press, Rockland Maine 2005; (2) Original Record of Maine Towns & Cities Town Records of Embden, Disk 1 Page 103, Picton Press, Rockland Maine Copyright 2005.
Marriage: (1) Original Record of Maine Towns & Cities Town Records of Embden, Disk 1 Page 370, Picton Press, Rockland Maine 2005; (2) "Embden Town of Yore" by Ernest George Walker, Page 707, Published by Independent-Reporter Company, Skowhegan, Maine, 1929.
Death: (1) Record of Death, Maine Vital Records; (2) Gravestone.
Graveyard: (1) Burial Records, Sunset Cemetery, North Anson, Maine; (2) "Maine Old Cemetery Association Special Publication Number 12, Edition No. 1: Series 1, 2 and 3", Page 168, Picton Press, Rockland, Maine, Copyright 2006; (3) Find A Grave, Memorial #91659820.

Sally R. Williams
Birth: Original Record of Maine Towns & Cities Town Records of Embden, Disk 1 Page 103, Picton Press, Rockland Maine Copyright 2005.
Death: Gravestone.
Graveyard: (1) Burial Records, Sunset Cemetery, North Anson, Maine; (2) "Maine Old Cemetery Association Special Publication Number 12, Edition No. 1: Series 1, 2 and 3", Page 168, Picton Press, Rockland, Maine, Copyright 2006; (3) Find A Grave, Memorial #91659829.

Baby Girl Williams
Birth:
Death: Gravestone.
Graveyard: (1) Burial Records, Sunset Cemetery, North Anson, Maine; (2) "Maine Old Cemetery Association Special Publication Number 12, Edition No. 1: Series 1, 2 and 3", Page 168, Picton Press, Rockland, Maine, Copyright 2006; (3) Find A Grave, Memorial #130464843.

Historical Accounts: (1) 1850 United States Federal Census for Embden, Somerset, Maine; (2) 1870 United States Federal Census for Embden, Somerset, Maine, Page 9; (3) 1880 United States Federal Census for Embden, Somerset, Maine, Page 15; (4) 1900 United States Federal Census for Embden, Somerset, Maine, Page 3.

Joanna Dean Williams
(1811 - 1878)

The third child of John Williams and his first wife Sally Maynard was Joanna Dean who was born in Anson, Somerset, Maine on October 29, 1811.

Sometime in 1831, the exact date and place are not known, an unmarried Joanna Dean gave birth to a daughter Minerva Violetta in Anson. The name of the father has not been found and Minerva Violetta used Williams as her last name.

Minerva Violetta	b. 1831	d. November 6, 1913

At age twenty-two, on December 13, 1833, Joanna Dean was married to Dennis B. Taylor, age twenty-four, in Industry, Franklin, Maine by Samuel Shaw, a Justice of the Peace. Dennis B., the son of Joseph Taylor and Abigail Selden, was born on November 9, 1809 in Starks, Somerset, Maine.

Joanna Dean and Dennis B. followed in a Williams' family tradition and had a large family of eleven children.

Benjamin	b. July 12, 1836	d. February 8, 1914
Asa	b. 1838	d. 1875
Alvah	b. 1840	d April 14, 1873
Rufus M.	b. December 30, 1843	d. August 17, 1877
Abigail M.	b. February 2, 1847	d. March 24, 1882
Susan A. (a twin)	b. January 1, 1848	d. April 27, 1875
Isaiah (a twin)	b. January 1, 1848	d. May 30, 1930
Stilman	b. November 8, 1851	d. January 2, 1873
Havilla	b. March 15, 1854	d. 1951
Josephine	b March 22, 1857	d. April 10, 1901
Rose Ellen	b. May 8, 1863	d. July 21, 1946

When the 1850 United States Federal Census was taken, Joanna Dean, Dennis B. and their children were recorded as living in Lexington, Somerset, Maine where Dennis B. was working as a "farmer".

Ten years later the 1860 United States Federal Census recorded that Joanna Dean, Dennis B. and their family had moved and were then living at the Sandy River Plantation in Franklin, Maine where Dennis B. was employed as a "laborer".

At the time of the 1870 United States Federal Census Joanna Dean and Dennis B. had made their final move to Rangeley, Franklin, Maine where Dennis B. was once again "farming".

Joanna Dean died in Rangeley at the age of sixty-six in 1878. The exact date and cause of her death have not been found. She was buried in the Dennis B. Taylor family plot at the Wilbur Cemetery in Rangeley.

In the 1880 United States Federal Census Dennis B. was recorded as living with his daughter, Josephine (Taylor) Wilbur, and her family in Rangeley.

Dennis B. outlived his wife by twelve years, dying in Rangeley of an unknown cause on August 3, 1890 at the age of eighty. He too was buried in his family plot in Rangeley at the Wilbur Cemetery.

Gravestone for Joanna Dean Williams and Dennis B. Taylor
(Photograph Courtesy of Gail Kelly)

SOURCES:

Joanna Dean Williams
Birth: (1) Original Record of Maine Towns & Cities Town Records of Embden, Disk 2 Page 21, Picton Press, Rockland Maine Copyright 2005; (2) Original Record of Maine Towns & Cities Town Records of Embden, Disk 2 Page 118, Picton Press, Rockland Maine Copyright 2005; (3) Original Record of Maine Towns & Cities, Town of Rangeley, Maine, Page 32, Picton Press, Rockland Maine 2005.
Death:
Graveyard: (1) "Wilbur Cemetery, Rangeley, Franklin, Maine, Gravestones", Copied August 1981 by George & Janet Thompson; (2) Find A Grave, Memorial #101210302.

Dennis B. Taylor
Birth: (1) Original Record of Maine Towns & Cities Town Records of Starks, Page 135, Picton Press, Rockland Maine Copyright 2005; (2) Original Record of Maine Towns & Cities, Town of Rangeley, Maine, Page 32, Picton Press, Rockland Maine 2005.
Marriage: (1) Record of a Marriage, Maine Vital Records; (2) Edmund West, comp., "Family Data Collection - Individual Records ", [database on-line], Provo, UT, USA: Ancestry.com Operations Inc, 2000.
Death: (1) Record of a Death, Maine Vital Records; (2) "Vital Records of Rangeley, Maine", Compiled and Edited by Jacqueline F. Chamberlain, Page 13, Picton Press, Rockland Maine 2008; (3) Original Record of Maine Towns & Cities, Town of Rangeley, Maine, Page 32, Picton Press, Rockland Maine 2005.
Graveyard: (1) "Wilbur Cemetery, Rangeley, Franklin, Maine, Gravestones", Copied August 1981 by George & Janet Thompson; (2) Find A Grave, Memorial #101210254.

Historical Accounts: (1) 1850 United States Federal Census for Lexington, Somerset, Maine; (2) 1860 United States Federal Census for Sandy River Plantation, Franklin, Maine, Pages 79 & 80; (3) 1870 United States Federal Census for Rangeley, Franklin, Maine, Pages 3 & 4; (4) 1880 United States Federal Census for Rangeley, Franklin, Maine, Page 10.

Sarah Whitney Williams
(1813 - 1871)

Sarah Whitney was the fourth child of John Williams and his first wife Sally Maynard. She was born in Embden, Somerset, Maine on October 1, 1813.

On April 2, 1839, at age twenty-six, Sarah Whitney married James R. Foss, age twenty-four, in Embden. The ceremony was performed by her uncle Caleb Williams who was a local Justice of the Peace. James R., the son of Ichabod Foss and Sarah Rowe, was born in Brighton, Somerset, Maine on February 17, 1815.

Sarah Whitney and James R. had six children.

Elfin J.	b. March 12, 1840	d. July 7, 1863
Sally W.	b. January 1842	d. November 19, 1875
John W.	*b. November 3, 1843*	*d. November 20, 1862*
Adeline R.	*b. 1848*	*d. February 5, 1871*
Kinsley Wyman	b. October 14, 1849	d. 1939
Mortimer Bodwell	b. March 18, 1855	d. March 18, 1922

In the 1850 United States Federal Census Sarah Whitney, James R. and their family were listed as living in Embden. They lived on and worked the ancestral farm of James R.'s father located on Lot 124 in Embden.

Just four years after the 1850 census, James R. died on August 8, 1854, of a cause not known, at the age of thirty-nine. He was buried in the family plot at the Moulton Cemetery in Embden.

On September 10, 1862, at age eighteen, Sarah Whitney and James R.'s third child John W. enlisted in the Union Army joining Company A, 28th Infantry of the Maine Volunteers. Two months later, while stationed in New York, and just after his nineteenth birthday, he contracted "typhoid fever" and died on November 20, 1862. His body was transported back to Embden where he was buried alongside his father in the family plot at the Moulton Cemetery.

The 1870 United States Federal Census listed Sarah Whitney living on a farm in Embden with two of her children, Adeline R. and Mortimer Bodwell. It is presumed to be the same property that John R. inherited from his father.

On February 5, 1871 the fourth child of Sarah Whitney and James R., Adeline R., died of a cause not found in Embden at the age of twenty-three. At the time of her death she was unmarried and did not have any children. Adeline R. was also buried in the Moulton Cemetery in Embden.

Sarah Whitney lived until she was fifty-eight, passing away in Embden on

December 2, 1871. Her cause of death has not been found. She too was buried in the family plot at the Moulton Cemetery in Embden.

**Gravestones for Sarah Whitney Williams (top left), James R. Foss (top right)
and John W. Foss (bottom)**
(Photographs Courtesy of Francine York)

SOURCES:

Sarah Whitney Williams
Birth: (1) Original Record of Maine Towns & Cities Town Records of Embden, Dick 2 Page 118, Picton Press, Rockland Maine, Copyright 2005; (2) Original Record of Maine Towns & Cities Town Records of Embden, Disk 2 Page 21, Picton Press, Rockland Maine, Copyright 2005.
Death: (1) "South of Lost Nation" by Ernest George Walker, Page 66, Washington, D.C., July 4, 1939, Retyped in 1994-1995 by Dean Lyons for the Embden Historical Society; (2) Gravestone.
Graveyard: (1) "Maine Old Cemetery Association Special Publication Number 12, Edition No. 1: Series 1, 2 and 3", Page 649, Picton Press, Rockland, Maine, Copyright 2006; (2) "South of Lost Nation" by Ernest George Walker, Page 66, Washington, D.C., July 4, 1939, Retyped in 1994-1995 by Dean Lyons for the Embden Historical Society; (3) Find A Grave, Memorial #118345122.

James R. Foss
Birth: "South of Lost Nation" by Ernest George Walker, Page 66, Washington, D.C., July 4, 1939, Retyped in 1994-1995 by Dean Lyons for the Embden Historical Society.
Marriage: (1) Original Record of Maine Towns & Cities Town Records of Embden, Dick 2 Page 370, Picton Press, Rockland Maine, Copyright 2005; (2) "Embden Town of Yore" by Ernest George Walker, Page 708, Published by Independent-Reporter Company, Skowhegan, Maine, 1929.
Death: (1) "South of Lost Nation" by Ernest George Walker, Page 66, Washington, D.C., July 4, 1939, Retyped in 1994-1995 by Dean Lyons for the Embden Historical Society; (2) Gravestone.
Graveyard: (1) "Maine Old Cemetery Association Special Publication Number 12, Edition No. 1: Series 1, 2 and 3", Page 649, Picton Press, Rockland, Maine, Copyright 2006; (2) "South of Lost Nation" by Ernest George Walker, Page 66, Washington, D.C., July 4, 1939; (3) Find A Grave, Memorial #118345063.

John W. Foss
Birth: "Maine, Veterans Cemetery Records 1676-1918," database with images, FamilySearch, (https://familysearch.org/ark:/61903/1:1: KXQC-TVY).
Death: (1) "Maine, Veterans Cemetery Records 1676-1918," database with images, FamilySearch, (https://familysearch.org/ark:/61903/1:1: KXQC-TVY); (2) "South of Lost Nation" by Ernest George Walker, Page 66, Washington, D.C., July 4, 1939, Retyped in 1994-1995 by Dean Lyons for the Embden Historical Society; (3) Gravestone.
Graveyard: (1) "Maine, Veterans Cemetery Records 1676-1918," database with images, FamilySearch, (https://familysearch.org/ark:/61903/1:1:KXQC-TVY); (2) "South of Lost Nation" by Ernest George Walker, Page 66, Washington, D.C., July 4, 1939, Retyped in 1994-1995 by Dean Lyons for the Embden Historical Society; (3) Find A Grave, Memorial #118345316.

Adeline R. Foss
Birth:
Death: "South of Lost Nation" by Ernest George Walker, Page 66, Washington, D.C., July 4, 1939, Retyped in 1994-1995 by Dean Lyons for the Embden Historical Society.
Graveyard: "South of Lost Nation" by Ernest George Walker, Page 66, Washington, D.C., July 4, 1939, Retyped in 1994-1995 by Dean Lyons for the Embden Historical Society.

Historical Accounts: (1) 1850 United States Federal Census for Embden, Somerset, Maine; (2) 1870 United States Federal Census for Embden, Somerset, Maine, Page 10; (3) "Embden Town of Yore" by Ernest George Walker, Page 449, Published by Independent-Reporter Company, Skowhegan, Maine, 1929; (4) "South of Lost Nation" by Ernest George Walker, Washington, D.C., July 4, 1939, Retyped in 1994-1995 by Dean Lyons for the Embden Historical Society.

Malissa M. Williams
(1836 - 1853)

The second child of John Williams and his second wife Belinda Wells was Malissa M. who was born on June 13, 1836 in Embden, Somerset, Maine.

Malissa M., at age fifteen, married Ezra Crosby, age thirty, on May 27, 1852 in Embden. Ezra, born November 26, 1822, was the son of Robert Crosby and Nancy Clark of Starks, Somerset, Maine. Additionally, besides getting married in 1852, Ezra served as the Postmaster for Embden Central during that year.

Tragically, just a little over ten months after her marriage, Malissa M. died on April 8, 1853 at the age of sixteen without issue. The cause and place of her death are not known. Malissa M. was buried in the Hodgdon Cemetery in Embden.

Ezra went on to marry Malissa M.'s younger sister, Fanny W. on December 10, 1871. After Fanny W.'s death in 1875 he married one other time and had a family. He died of "heart disease" on June 8, 1903 at age eighty-one in Madison, Somerset, Maine and was buried in the Maplewood Cemetery in Fairfield, Somerset, Maine.

SOURCES:

Malissa M. Williams
Birth: (1) Original Record of Maine Towns & Cities Town Records of Embden, Disk 1, Page 118, Picton Press, Rockland Maine, Copyright 2005; (2) Original Record of Maine Towns & Cities Town Records of Embden, Disk 2 Page 21, Picton Press, Rockland Maine, Copyright 2005.
Death: "Maine Old Cemetery Association Special Publication Number 12, Edition No. 1: Series 1, 2 and 3", Page 646, Picton Press, Rockland, Maine, Copyright 2006.
Graveyard: "Maine Old Cemetery Association Special Publication Number 12, Edition No. 1: Series 1, 2 and 3", Page 646, Picton Press, Rockland, Maine, Copyright 2006.

Ezra Crosby
Birth: "The Dinsmore Genealogy from about 1620 to 1925", by Sarah Marita Houghton Savage, Page 120, Printed by the Knowlton & McLeary Company, Farmington, Maine, 1927.
Marriage: (1) "Maine, Marriages, 1771-1907," index, FamilySearch, (https://familysearch.org/pal:/MM9.1.1 /F462-G4H); (2) "Embden Town of Yore" by Ernest George Walker, Page 714, Published by Independent-Reporter Company, Skowhegan, Maine, 1929.
Death: Record of a Death, Maine Vital Records.
Graveyard: "Maine Old Cemetery Association Special Publication Number 12, Edition No. 1: Series 1, 2 and 3", Page 746, Picton Press, Rockland, Maine, Copyright 2006.

Historical Account: "The Maine Register and State Reference Book, 1852", Page 247, Published by Master, Smith & Co., Hallowell Maine, 1852.

Fanny W. Williams
(1838 - 1875)

Fanny W. was the third child of John Williams and his second wife Belinda Wells. She was born on November 19, 1838 in Embden, Somerset, Maine.

At age twenty-two, on August 30, 1861, Fanny W. was married to Tilson T. Whitcomb, age twenty-six, in Embden by Ozias H. McFadden, a Justice of the Peace. Tilson T., born on May 23, 1835, was the son of Roswell Whitcomb and Sylvia D. Whitcomb of Norridgewock, Somerset, Maine.

Fannie W. and Tilson T. had just one child.

Lilla P.   b. 1862   d.

Prior to their marriage Tilson T. worked as a "farm laborer", as noted in the 1850 United States Federal Census for Skowhegan, Somerset, Maine, and Fanny W. worked as a "domestic", as recorded in the 1860 United States Federal Census for Embden.

On August 14, 1862, Tilson T. enlisted as a Private in Company A, 16th Maine Infantry Regiment of the Union Army. In 1864 he was captured during a battle near Petersburg, West Virginia by troops of the Confederate Army and was subsequently imprisoned in the notorious Confederate Prison at Salisbury, Rowen, North Carolina. Tilson T. died at that prison on January 15, 1865, at the age of thirty and holding the rank of Corporal. His cause of death and place of burial are unknown at this time.

After the death of her husband Tilson T., Fanny W. applied for his military pension on May 15, 1865.

Fanny W., at the age of twenty-seven, was married to her second husband Jacob Cates, age fifty-five, in Anson, Somerset, Maine on October 10, 1866 by Ozias H. McFadden. Jacob, the son of John Cates and Elizabeth Roberts, was born in Brooks, Waldo, Maine on July 4, 1811. There is no record of Fanny W. and Jacob ever having children.

Records show that Fanny W. and Jacob were divorced sometime between the date of their marriage and March 29, 1869, when Jacob married his third wife. Jacob died of an unknown cause on October 13, 1884 in Parkman, Piscataquis, Maine at the age of seventy-three. He was buried in the Pingree Center Cemetery in Parkman.

The 1870 United States Federal Census recorded Fanny W. and her daughter Lilla P. as living in Fairfield, Somerset, Maine where Fanny W. was working as a "seamstress".

On December 10, 1871 Fanny W., age thirty-three, was married to her third husband Ezra Crosby, age forty-nine, in Fairfield by S. S. Chapman, a Justice of the Peace. Ezra was also the widower of Fanny W.'s older sister Malissa M. Williams. The son of Robert Crosby and Nancy Clark, Ezra was born in Starks, Somerset, Maine on November 26, 1822.

Fanny W. died on February 5, 1875 at the age of thirty-six. The exact place and cause of her death are not known. She was buried in the Maplewood Cemetery in Fairfield.

Ezra went on to marry a third time and had a family with that wife. He died at age eighty-one in Madison, Somerset, Maine of "heart disease" on June 8, 1903. He was buried in Fairfield at the Maplewood Cemetery with his second wife Fanny W.

Gravestone for Fanny W. Williams and Ezra Crosby
Full View (left) and Close-up (right)
(Photographs from the Collection of Jeffrey Nelson Williams and Jacqueline Pon Williams)

SOURCES:

Fanny W. Williams
Birth:
Death: (1) "Maine Old Cemetery Association Special Publication Number 12, Edition No. 1: Series 1, 2 and 3", Page 746, Picton Press, Rockland, Maine, Copyright 2006; (2) Gravestone.

Graveyard: (1) Burial Records for the Maplewood Cemetery, Public Works Department, Town of Fairfield, Maine; (2) Maine Old Cemetery Association Special Publication Number 12, Edition No. 1: Series 1, 2 and 3", Page 746, Picton Press, Rockland, Maine, Copyright 2006.

Tilson T. Whitcomb
Birth: Original Record of Maine Towns & Cities, Town of Moscow, Page 47, Picton Press, Rockland Maine, Copyright 2005.
Marriage: (1) Original Record of Maine Towns & Cities Town Records of Embden, Disk 2, Page 89, Picton Press, Rockland Maine Copyright 2005; (2) "Maine, Marriages, 1771-1907," index, Family Search (https://familysearch.org/ pal:/MM9.1.1/F462-PMF); (3) "Embden Town of Yore" by Ernest George Walker, Page 718, Published by Independent-Reporter Company, Skowhegan, Maine, 1929.
Death: "Report of the Maine Commissions on the Monument Erected at Salisbury, North Carolina 1908", Sentinel Publishing Company, Waterville Maine, 1908.
Graveyard:

Jacob Cates
Birth:
Marriage: (1) Original Record of Maine Towns & Cities Town Records of Anson, Disk 1, Page 96, Picton Press, Rockland Maine, Copyright 2005; (2) "Maine, Marriages, 1771-1907," index, Family Search, (https://familysearch.org/pal:/MM9.1.1/F4X6-QPR).
Death: Gravestone.
Graveyard: Find A Grave, Memorial #41993556.

Ezra Crosby
Birth: "The Dinsmore Genealogy from about 1620 to 1925", by Sarah Marita Houghton Savage, Printed by the Knowlton & McLeary Company, Farmington, Maine, 1927, Page 120.
Marriage: Record of Marriage, Maine Vital Records.
Death: (1) Record of a Death, Maine Vital Records; (2) Gravestone.
Graveyard: (1) Burial Records for the Maplewood Cemetery, Public Works Department, Town of Fairfield, Maine; (2) "Maine Old Cemetery Association Special Publication Number 12, Edition No. 1: Series 1, 2 and 3", Page 746, Picton Press, Rockland, Maine, Copyright 2006.

Historical Accounts: (1) 1860 United States Federal Census for Embden, Somerset, Maine, Page 61; (2) 1870 United States Federal Census for Fairfield, Somerset, Maine, Page 111; (3) "The Sixteenth Maine Regiment in the War of the Rebellion 1861-1865" by Major Abner Ralph Small, B. Thurston & Company, Portland Maine, 1886; (4) US Civil War Pension Index; General Index to Pension Files, 1861-1934.

Daniel Kingman Williams
(1840 - 1918)

The fourth child of John Williams and his second wife Belinda Wells was Daniel Kingman who was born in Embden, Somerset, Maine on November 18, 1840.

Daniel Kingman Williams
(Photograph from The Independent Reporter, Skowhegan, Maine, July 26, 1918)

On October 13, 1862, Daniel Kingman enlisted as a Private in Company A, 28th Maine Infantry Regiment of the Union Army. He was discharged from service on August 31, 1863.

Daniel Kingman, age twenty-three, was married to Margaret Berry, age sixteen, on February 12, 1864 in Embden by Ozias H. McFadden, a Justice of the Peace. Margaret, the daughter of Michael F. Berry and Abigail Burns, was born in Embden on August 6, 1847.

During their marriage Daniel Kingman and Margaret had six children.

Charles Lester	b. July 1, 1866	d. May 20, 1950
Olon E.	*b. July 10, 1870*	*d. December 30, 1890*
Chester Kingman	b. October 28, 1872	d. April 1, 1922
Cora Vesta	b. July 19, 1874	d. March 6, 1913
Palmer Allen	b. May 14, 1878	d. February 3, 1940
Guy Floyd	b. June 24, 1884	d. November 23, 1959

When the 1870 United States Federal Census was taken for Embden, on July 19, 1870, Daniel Kingman and Margaret were recorded as having an infant son Albert E. It is believed that the boy Albert E. listed in the 1870 census was

Daniel Kingman and Margaret's son Olon E. who was born days before that census was taken.

On December 16, 1878 Daniel Kingman was made a Mason of Keystone Lodge No. 80 in Solon, Somerset, Maine.

In the 1880 United States Federal Census Daniel Kingman, Margaret and their children were recorded as still living in Embden, with Daniel Kingman's occupation being listed as a "farmer".

The 1890 Census of Union Veterans and Widows of the Civil War reported Daniel Kingman as having a service related disability of "chronic diarrhea from malarial poison"

The third child of Daniel Kingman and Margaret, Olon E., died on December 30, 1890 at the age of twenty having never married. The cause and place of his death have not been found. He was buried in the family plot that his father purchased at the Sunset Cemetery in North Anson, Somerset, Maine.

Gravestone for Olon E. Williams
(Photograph from the Collection of Jeffrey Nelson Williams and Jacqueline Pon Williams)

Daniel Kingman, Margaret and their children as still living and farming in Embden when the 1900 United States Federal Census was taken.

At the time of the 1910 United States Federal Census Daniel Kingman, Margaret and their family had moved to North Anson where he and his son,

Guy Floyd, had purchased the Hutchins mansion on Upper Maine Street.

On July 18, 1918, at the age of seventy-seven, Daniel Kingman died suddenly in North Anson of "myocarditis" in the field in back of his house where he had been mowing. Funeral services for Daniel Kingman were held at his home at 3:00 P.M. on Saturday, July 20th with Reverend T. B. Hatt of Bingham, Somerset, Maine officiating. In his obituary Daniel Kingman was referred to as "a large souled man, and his charity and sympathy were extended to all" and that he "was a particularly thoughtful man in his family, a good neighbor, kind friend, and most highly respected citizen". He was buried in his family plot at the Sunset Cemetery in North Anson. At the time of his death Daniel Kingman was still an active member of the Keystone Masonic Lodge, No. 80 in Solon and a member of the Order of the Eastern Star.

Shortly after Daniel Kingman's death, Margaret, on August 14, 1918, applied for and received his military pension. She was recorded as living with her son Guy Floyd and his family in North Anson when the 1920 United States Federal Census was taken.

Margaret survived her husband by almost six years dying of an unknown cause at age seventy-six on May 22, 1924 in North Anson. She too was buried in the family plot at the Sunset Cemetery.

Gravestone for Daniel Kingman Williams and Margaret Berry
(Photograph from the Collection of Jeffrey Nelson Williams and Jacqueline Pon Williams)

SOURCES:

Daniel Kingman Williams
Birth: (1) Obituary, The Independent Reporter, Skowhegan, Somerset, Maine, July 26, 1918, Page 4; (2) Edmund West, comp., "Family Data Collection - Individual Records", [database on-line]. Provo, UT, USA: Ancestry.com Operations Inc., 2000.
Death: (1) Record of a Death, Maine Vital Records; (2) "South of Lost Nation" by Ernest George Walker, Page 85, Washington, D.C., July 4, 1939, Retyped in 1994-1995 by Dean Lyons for the Embden Historical Society; (3) Obituary, The Independent Reporter, Skowhegan, Somerset, Maine, July 26, 1918, Page 4.
Graveyard: (1) Burial Records, Sunset Cemetery, North Anson, Maine; (2) "Maine Old Cemetery Association Special Publication Number 12, Edition No. 1: Series 1, 2 and 3", Page 167, Picton Press, Rockland, Maine, Copyright 2006; (3) Find A Grave, Memorial #91659782.

Margaret Berry
Birth: "South of Lost Nation" by Ernest George Walker, Page 23, Washington, D.C., July 4, 1939, Retyped in 1994-1995 by Dean Lyons for the Embden Historical Society.
Marriage: (1) Original Record of Maine Towns & Cities Town Records of Embden, Disk 2, Page 94, Picton Press, Rockland Maine, Copyright 2005; (2) "Maine, Marriages, 1771-1907," index, Family Search, (https:// familysearch.org/pal:/ MM9.1.1/F462-PQZ); (3) "Embden Town of Yore" by Ernest George Walker, Page 720, Published by Independent-Reporter Company, Skowhegan, Maine, 1929; (4) "South of Lost Nation" by Ernest George Walker, Page 23, Washington, D.C., July 4, 1939, Retyped in 1994-1995 by Dean Lyons for the Embden Historical Society.
Death:
Graveyard: (1) Burial Records, Sunset Cemetery, North Anson, Maine; (2) "Maine Old Cemetery Association Special Publication Number 12, Edition No. 1: Series 1, 2 and 3", Page 167, Picton Press, Rockland, Maine, Copyright 2006; (3) Find A Grave, Memorial #91659787.

Olon E. Williams
Birth:
Death: (1) "South of Lost Nation" by Ernest George Walker, Page 85, Washington, D.C., July 4, 1939, Retyped in 1994-1995 by Dean Lyons for the Embden Historical Society; (2) Gravestone.
Graveyard: (1) Burial Records, Sunset Cemetery, North Anson, Maine; (2) "Maine Old Cemetery Association Special Publication Number 12, Edition No. 1: Series 1, 2 and 3", Page 167, Picton Press, Rockland, Maine, Copyright 2006; (3) Find A Grave, Memorial #91659793.

Historical Accounts: (1) 1870 United States Federal Census for Embden, Somerset, Maine, Page 7; (2) 1880 United States Federal Census for Embden, Somerset, Maine; (3) 1890 Census of Union Veterans and Widows of the Civil War for Embden, Page 1; (4) 1900 United States Federal Census for Embden, Somerset, Maine, Page 2; (5) 1910 United States Federal Census for North Anson, Somerset, Maine, Page 7B; (6) 1920 United States Federal Census for Anson, Somerset, Maine, Page 7B; (7) "U.S. Civil War Soldier Records and Profiles, 1861-1865", (database on-line), Ancestry.com Operations, Inc., 2009; (8) "South of Lost Nation" by Ernest George Walker, Page 85, Washington, D.C., July 4, 1939, Retyped in 1994-1995 by Dean Lyons for the Embden Historical Society; (9) Obituary for Daniel Kingman Williams, The Independent Reporter, Skowhegan, Somerset, Maine, July 26, 1918, Page 4.

Belinda Adelaide Williams
(1844 - 1890)

The fifth child, Belinda Adelaide (commonly known as Adelaide Belinda), of John Williams and his second wife Belinda Wells was born in Embden, Somerset, Maine on January 25, 1844.

When the 1860 United States Federal Census was taken Belinda Adelaide was recorded as living with her parents in Embden and working as a "domestic".

At the age of twenty-two, on August 18, 1866, Belinda Adelaide was married to James E. Morse, age twenty-seven, by A. R. Sylvester, a clergyman, in Fairfield, Somerset, Maine. James E., the son of Thomas Morse and Mary B. Nichols, was born in Industry, Franklin, Maine on December 12, 1838. No record has been found providing evidence that Belinda Adelaide and James E. ever had a child together.

The 1870 United States Federal Census recorded Belinda Adelaide, James E. and James E.'s daughter from a prior marriage, Esther (listed as Etta), living in Fairfield where James E. was working as a "shoemaker".

When the 1880 United States Federal Census was taken Belinda Adelaide and her step-daughter Esther were still living in Fairfield. Belinda Adelaide's occupation was recorded as "keeping a boarding house". The whereabouts of James E. at the time of that census has not been found.

Two years later, in September 1882, Belinda Adelaide and James E. were divorced in Somerset County, Maine.

Belinda Adelaide died on May 28, 1890 at the age of forty-six. The exact cause and place of her death has not been found. She was buried in the Maplewood Cemetery in Fairfield.

James E. outlived his ex-wife by thirty-two years dying on August 1, 1922. The place and cause of his death are also not known. He was buried in the Harmony Cemetery in Georgetown, Essex, Massachusetts.

Gravestone for Belinda Adelaide Williams
(Photograph from the Collection of Jeffrey Nelson Williams and Jacqueline Pon Williams)

SOURCES:

Belinda Adelaide Williams
Birth: Gravestone.
Death: (1) "Maine Old Cemetery Association Special Publication Number 12, Edition No. 1: Series 1, 2 and 3",
Page 827, Picton Press, Rockland, Maine, Copyright 2006; (2) Gravestone.
Graveyard: (1) Burial Records for the Maplewood Cemetery, Public Works Department, Town of Fairfield,
Maine; (2) "Maine Old Cemetery Association Special Publication Number 12, Edition No. 1: Series 1, 2 and 3",
Page 827, Picton Press, Rockland, Maine, Copyright 2006; (3) Find A Grave, Memorial #88597727.

James E. Morse
Birth: "U.S. National Homes for Disabled Volunteer Soldiers, 1866-1938", Page 13747, [database on-line].
Provo, UT, USA: Ancestry.com Operations Inc., 2007.
Marriage: Record of Marriage, Maine Vital Records.
Divorce: "Maine, Divorce Records, 1798-11891," (database on-line), Provo, UT, USA: Ancestry.com Operations,
Inc., 2011.
Death: "U.S., Civil War Soldier Records and Profiles, 1861-1865", [database on-line]. Provo, UT, USA:
Ancestry.com Operations Inc, 2009.
Graveyard: Find A Grave, Memorial #125750902.

Historical Accounts: (1) 1860 United States Federal Census for Embden, Somerset, Maine, Page 61; (2) 1870
United States Federal Census for Fairfield, Somerset, Maine, Page 41; (3) 1880 United States Federal Census for
Fairfield, Somerset, Maine; Page 17.

Cyrus A. Williams
(1847 - 1887)

Cyrus A. was the sixth child of John Williams and his second wife Belinda Wells. He was born on January 14, 1847 in Embden, Somerset, Maine.

In the 1870 United States Federal Census taken on June 20, 1870, Cyrus A. was recorded as working as a "tailor" and living with his cousin Lucy Ellen (Williams) McIntire and her husband Charles B. McIntire in Solon, Somerset, Maine.

A few months later on November 12, 1870, at age twenty-three, Cyrus A. and Lucy Ann Holway, age twenty-one, filed their intentions to be married with the Town Clerk of Bingham, Somerset, Maine. A Certificate of Marriage was issued to them six days later, on November 18, 1870, in Bingham. Lucy Ann, born on January 8, 1849, was the daughter of Ansel Holway and Betsey McIntire of Bingham. Cyrus A. and Lucy Ann did not have any children during their marriage.

By the time the 1880 United States Federal Census was taken, Cyrus A. and Lucy Ann were recorded as living in Fairfield, Somerset, Maine. In that census Cyrus A.'s occupation was listed as a "confectionary dealer".

Sometime between the taking of the 1880 census and 1887 Cyrus A. and Lucy Ann moved to Somerville, Middlesex, Massachusetts where on June 12, 1887, at the age of forty, Cyrus A. died of "paralysis". His death certificate indicated that was he was working there as a "salesman". Cyrus A.'s body was returned to Maine where he was buried in the Maplewood Cemetery in Fairfield.

Two years later, on June 13, 1889, Lucy Ann married her second husband James Hayward Mills in Somerville. James Hayward, the son of William Mills and Elizabeth A. Cutts, was born in Cambridge, Middlesex, Massachusetts on January 8, 1837. Lucy Ann and James Hayward did not have any children during their marriage.

A little over five years later, on November 4, 1894, James Hayward died in Somerville of "heart failure". His body was taken to Maine where he was buried in the Maplewood Cemetery in Fairfield.

Lucy Ann was listed in the 1900 and 1910 United States Federal Census' as a widow living in Somerville where she was working as a "seamstress".

By the time the 1920 United States Federal Census was taken Lucy Ann was living in Oakland, Kennebec, Maine with her aunt Elizabeth McIntire.

At the time of the 1930 United States Federal Census Lucy Ann had moved back to Fairfield where she was living at #6 on the Kelly Street Extension. She died four years later, in 1934, at the age of eighty-four. The exact date, location and cause of her death have not been found. She too was buried in the Maplewood Cemetery in Fairfield.

Gravestone for Cyrus A. Williams, Lucy Ann Holway & James Hayward Mills
Front View (top left) and Back View (top right)

Headstones for Cyrus A. Williams (middle left), Lucy Ann Holway (middle right)
and James Hayward Mills (bottom)

(Photographs from the Collection of Jeffrey Nelson Williams and Jacqueline Pon Williams)

SOURCES:

Cyrus A. Williams
Birth:
Death: "Massachusetts, Death Records, 1841-1915", [database on-line], Provo, UT, USA: Ancestry.com Operations, Inc., 2013, Deaths Registered in the City of Somerville for the Year 1887.
Graveyard: (1) Burial Records for the Maplewood Cemetery, Public Works Department, Town of Fairfield, Maine; (2) "Maine Old Cemetery Association Special Publication Number 12, Edition No. 1: Series 1, 2 and 3", Page 825, Picton Press, Rockland, Maine, Copyright 2006; (3) Find A Grave, Memorial #88597563.

Lucy Ann Holway
Birth: "Maine, Births and Christenings, 1739-1900," index, FamilySearch, (https://familysearch.org/pal: /MM9.1.1/F439-YZG).
Marriage: (1) Original Record of Maine Towns & Cities, Town of Bingham, Page 202, Picton Press, Rockland Maine, Copyright 2005; (2) "Maine, Marriages, 1771-1907," index, Family Search, (https://familysearch.org/pal:/ MM9.1.1/F4F1-MHW).
Death:
Graveyard: (1) Burial Records for the Maplewood Cemetery, Public Works Department, Town of Fairfield, Maine; (2) "Maine Old Cemetery Association Special Publication Number 12, Edition No. 1: Series 1, 2 and 3", Page 825, Picton Press, Rockland, Maine, Copyright 2006; (3) Find A Grave, Memorial #88597538.

James Hayward Mills
Birth: "Massachusetts, Mason Membership Cards, 1733-1990", [database on-line]. Provo, UT, USA: Ancestry.com Operations, Inc., 2013.
Marriage: "Massachusetts, Marriage Records, 1840-1915", [database on-line], Provo, UT, USA: Ancestry.com Operations, Inc., 2013, Marriages Registered in the City of Somerville for the Year 1889, Page 258.
Death: "Massachusetts, Death Records, 1841-1915", [database on-line], Provo, UT, USA: Ancestry.com Operations, Inc., 2013, Deaths Registered in the City of Somerville for the Year 1894.
Graveyard: (1) Burial Records for the Maplewood Cemetery, Public Works Department, Town of Fairfield, Maine; (2) "Maine Old Cemetery Association Special Publication Number 12, Edition No. 1: Series 1, 2 and 3", Page 825, Picton Press, Rockland, Maine, Copyright 2006; (3) Find A Grave, Memorial #88597385.

Historical Accounts: (1) 1870 United States Federal Census for Solon, Somerset, Maine, Page 22; (2) 1880 United States Federal Census for Fairfield, Somerset, Maine, Page 13; (3) 1900 United States Federal Census for Somerville, Middlesex, Massachusetts, Page 10; (4) 1910 United States Federal Census for Somerville, Middlesex, Massachusetts, Page 20A; (5) 1920 United States Federal Census for Oakland, Kennebec, Maine, Page 24B; (6) 1930 United States Federal Census for Fairfield, Somerset, Maine, Page 24B.

Isaac Palmer Williams
(1849 - 1874)

The seventh child of John Williams and his second wife Belinda Wells was Isaac Palmer. He was born in Embden, Somerset, Maine in June of 1849.

When the 1850 and 1860 United States Federal Census' were taken Isaac Palmer (commonly known as Palmer) was living with his parents on their farm in Embden.

At the time of the 1870 United States Federal Census Isaac Palmer was recorded as living with his brother Daniel Kingman Williams and his family in Embden. In that census Isaac Palmer was working as a "farm laborer" on his brother's, Daniel Kingman's, farm.

Isaac Palmer died on August 12, 1874 at the age of twenty-five without having married or having had any children. The exact place and cause of his death have not been found. He was buried in the John Williams family plot at the Pleasantdale Cemetery in Embden.

Gravestone for Isaac Palmer Williams
(Photograph from the Collection of Jeffrey Nelson Williams and Jacqueline Pon Williams)

SOURCES:

Isaac Palmer Williams
Birth:
Death: (1) "Faylene Hutton Cemetery Collection, 1780-1980, Accession #5030", FamilySearch, (https://familysearch.org/ark:/61903/1.1/QKM1-W29W); (2) Gravestone.
Graveyard: (1) "Pleasantdale Cemetery" complied by Nancy Hamlin Davis and Ruth Hamlin, Record 129, Old Canada Road Historical Society; (2) Find A Grave, Memorial #118445664

Historical Accounts: (1) 1850 United States Federal Census for Embden, Somerset, Maine; (2) 1860 United States Federal Census for Embden, Somerset, Maine, Page 61; (3) 1870 United States Federal Census for Embden, Somerset, Maine, Page 8.

Alvin Williams
(1814 - 1842)

Alvin, the second child of Richard Williams and Abigail Rowe, was born on August 15, 1814 in Concord, Somerset, Maine.

In the 1840 United States Federal Census of Concord Alvin was recorded as the head of his own household.

One year later, on May 15, 1841 Alvin, at the age of twenty-six, and Lydia Cain of Sydney, Kennebec, Maine published their intentions to marry with the Town Clerk of Concord. The date and place of their subsequent marriage, as well as Lydia's date of birth and the names of her parents, are not known.

Alvin died a short time later on March 18, 1842 at the age of twenty-seven. The place and cause of his death have not been found. He was buried alongside his sister Elvira in the Richard Williams family plot at the Pleasantdale Cemetery in Embden, Somerset, Maine.

Additional information regarding the life and death of Lydia has not been found.

Gravestone for Alvin Williams
(Photograph from the Collection of Jeffrey Nelson Williams and Jacqueline Pon Williams)

SOURCES:

Alvin Williams
Birth: (1) Original Record of Maine Towns & Cities, Town of Concord, Page 83, Picton Press, Rockland Maine, Copyright 2005; (2) "Maine Births and Christenings 1739-1900," index Family Search, (https://familysearch.org /pal:/MM9.1.1 /F4Q4-RQF).
Death: Gravestone.
Graveyard: (1) "Pleasantdale Cemetery" complied by Nancy Hamlin Davis and Ruth Hamlin, Record 129, Old Canada Road Historical Society; (2) Find A Grave, Memorial #118443423.

Lydia Cain
Birth:
Marriage: (1) Original Record of Maine Towns & Cities Town Records of Concord, Page 138, Picton Press, Rockland Maine 2005.
Death:
Graveyard:

Historical Accounts: 1840 United States Federal Census for Concord, Somerset, Maine.

Luther Williams
(1816 - 1870)

The third child of Richard Williams and Abigail Rowe was Luther. He was born in Concord, Somerset, Maine on October 23, 1816.

When the 1840 United States Federal Census of Concord was taken, Luther was recorded as the head of his own household.

It is believed that sometime after the 1840 census was taken Luther moved to Lynn, Essex, Massachusetts where on January 22, 1845, at the age of twenty-eight, Luther married Rebecca Silsbee, age twenty-six. Rebecca, the daughter of Henry Silsbee and Miriam Gould, was born on October 2, 1818 in Lynn.

Luther and Rebecca had five children.

Sumner Gould	b. November 12, 1845	d. May 15, 1899
Maria Silsbee	*b. May 6, 1849*	*d. August 3, 1865*
Henry Stillman	b. February 26, 1851	d. November 26, 1901
Mary Ann	*b. January 14, 1853*	*d. August 20, 1859*
Alden Burrill	*b. November 6, 1855*	*d. November 21, 1859*

In the 1850 United States Federal Census and the 1855 Massachusetts State Census taken on August 21, 1855, Luther was recorded as working as a "farmer" and living with his family in Lynn.

In 1859 two of Luther and Rebecca's children died in Lynn at young ages. Mary Ann was six years eight months when she died of "dropsy" on August 20, 1859 and Alden Burrill was four years old when he died of "dropsy of the brain" three months later on November 21, 1859. Both children were buried in the Luther Williams family lot, Plot #595 on Locust Avenue, at the Pine Grove Cemetery in Lynn. Mary Ann is buried there in Grave 4 and Alden Burrill is buried in Grave 2.

The 1860 United States Federal Census for Lynn recorded Luther, Rebecca and their children as still living and farming there.

On August 3, 1865 Maria Silsbee, the second child of Luther and Rebecca, died at the age of sixteen. The place and cause of her death have not been found. She was buried in Plot #595, Grave 6 at the Pine Grove Cemetery in Lynn.

Luther died of "consumption" on April 23, 1870 in Solon, Somerset, Maine at the age of fifty-three. His body was returned to Massachusetts and was buried in Plot #595, Grave 8, his family lot, at the Pine Grove Cemetery in Lynn.

When the 1870 United States Federal Census was taken on June 6, 1870, Rebecca had moved and was recorded as living on a farm in Solon with her son, Henry Stillman.

By the time the 1880 United States Federal Census was taken, Rebecca had moved again and was living in Lewiston, Androscoggin, Maine with her first son, Sumner Gould, and his family.

Rebecca outlived Luther by more than twenty-three years, dying on August 6, 1897 of an unknown cause at the age of seventy-eight in Lewiston. Her body was returned to Massachusetts where she was buried in Lynn at the Pine Grove Cemetery in Plot #595, Grave 10.

SOURCES:

Luther Williams
Birth: (1) Original Record of Maine Towns & Cities, Town of Concord, Page 83, Picton Press, Rockland Maine, Copyright 2005; (2) "Maine Births and Christenings 1739-1900," index Family Search, (https://familysearch.org /pal:/MM9.1.1 /F4Q4-RQV).
Death: United States Federal Census Mortality Schedule for Solon, Somerset, Maine, for the year ending June 30, 1870, Page 1.
Graveyard: Find A Grave, Memorial #46645081.

Rebecca Silsbee
Birth: "Massachusetts, Town and Vital Records, 1620-1988", [database on-line], Provo, UT, USA: Ancestry.com Operations, Inc., 2011, Lynn Births, Page 369.
Marriage: "Massachusetts, Town and Vital Records, 1620-1988", [database on-line], Provo, UT, USA: Ancestry.com Operations, Inc., 2011, Lynn Marriages, Page 397.
Death: (1) Record of a Death, Maine Vital Records; (2) Death Notice, Lewiston Evening Journal, Lewiston, Maine, Saturday, August 7, 1897, Page 11.
Graveyard: Find A Grave, Memorial #46645118.

Maria Silsbee Williams
Birth: (1) "Massachusetts, Town and Vital Records, 1620-1988", [database on-line], Provo, UT, USA: Ancestry.com Operations, Inc., 2011, Lynn Births, Page 369; (2) Lynn Massachusetts, Town Records, for the year 1848 from May 14 and for the year 1849, Page 7 Number 298.
Death:
Graveyard: Find A Grave, Memorial #46646188.

Mary Ann Williams
Birth: "Massachusetts, Birth Records, 1840-1915", [database on-line], Provo, UT, USA: Ancestry.com Operations, Inc., 2013, Births in the Town of Lynn for the year 1853, Page 210.
Death: (1) "Massachusetts, Death Records, 1841-1915", [database on-line], Provo, UT, USA: Ancestry.com Operations, Inc., 2013; (2) United States Federal Census Mortality Schedule for Lynn, Middlesex, Massachusetts for the year ending June 30, 1860, Page 1.
Graveyard: Find A Grave, Memorial #46645045.

Alden Burrill Williams
Birth: Massachusetts Birth Records registered in Lynn Massachusetts for the year 1855, Page 202 Number 450.
Death: "Massachusetts, Death Records, 1841-1915", [database on-line], Provo, UT, USA: Ancestry.com Operations, Inc., 2013.
Graveyard: Find A Grave, Memorial #46644964.

Historical Accounts: (1) 1840 United States Federal Census for Concord, Somerset, Maine; (2) 1850 United States Federal Census for Lynn, Essex, Massachusetts; (3) 1855 Massachusetts State Census for Lynn, Essex, Massachusetts; (4) 1860 United States Federal Census for Lynn, Essex, Massachusetts, Page 122; (5) 1870 United States Federal Census for Solon, Somerset, Maine, Page 1; (6) 1880 United States Federal Census for Lewiston, Androscoggin, Maine, Page 6.

Mary Ann Williams
(1819 - 1888)

Mary Ann, the fourth child of Richard Williams and Abigail Rowe, was born on November 24, 1819 in Concord, Somerset, Maine.

On September 16, 1841 Mary Ann, age twenty-one, and Ezra McIntire Fletcher, age twenty-six, published their intentions to marry with the Town Clerk of Concord. The date and place of their subsequent marriage have not been found. Ezra McIntire, born on November 13, 1814, was the son of Asa Fletcher and Lydia McIntire of Moscow, Somerset, Maine.

During their marriage Mary Ann and Ezra McIntire had seven children.

Clara A.	b. July 31, 1843	d. February 15, 1918
Charles Henry	b. July 4, 1845	d. March 16, 1890
Luther W.	b. October 6, 1847	d. January 1924
Sarah F.	*b. June 10, 1850*	*d. June 7, 1866*
Ella May	b. November 19, 1856	d. December 11, 1941
Alice Alberta	b. June 6, 1859	d. February 16, 1893
Fred William	b. March 17, 1865	d. June 6, 1940

In the 1850 and 1860 United States Federal Census' Mary Ann, Ezra McIntire and their children were recorded as living in Solon, Somerset, Maine where Ezra McIntire was "farming".

Sarah F., the fourth child of Mary Ann and Ezra McIntire, died on June 7, 1866 at the age of fifteen. The location and cause of her death are not known. She was buried in the Ezra McIntire Fletcher family plot in in Solon at the Village Cemetery.

Headstone for Sarah F. Fletcher
(Photograph from the Collection of Jeffrey Nelson Williams and Jacqueline Pon Williams)

When the 1870 and 1880 United States Federal Census' were taken for Solon, Mary Ann, Ezra McIntire and their children were recorded as still living there and working their farm.

On July 27, 1888 Mary Ann, at the age of sixty-eight, died of an unknown cause in Solon. She was buried in the family plot at the Village Cemetery in Solon.

Ezra McIntire outlived his wife by a little more than five years, dying suddenly at age seventy-eight, of "heart disease", on August 2, 1893 in Auburn, Androscoggin, Maine where he was visiting his daughter Ella May (Fletcher) Foss. His body was transported back to Solon where he was buried with his wife and children in the Village Cemetery.

The estate of Ezra McIntire, after funeral and probate costs, was valued at $1,308.01. It was distributed five ways. One-fifth was given to each of his surviving children and one-fifth was given to the children of his late son Charles Henry.

Fletcher Family Monument
Front View (top left) and Back View (top right)
Headstones for Mary Ann Williams (bottom left) and Ezra McIntire Fletcher (bottom right)
(Photographs from the Collection of Jeffrey Nelson Williams and Jacqueline Pon Williams)

SOURCES:

Mary Ann Williams
Birth: (1) "Maine Births and Christenings 1739-1900," index Family Search, (https://familysearch.org/pal:/MM9.1.1/F4CT-MJM); (2) Original Record of Maine Towns & Cities Town Records of Concord, Page 83, Picton Press, Rockland Maine, Copyright 2005.
Death:
Graveyard: Find A Grave, Memorial #94737510.

Ezra McIntire Fletcher
Birth: (1) Original Record of Maine Towns & Cities Town Records of Moscow, Page 12, Picton Press, Rockland Maine, Copyright 2005; (2) "Maine Births and Christenings 1739-1900," index Family Search, (https://familysearch.org/pal:/MM9.1.1/F4QH-BYY).
Marriage: Original Record of Maine Towns & Cities Town Records of Concord, Page 138, Picton Press, Rockland Maine, Copyright 2005.
Death: (1) Record of a Death, Maine Vital Records; (2) Death Notice, Lewiston Evening Journal, Lewiston, Maine, Thursday, August 3, 1893, Page 5.
Graveyard: Find A Grave, Memorial #94737500.

Sarah F. Fletcher
Birth:
Death:
Graveyard: Find A Grave, Memorial #94737531.

Historical Accounts: (1) 1850 United States Federal Census for Solon, Somerset, Maine; (2) 1860 United States Federal Census for Solon, Somerset, Maine, Page 43; (3) 1870 United States Federal Census for Solon, Somerset, Maine, Page 1; (4) 1880 United States Federal Census for Solon, Somerset, Maine, Page 1; (5) "Maine, Wills and Probate Records, 1584-1999", [database on-line]. Provo, UT, USA: Ancestry.com Operations Inc, 2015.

Calvin Williams
(1829 - 1896)

Calvin was the sixth child of Richard Williams and Abigail Rowe. He was born in Concord, Somerset, Maine on May 25, 1829.

During the years before his marriage, Calvin spent some time in Massachusetts and by the time the 1850 United States Federal Census was taken he had returned to Concord to live with his parents. It was said that after his return Calvin was a little more liberal than his stern Methodist parents.

At the age of twenty-one, Calvin and Susan Clark Wells, age twenty, filed their intentions to marry with the Town Clerk of Embden, Somerset, Maine on July 29, 1850. They were subsequently married in Embden on August 4, 1850 by Daniel Witham, a Justice of the Peace. Susan Clark, the daughter of Ralph Wells and Mercy Clark, was born on October 8, 1829 in Embden.

Calvin and Susan Clark had eight children together.

James Leon	b. April 21, 1852	d. February 23, 1932
Charles Osmund	b. May 21, 1854	d. August 3, 1885
Emma Delia	b. April 11, 1856	d. November 28, 1955
Jessie Viola	b. July 1858	d. June 29, 1936
Calvin Milton	b. February 1861	d. 1955
Andrew J.	b. April 6, 1864	d. July 22, 1943
Malon	b. 1868	d. February 28, 1892
Herbert	b. May 1870	d. August 18, 1893

In his book "The Life and Work of James Leon Williams" George Wood Clap remarked that the Calvin Williams household was one where reading was favored. Calvin was known to receive the weekly "Maine Farmer" and Susan Clark received "Godey's Lady Book" every month.

When the 1860 United States Federal Census was taken for Concord, Calvin and his family were living on a farm. After Calvin's mother's death in 1863, his father, Richard Williams, moved in to live with him and his family.

In the later 1860's Calvin left the family farm and moved his family to Skowhegan, Somerset, Maine. Two years after that move, the family once again relocated, this time to Vassalboro, Kennebec, Maine.

At the time of the 1870 United States Federal Census Calvin, Susan Clark and their family were recorded as living in Vassalboro, with Calvin's occupation listed as a "woolen factory employee".

The 1880 United States Federal Census recorded Calvin, Susan Clark and their last three children, Andrew J., Malon and Herbert, living in Vassalboro and Calvin still working in a "woolen mill".

Calvin died on April 19, 1896 at age sixty-six in North Vassalboro, Kennebec, Maine. His cause of death was listed as the "effect of a combination of diseases". He was buried in the North Vassalboro Village Cemetery in North Vassalboro.

Susan Clark survived her husband by nine years and eight days, dying on April 27, 1905 at the age of seventy-five while living at 12 Pleasant Street in Rochester, Strafford, New Hampshire. Her cause of death was listed as "pulmonary tuberculosis". Susan Clark's body was returned to Maine and where she was buried next to her husband in the North Vassalboro Village Cemetery in North Vassalboro.

Gravestones for Calvin Williams (left) and Susan Clark Wells (right)
(Photographs from the Collection of Jeffrey Nelson Williams and Jacqueline Pon Williams)

SOURCES:

Calvin Williams
Birth: Edmund West, comp., "Family Data Collection - Individual Records", [database on-line], Provo, UT, USA: Ancestry.com Operations Inc, 2000.
Death: (1) Record of a Death, Maine Vital Records; (2) Gravestone.
Graveyard: Find A Grave, Memorial #17368548.

Susan Clark Wells
Birth: (1) Original Record of Maine Towns & Cities, Town of Embden, Disk 1, Page 106, Picton Press, Rockland Maine, Copyright 2005; (2) Original Record of Maine Towns & Cities, Town of Embden, Disk 2, Page 20, Picton Press, Rockland Maine, Copyright 2005.
Marriage: (1) Original Record of Maine Towns & Cities, Town of Embden, Disk 2, Page 65, Picton Press, Rockland Maine, Copyright 2005; (2) "Maine, Marriages, 1771-1907," index, Family Search, (https://familysearch.org/pal: /MM9.1.1/F462-GQB).
Death: (1) Record of a Death, Maine Vital Records; (2) "New Hampshire Death and Burial Records Index, 1654-1949," [database on-line], Provo, UT, USA: Ancestry.com Operations, Inc., 2011; (3) Gravestone.
Graveyard: Find A Grave, Memorial #17368588.

Historical Accounts: (1) 1850 United States Federal Census for Concord, Somerset, Maine; (2) 1860 United States Federal Census for Concord, Somerset, Maine, Page 65; (3) 1870 United States Federal Census for Vassalboro, Kennebec, Maine, Page 28; (4) 1880 United States Federal Census for Vassalboro, Kennebec, Maine, Page 41; (5) "The Life and Work of James Leon Williams" by George Wood Clapp, Published by The Dental Digest, New York, USA 1925.

Otis Isaac Williams
(1818 - 1878)

The second child of Isaac Otis Williams and Rachel S. Heald was Otis Isaac who was born on November 6, 1818 in Somerset County, Maine.

At age twenty-three, on September 20, 1843, Otis Isaac was married to Martha A. Somerby, age fourteen, in Solon, Somerset, Maine by John Pierce, a Justice of the Peace. Martha A., the daughter of Robert Somerby and Eleanor Bean, was born in Caratunk, Somerset, Maine. There are two data points for her date of birth, her death record indicates she was born on April 30, 1827 and her gravestone indicates she was born on May 26, 1827. Which, if either, is the correct date is not known.

Martha A. Somerby
(Photograph Courtesy of Carolann Sheppard)

During their marriage Otis Isaac and Martha A. had six children.

Vesta Victoria	b. October 24, 1844	d. December 18, 1904
Mary Ellen	b. February 14, 1846	d. March 26, 1912
Rachel Violet	b. August 1847	d. November 11, 1900
Rose L.	b. August 1850	d. December 2, 1933
Ada M.	b. April 18, 1857	d. August 14, 1934
Lillian E.	b. October 1859	d. January 9, 1930

In the 1850 United States Federal Census Otis Isaac, Martha A. and their first three children were recorded as living in No. 1, Range 2, West Kennebec River, Somerset, Maine, with Otis Isaac's occupation being listed as a "laborer".

Otis Isaac, Martha A. and their children were listed as living in Pleasant

Ridge, Somerset, Maine in the 1860 United States Federal Census. Otis Isaac's occupation was recorded as a "farmer".

Sometime between 1861 and 1865 during the United States Civil War, Otis Isaac served as a Private in Company C of the 29th Regiment of the Maine Infantry for the Union Army.

The 1870 United States Federal Census recorded Otis Isaac, Martha A. and their three youngest children as living on the family farm in Pleasant Ridge.

On July 17, 1878, at the age of fifty-eight, Otis Isaac passed away. The cause and place of his death have not been found. He was buried in the Bingham Village Cemetery in Bingham, Somerset, Maine.

When the 1880 United States Federal Census was taken Martha A., then age fifty-three, was still living in Pleasant Ridge. In that census she was listed as working as a "housekeeper".

Martha A. outlived her husband by almost fourteen years, dying in Pleasant Ridge on April 12, 1892 at the age of sixty-four from "carcinoma of the womb". She was buried in Bingham next to her husband in the Bingham Village Cemetery.

Gravestones for Otis Isaac Williams (left) and Martha A. Somerby (right)
(Photographs from the Collection of Jeffrey Nelson Williams and Jacqueline Pon Williams)

SOURCES:

Otis Isaac Williams

Birth: (1) Original Record of Maine Towns & Cities, Town of Bingham, Page 24, Picton Press, Rockland Maine, Copyright 2005; (2) Original Record of Maine Towns & Cities, Town of Moscow, Page 49, Picton Press, Rockland Maine, Copyright 2005. (3) "Maine, Births and Christenings, 1739-1900," index, FamilySearch, (https://familysearch.org/pal:/MM9.1.1/F4QC-3HN); (4) Listing of family births and deaths from the Gilman L. Williams family archives from the collection of SullyJ; (5) Gravestone.

Death: Gravestone.

Graveyard: (1) "Maine Old Cemetery Association Special Publication Number 12, Edition No. 1: Series 1, 2 and 3", Page 335, Picton Press, Rockland, Maine, Copyright 2006; (2) "Bingham Village Cemetery" by Nancy Hamlin Davis and Ruth Hamlin, Old Canada Road Historical Society; (3) Find A Grave, Memorial #81805400.

Martha A. Somerby

Birth: (1) Record of a Death, Maine Vital Records; (2) Gravestone.

Marriage: Original Record of Maine Towns & Cities, Town of Solon, Page 89, Picton Press, Rockland Maine, Copyright 2005.

Death: (1) Record of a Death, Maine Vital Records; (2) Gravestone.

Graveyard: (1) "Maine Old Cemetery Association Special Publication Number 12, Edition No. 1: Series 1, 2 and 3", Page 334, Picton Press, Rockland, Maine, Copyright 2006; (2) "Bingham Village Cemetery" by Nancy Hamlin Davis and Ruth Hamlin, Old Canada Road Historical Society; (3) Find A Grave, Memorial #81805416.

Historical Accounts: (1) 1850 United States Federal Census for No. 1, Range 2, West Kennebec River, Somerset Maine; (2) 1860 United States Federal Census for Pleasant Ridge, Somerset, Maine, Page 11; (3) 1870 United States Federal Census for Pleasant Ridge, Somerset, Maine, Page 1; (4) 1880 United States Federal Census for Pleasant Ridge, Somerset, Maine, Page 6; (5) "United States Civil War Index" index, FamilySearch, (https://familysearch.org/pal:/MM9.1.1/FS4T-ZMX).

Eli S. Williams
(1821 - 1884)

Eli S. was the third child of Isaac Otis Williams and Rachel S. Heald and the second child they had named Eli. He was born in Moscow, Somerset, Maine on April 13, 1821. (Note: Although his gravestone indicates his date of birth as December 22, 1820, the Moscow and other official records reviewed indicate that he was born on April 13, 1821)

In the 1850 United States Federal Census Eli S., age twenty-nine, was recorded as living with his parents in Moscow and working as a "farmer".

On May 3, 1853, at age thirty-two, Eli S. was married to Sybil M. Hunnewell, age twenty-six, in Moscow. Sybil M., the daughter of Ebenezer Hunnewell and Abigail Thompson of Moscow, was born on February 8, 1827.

Eli S. and Sybil M. had seven children.

Nancy	b. June 18, 1855	d. June 19, 1920
Juliette E.	b. December 23, 1856	d. January 15, 1942
Josephine C.	b. March 15, 1858	d. June 4, 1935
Orlando G.	*b. October 1858*	*d. April 5, 1864*
Milford G.	*b. August 1859*	*d. April 9, 1864*
Naomi May	b. July 10, 1862	d. April 13, 1920
Frank W.	b. December 10, 1864	d. 1913

The 1860 United States Federal Census recorded Eli S., Sybil M. and their children living in Moscow. Eli S.'s occupation was still listed as a "farmer".

In 1864 two of Eli S. and Sybil M.'s children died at young ages. Their fourth child Orlando G. died at the age of five years six months on April 5th, and four days later on April 9th their fifth child Milford G. died at four years eight months. The causes and places of their deaths have not been found. Their two sons were buried in the Eli S. Williams plot at the Bingham Village Cemetery in Bingham, Somerset, Maine.

When the 1870 and 1880 United States Federal Census' were taken, Eli S. and Sybil M. were recorded as still living in Moscow with Eli S.'s occupation being listed as a "farmer".

Eli S. died on October 26, 1884 at the age of sixty-three. His place and cause of death are not known. He was buried in his family plot in Bingham at the Bingham Village Cemetery.

Sybil M. survived her husband by a little more than fourteen years dying on November 6, 1898, at the age of seventy-one, in Lewiston, Androscoggin,

Maine. Her cause of death was listed as "pulmonary congestion". Sybil M.'s body was taken back to Bingham where she was buried in the family plot at the Bingham Village Cemetery.

Gravestones for Orlando G. Williams (top left), Milford G. Williams (top right) and Eli S. Williams and Sybil M. Hunnewell (bottom)
(Photographs from the Collection of Jeffrey Nelson Williams and Jacqueline Pon Williams)

SOURCES:

Eli S. Williams
Birth (1) Original Record of Maine Towns & Cities, Town of Moscow, Page 49, Picton Press, Rockland Maine, Copyright 2005; (2) "Maine, Births and Christenings, 1739-1900," index, FamilySearch, (https://familysearch.org /pal:/MM9.1.1/F4QC-3HK); (3) Listing of family births and deaths from the Gilman L. Williams family archives from the collection of SullyJ.
Death: Gravestone.
Graveyard: (1) "Maine Old Cemetery Association Special Publication Number 12, Edition No. 1: Series 1, 2 and 3", Page 334, Picton Press, Rockland, Maine, Copyright 2006; (2) "Bingham Village Cemetery" by Nancy Hamlin Davis and Ruth Hamlin, Old Canada Road Historical Society; (3) Find A Grave, Memorial #82062867.

Sybil M. Hunnewell
Birth: Original Record of Maine Towns & Cities, Town of Moscow, Page 20, Picton Press, Rockland Maine, Copyright 2005.
Marriage: (1) "Maine, Marriages, 1771-1907," index, FamilySearch, (https://familysearch.org/pal:/MM9.1.1 /F4FK-NQB); (2) Original Record of Maine Towns & Cities, Town of Moscow, Page 59, Picton Press, Rockland Maine, Copyright 2005; (3) Original Record of Maine Towns & Cities, Town of Moscow, Page 62, Picton Press, Rockland Maine, Copyright 2005.
Death: (1) Record of a Death, Maine Vital Records; (2) Gravestone.
Graveyard: (1) "Maine Old Cemetery Association Special Publication Number 12, Edition No. 1: Series 1, 2 and 3", Page 334, Picton Press, Rockland, Maine, Copyright 2006; (2) "Bingham Village Cemetery" by Nancy Hamlin Davis and Ruth Hamlin, Old Canada Road Historical Society; (3) Find A Grave, Memorial #82063045.

Orlando G. Williams
Birth:
Death: Gravestone.
Graveyard: (1) "Maine Old Cemetery Association Special Publication Number 12, Edition No. 1: Series 1, 2 and 3", Page 334, Picton Press, Rockland, Maine, Copyright 2006; (2) "Bingham Village Cemetery" by Nancy Hamlin Davis and Ruth Hamlin, Old Canada Road Historical Society; (3) Find A Grave, Memorial #82063072.

Milford G. Williams
Birth:
Death: Gravestone.
Graveyard: (1) "Maine Old Cemetery Association Special Publication Number 12, Edition No. 1: Series 1, 2 and 3", Page 334, Picton Press, Rockland, Maine, Copyright 2006; (2) "Bingham Village Cemetery" by Nancy Hamlin Davis and Ruth Hamlin, Old Canada Road Historical Society; (3) Find A Grave, Memorial #82063104.

Historical Accounts: (1) 1850 United States Federal Census for Moscow, Somerset, Maine; (2) 1860 United States Federal Census for Moscow, Somerset, Maine, Page 53; (3) 1870 United States Federal Census for Moscow, Somerset, Maine, Page 10; (4) 1880 United States Federal Census for Moscow, Somerset, Maine, Page 11.

Mary Jane Williams
(1824 - 1887)

The fourth child of Isaac Otis Williams and Rachel S. Heald was Mary Jane who was born on February 24, 1824 in Moscow, Somerset, Maine.

At age twenty-four, on May 3, 1848, Mary Jane and Eber Steward, age twenty-seven, filed their intentions to marry with the Town Clerk in Moscow. They were subsequently married on May 17, 1848 in Moscow by J. D. Hill, a Justice of the Peace. Eber, the son of Eli Steward and Betsey Blagden, was born in Maine around 1818. The exact date and place of his birth have not been found.

During their marriage Mary Jane and Eber had two children.

Frances J.	*b. July 31, 1848*	*d. April 2, 1849*
Gustavus A.	*b. January 18, 1850*	*d. March 3, 1864*

The first child of Mary Jane and Eber, Frances J., died on April 2, 1849 when she was eight months two days old. The place and cause of her death have not been found. She was buried in Lot 14 at the North Cemetery in Skowhegan, Somerset, Maine.

Gravestone for Frances J. Steward
(Photograph Courtesy of Gail Kelly)

When the 1850 United States Federal Census was taken Mary Jane, Eber and their second child, Gustavus A., were recorded as living in Moscow where Eber was "farming".

At the time of the 1860 United States Federal Census Mary Jane, Eber and Gustavus A. had moved to Skowhegan. Eber did not have an occupation recorded in that census.

Eber died in Skowhegan of an unknown cause on October 12, 1861 at the age of forty-three. He was also buried at the North Cemetery in Skowhegan in Lot 14 alongside his daughter.

On March 3, 1864 Gustavus A., the second child of Mary Jane and Eber, died at the age of fourteen years one month and two days. The cause and location of his death are not known. He too was buried in Lot 14 at the North Cemetery in Skowhegan.

Gravestones for Eber Steward (left) and Gustavus A. Steward (right)
(Photographs Courtesy of Gail Kelly)

Mary Jane, at age forty-two and the widower George W. Blackwell, age fifty-three, filed their intentions to be married in Skowhegan on October 10, 1866. The exact date of their subsequent marriage is not known. George W., the son of Heman Blackwell and Contentment Landers, was born in Maine around 1813. The exact place and date of his birth has not been found. Mary Jane and George W. did not have any children together.

The 1870 United States Federal Census recorded Mary Jane, George W. and two children from his first marriage living in Skowhegan. Ten years later when the 1880 United States Federal Census was taken Mary Jane and George W. had moved to Madison, Somerset, Maine where George W. was "farming".

Mary Jane died on September 26, 1887 at the age of sixty-three. Her cause and place of death have not been found. She was buried alongside her first husband Eber Steward and their two children in Lot 14 at the North Cemetery in Skowhegan.

Gravestone for Mary Jane Williams
(Photograph Courtesy of Gail Kelly)

Additional information on the life and death of George W. could not be found.

SOURCES:

Mary Jane Williams
Birth: (1) Original Record of Maine Towns & Cities, Town of Moscow, Page 49, Picton Press, Rockland Maine, Copyright 2005; (2) "Maine, Births and Christenings, 1739-1900," index, FamilySearch, (https://familysearch.org /pal:/MM9.1.1/F4QC-3Z9); (3) Listing of family births and deaths from the Gilman L. Williams family archives from the collection of SullyJ.
Death: (1) Burial Records, North Cemetery, Skowhegan, Somerset, Maine, Cemeteryfind.com; (2) Gravestone.
Graveyard: (1) Burial Records, North Cemetery, Skowhegan, Somerset, Maine, Cemeteryfind.com; (2) Find A Grave, Memorial #135054089.

Eber Steward
Birth:
Marriage: (1) Original Record of Maine Towns & Cities, Town of Moscow, Page 101, Picton Press, Rockland Maine, Copyright 2005; (2) Original Record of Maine Towns & Cities, Town of Moscow, Page 103, Picton Press, Rockland Maine, Copyright 2005; (3) "Maine, Marriages, 1771-1907," database, FamilySearch, (https:// familysearch. org/ark:/61903 /1:1: F4XF-FXT).
Death: (1) Burial Records, North Cemetery, Skowhegan, Somerset, Maine, Cemeteryfind.com; (2) Gravestone.
Graveyard: (1) Burial Records, North Cemetery, Skowhegan, Somerset, Maine, Cemeteryfind.com; (2) Find A Grave, Memorial #135054086.

Frances J. Steward
Birth: Burial Records, North Cemetery, Skowhegan, Somerset, Maine, Cemeteryfind.com.
Death: (1) Burial Records, North Cemetery, Skowhegan, Somerset, Maine, Cemeteryfind.com; (2) Gravestone.
Graveyard: (1) Burial Records, North Cemetery, Skowhegan, Somerset, Maine, Cemeteryfind.com; (2) Find A Grave, Memorial #135054092.

Gustavus A. Steward
Birth: Burial Records, North Cemetery, Skowhegan, Somerset, Maine, Cemeteryfind.com.
Death: (1) Burial Records, North Cemetery, Skowhegan, Somerset, Maine, Cemeteryfind.com; (2) Gravestone.
Graveyard: (1) Burial Records, North Cemetery, Skowhegan, Somerset, Maine, Cemeteryfind.com; (2) Find A Grave, Memorial #135054090.

George W. Blackwell
Birth:
Marriage; (1) "Vital Records of Skowhegan Maine", Compiled by Sally Furber Nelson, Page 239, Picton Press, Rockland Maine August 2010; (2) "Maine, Marriages, 1771-1907," index, FamilySearch, (https://familysearch. org /pal:/MM9.1.1/F4FB-RJV).
Death:
Graveyard:

Historical Accounts: (1) 1850 United States Federal Census for Moscow, Somerset, Maine; (2) 1860 United States Federal Census for Skowhegan, Somerset, Maine, Page 51; (3) 1870 United States Federal Census for Skowhegan, Somerset, Maine, Page 3; (4) 1880 United States Federal Census for Madison, Somerset, Maine, Page 16.

Ephraim H. Williams
(1826 - 1895)

Ephraim H. was the fifth child of Isaac Otis Williams and Rachel S. Heald. He was born in Moscow, Somerset, Maine on March 19, 1826.

In the 1850 United States Federal Census Ephraim, at age twenty-three, was recorded as living with his parents in Moscow and working as a "farmer".

Shortly after the 1850 census was taken, on October 17, 1852, Ephraim H., age twenty-six, and Abigail J. Mullen, age twenty-three, registered their marriage with the Town Clerk of Moscow. The exact date and place of their marriage has not been found. Born on June 28, 1829, Abigail J. was the daughter of Daniel Lee and Abigail Mullen of Concord, Somerset, Maine.

Ephraim H. and Abigail J. had seven children together.

Flavilla	*b. July 12, 1859*	*d. May 30, 1860*
Flora	*b. March 17, 1861*	*d. August 17, 1865*
Ozias	b. April 3, 1863	d. January 16, 1937
Gilman	b. September 25, 1865	d. January 19, 1937
Manley	b. November 7, 1867	d. February 13, 1937
William Ephraim	b. September 27, 1869	d. December 30, 1931
Flora F.	b. August 28, 1873	d. November 30, 1940

On May 30, 1860 Flavilla, the first child of Ephraim H. and Abigail J., died in Moscow of "dropsy" at the age of ten months seventeen days old. She was buried in the Bingham Village Cemetery in Bingham, Somerset, Maine.

In the 1860 United States Federal Census, which was taken on June 25th of that year, Ephraim H., Abigail J. and their children were recorded as living and farming in Moscow.

The second daughter of Ephraim H. and Abigail J., Flora died on August 17, 1865 at the age of four years and six months. Her place and cause of death are not known. She too buried in the Bingham Village Cemetery in Bingham next to her sister.

By the time the 1880 United States Federal Census was taken, Ephraim H., Abigail J. and their family had moved to Riverton Township, Floyd, Iowa where Ephraim H. was again "farming".

On April 26, 1895, at the age of sixty-nine, Ephraim H. died of a cause unknown in Chickasaw Township, Chickasaw County, Iowa. He was buried in Lot 4, Block 50 at the Greenwood Cemetery in Nashua, Chickasaw, Iowa.

On July 18, 1896 at age sixty-seven, Abigail J. was married to her second husband Joseph H. Beckwith, age seventy-five in Floyd County Iowa. Joseph H., the son of Dyer Beckwith and Susannah Bartholomew, was born on June 1, 1821 in Whitehall, Washington, New York. Less than two years after their marriage, on June 17, 1898, Joseph H. died at the age of seventy-six of an unknown cause in Charles City, Floyd, Iowa. He was buried in the Beckwith Cemetery in Nilesville, Floyd, Iowa.

Abigail J. was recorded as living with her son, Ozias, and his family in Chickasaw Township when the 1900 and 1910 United States Federal Census' were taken.

On April 9, 1912 Abigail J. died of an unknown cause, at the age of eighty-two, in Chickasaw Township. She had been confined to her bed for two years after suffering a broken bone in a fall. On the following day, April 10th, her funeral was held and she was interred in the Greenwood Cemetery in Nashua.

Gravestones for Flavilla Williams (left) and Flora Williams (right)
(Photographs from the Collection of Jeffrey Nelson Williams and Jacqueline Pon Williams)

SOURCES:

Ephraim H. Williams
Birth: (1) Original Record of Maine Towns & Cities, Town of Moscow, Page 49, Picton Press, Rockland Maine, Copyright 2005; (2) Listing of family births and deaths from the Gilman L. Williams family archives from the collection of SullyJ.
Death: (1) "Iowa, Cemetery Records, 1662-1999", [database on-line]. Provo, UT, USA: Ancestry.com Operations Inc., 2000; (2) Greenwood Cemetery Records, (http://iagenweb.org/chickasaw/cemetery/ Greenwoodtz.htm).
Graveyard: (1) "Iowa, Cemetery Records, 1662-1999", [database on-line]. Provo, UT, USA: Ancestry.com Operations Inc., 2000; (2) Greenwood Cemetery Records, (http://iagenweb.org/chickasaw/cemetery/ Greenwoodtz.htm); (3) Find A Grave, Memorial #155176917.

Abigail J. Mullen
Birth:
Marriage: (1) Original Record of Maine Towns & Cities, Town of Moscow, Page 110, Picton Press, Rockland Maine, Copyright 2005; (2) "Maine, Marriages, 1771-1907," index, FamilySearch, (https://familysearch.org/pal: /MM9.1.1/F4FK-NQB).
Death: (1) Obituary, The Nashua Reporter, Nashua, Iowa, Thursday, April 11, 1912, Page 1; (2) "Iowa, Deaths and Burials, 1850-1990", FamilySearch, (https://familysearch.org/pal:/MM9.1.1/XVHT-X8Q).
Graveyard: (1) "Iowa, Deaths and Burials, 1850-1990", FamilySearch, (https://familysearch.org/pal:/MM9.1.1 /XVHT-X8Q); (2) Find A Grave, Memorial #155178072.

Flavilla Williams
Birth:
Death: (1) United States Federal Census Mortality Schedule for the year ending June 1860 for Somerset County, Maine, Page 1; (2) Gravestone.
Graveyard: (1) "Maine Old Cemetery Association Special Publication Number 12, Edition No. 1: Series 1, 2 and 3", Page 334, Picton Press, Rockland, Maine, Copyright 2006; (2) "Bingham Village Cemetery" by Nancy Hamlin Davis and Ruth Hamlin, Old Canada Road Historical Society; (3) Find A Grave, Memorial #82115408.

Flora Williams
Birth:
Death: Gravestone.
Graveyard: (1) "Maine Old Cemetery Association Special Publication Number 12, Edition No. 1: Series 1, 2 and 3", Page 334, Picton Press, Rockland, Maine, Copyright 2006; (2) "Bingham Village Cemetery" by Nancy Hamlin Davis and Ruth Hamlin, Old Canada Road Historical Society; (3) Find A Grave, Memorial #82101144.

Joseph H. Beckwith
Birth: "Iowa, Cemetery Records, 1662-1999", [database on-line]. Provo, UT, USA: Ancestry.com Operations Inc., 2000.
Marriage: "Iowa, County Marriages, 1838-1934," index, FamilySearch, (https://familysearch.org/pal: /MM9.1.1 /KC4C-T29).
Death: "Iowa, Cemetery Records, 1662-1999", [database on-line]. Provo, UT, USA: Ancestry.com Operations Inc., 2000.
Graveyard: Find A Grave, Memorial #7755565.

Historical Accounts: (1) 1850 United States Federal Census for Moscow, Somerset, Maine; (2) 1860 United States Federal Census for Moscow, Somerset, Maine, Page 54; (3) 1880 United States Federal Census for Riverton Township, Floyd, Iowa, Page 18; (4) 1895 Iowa State Census for Chickasaw; (5) 1900 United States Federal Census for Chickasaw Township, Chickasaw, Iowa, Page 9; (6) 1910 United States Federal Census for Chickasaw Township, Chickasaw, Iowa, Page 7A.

Gilman L. Williams
(1828 - 1920)

Gilman L. was the sixth child of Isaac Otis Williams and Rachel S, Heald. He was born in Moscow, Somerset, Maine on January 5, 1828. (Note: Although the Moscow and other official records reviewed indicate that he was born on January 5, 1828 his gravestone indicates his date of birth as January 5, 1829)

In the 1850 United States Federal Census, Gilman L. was recorded as working as a "laborer" and living with his parents on their farm in Moscow.

On September 18, 1851 Gilman L., at the age of twenty-two, was married in Boston, Suffolk, Massachusetts to Mary Elizabeth Bickford age twenty-three, by Reverend Phineas Stow of the Seaman's Chapel. Their marriage record indicated that Gilman L. was working as a "carpenter" in Boston at that time. Mary Elizabeth, born on April 23, 1828 in Moscow, was the daughter of Rufus Bickford and Betsy Parsons.

Gilman L. Williams and Mary Elizabeth Bickford
(Photograph Courtesy of Jennifer Sullivan)

Gilman L. and Mary Elizabeth had five children together.

Edward Percy	*b. June 22, 1852*	*d. December 18, 1862*
Charles Henry	b. November 13, 1854	d. November 23, 1938
Emma Elizabeth	b. May 3, 1857	d. November 13, 1927
Freddie Gilman	*b. August 27, 1861*	*d. October 2, 1861*
Carrie L.	b. November 28, 1863	d. December 23, 1892

The 1855 Massachusetts State Census recorded Gilman L., Mary Elizabeth and their first two children, Edward Percy and Charles Henry, as living in Boston. Gilman L.'s occupation was listed as "ship joiner" in that census.

When the 1860 United States Federal Census and the 1865 Massachusetts State Census were taken Gilman L., Mary Elizabeth and their children had moved to Chelsea, Suffolk, Massachusetts where Gilman L. was listed as working as a "carpenter".

During the early 1860's while they were living in Chelsea, two of Gilman L. and Mary Elizabeth's children died at young ages. On October 2, 1861 their fourth child, Freddie Gilman died of "cholera infantum" at the age of one month eight days. Their first child Edward Percy died on December 18, 1862 of "scarlet fever" at the age of ten years and six months old. Both children were buried in their grandfather Rufus Bickford's lot at the Garden Cemetery in Chelsea.

By the time the 1870 United States Federal Census was taken Gilman L., Mary Elizabeth and their family had moved to Austin, Mower, Minnesota. They were recorded as still living in Austin in the 1865 Minnesota State Census. In both census documents Gilman L.'s occupation was listed as "carpenter".

Gilman L. and Mary Elizabeth had moved to Moody County in the Dakota Territory when the 1880 United States Federal Census was taken. On November 17, 1884 Gilman L. was granted 160 acres of land in the Dakota Territory under the 1882 Homestead Act. He subsequently sold this tract of land, on April 24, 1891, to a man named James Smith for the sum of $125.00.

At the time of both the 1900 United States Federal Census and 1905 South Dakota State Census Gilman L. and Mary Elizabeth were living in Egan, Moody, South Dakota (South Dakota was granted statehood in 1889). During that time Gilman L. continued to work as a "carpenter".

In recognition of their fiftieth wedding anniversary, Gilman L. and Mary Elizabeth held a celebration in their home in Egan on September 18, 1901 at 7:30 in the evening.

The 1910 United States Federal Census recorded Gilman L. and Mary Elizabeth as retired and living in the home of their daughter Emma Elizabeth (Williams) Kimball and her husband Frederick Rufus Kimball at 3001 DuPont Avenue in Minneapolis, Hennepin, Minnesota.

Mary Elizabeth died at the age of eighty-four on January 23, 1913 in Minneapolis. The exact cause and place of her death has not been found. She was buried in the Hillside Cemetery in Egan, Moody, South Dakota.

When the 1920 United States Federal Census was taken in January of that year Gilman L. had moved across the country with his daughter Emma Elizabeth (Williams) Kimball and her husband and was living with them in their home at 2529 East Broadway in Long Beach, Los Angeles, California.

Gilman L. was living back in the Minneapolis area when, at the age of ninety-two, he "dropped dead from the heat while waiting for a streetcar" on June 12, 1920. His funeral was held at 4:00 P.M. at the T. B. Johnson Funeral Home on Monday June 14th. Gilman L.'s body was transported to Egan where he was buried in Hillside Cemetery alongside his wife.

Gravestone for Gilman L. Williams and Mary Elizabeth Bickford (top)
Gravestone engraving (bottom)
(Photographs Taken by Find A Grave Member "Dells")

SOURCES:

Gilman L. Williams
Birth: (1) Original Record of Maine Towns & Cities, Town of Moscow, Page 49, Picton Press, Rockland Maine, Copyright 2005; (2) "Maine, Births and Christenings, 1739-1900," index, FamilySearch, (https://familysearch.org /pal:/MM9.1.1/F4QC-389); (3) Listing of family births and deaths from the Gilman L. Williams family archives from the collection of Jennifer Sullivan.
Death: (1) "Minnesota, Death Index, 1908-2002", (database on-line). Provo, UT, USA: Ancestry.com Operations, Inc., 2001; (2) "Minnesota, Deaths and Burials, 1835-1990," index, FamilySearch, (https://family search.org/ark:/ 61903/1.1: FD34-ZZF); (3) Listing of family births and deaths from the Gilman L. Williams family archives from the collection of Jennifer Sullivan; (4) Obituary, Star Tribune, Minneapolis, Minnesota, Sunday, June 13, 1920, Page 1; (4) Gravestone.
Graveyard: (1) Hillside Cemetery, Egan, Moody, South Dakota, www.southdakotagravestones.com; (2) Find A Grave, Memorial #55535537.

Mary Elizabeth Bickford
Birth: (1) "Maine, Births and Christenings, 1739-1900," index, FamilySearch, (https://family search.org/pal: /MM9.1.1/F4QC-SYL); (2) Gravestone.
Marriage: "Massachusetts, Town and Vital Records, 1620-1988", [database on-line], Provo, UT, USA: Ancestry.com Operations, Inc., 2011, Marriages registered in the City of Boston for the year 1851.
Death: (1) "Minnesota, Death Index, 1908-2002", (database on-line). Provo, UT, USA: Ancestry.com Operations, Inc., 2001; (2) Gravestone.
Graveyard: (1) Hillside Cemetery, Egan, Moody, South Dakota, www.southdakotagravestones.com; (2) Find A Grave, Memorial #55535555.

Edward Percy Williams
Birth: (1) "Massachusetts, Birth Records, 1840-1915", [database on-line], Provo, UT, USA: Ancestry.com Operations, Inc., 2013, Births registered in the City of Boston for the year 1852; (2) "Massachusetts, Town and Vital Records, 1620-1988", [database on-line], Provo, UT, USA: Ancestry.com Operations, Inc., 2011, Index to Births in Massachusetts 1851-1855.
Death: (1) "Massachusetts, Death Records, 1841-1915", [database on-line], Provo, UT, USA: Ancestry.com Operations, Inc., 2013, Deaths registered in the City of Chelsea for the year 1862; (2) "Massachusetts, Town and Vital Records, 1620-1988", [database on-line], Provo, UT, USA: Ancestry.com Operations, Inc., 2011, Index to Deaths in Massachusetts 1861-1865; (3) Obituary, Boston Daily Advertiser, Saturday, December 20, 1862.
Graveyard:

Freddie Gilman Williams
Birth:
Death: (1) "Massachusetts, Death Records, 1841-1915", [database on-line], Provo, UT, USA: Ancestry.com Operations, Inc., 2013, Deaths registered in the City of Chelsea for the year 1861; (2) "Massachusetts, Town and Vital Records, 1620-1988", [database on-line], Provo, UT, USA: Ancestry.com Operations, Inc., 2011, Index to Deaths in Massachusetts 1861-1865.
Graveyard:

Historical Accounts: (1) 1850 United States Federal Census for Moscow, Somerset, Maine, Page 8; (2) 1855 Massachusetts State Census for Boston, Suffolk, Massachusetts; (3) 1860 United States Federal Census for Chelsea, Suffolk, Massachusetts, Page 20; (4) 1865 Massachusetts State Census for Chelsea, Suffolk, Massachusetts; (5) 1870 United States Federal Census for Austin, Mower, Minnesota, Page 10; (6) 1875 Minnesota State Census; (7) 1880 United States Federal Census for Moody County, Dakota Territory, Page 25; (8) 1900 United States Federal Census for Egan, Moody, South Dakota, Page 1; (9) 1905 South Dakota State Census for Egan, Moody County, Cards 246 & 247; (10) 1910 United States Federal Census for Minneapolis, Hennepin, Minnesota, Page 4B; (11) 1920 United States Federal Census for Long Beach, Los Angeles, California, Page 14; (12) The United States of America, Homestead Certificate #4854; (13) Copy of 50th Anniversary Celebration Invitation for Gilman L. and Mary Elizabeth Williams from the collection of Jennifer Sullivan.

Henry Williams
(1832 -)

The seventh child, Henry, of Isaac Otis Williams and Rachel S. Heald was born on June 26, 1832 in Moscow, Somerset, Maine.

When the 1850 United States Federal Census was taken Henry, then age eighteen, was recorded as working as a "farmer" and living with his parents in Moscow.

At the time of the 1860 United States Federal Census Henry, age twenty-eight, had moved away from the family farm and was living with his brother Ephraim H. and his family in Moscow. Henry's occupation was listed as "farm laborer" in the census document.

Additional information regarding the life and death of Henry beyond that recorded in the 1860 census has not been found.

SOURCES:

Henry Williams
Birth: (1) Original Record of Maine Towns & Cities, Town of Moscow, Page 49, Picton Press, Rockland Maine, Copyright 2005; (2) "Maine, Births and Christenings, 1739-1900," index, FamilySearch, (https://familysearch.org /pal:/MM9.1.1/F4QC-38Q); (3) Listing of family births and deaths from the Gilman L. Williams family archives from the collection of SullyJ.
Death:
Graveyard:

Historical Accounts: (1) 1850 United States Federal Census for Moscow, Somerset, Maine; (2) 1860 United States Federal Census for Moscow, Somerset, Maine, Page 54.

Nancy Hale Williams
(1834 - 1904)

Nancy Hale, the eighth child of Isaac Otis Williams and Rachel S. Heald was born in Moscow, Somerset, Maine on July 19, 1834.

The 1850 United States Federal Census recorded Nancy Hale, then age sixteen, living with her parents on their farm in Moscow.

Sometime between 1850 and 1857 Nancy Hale married Daniel Stewart Churchill. The exact date and location are not known. Daniel Stewart was born in Maine on February 20, 1835 to Mr. Churchill and Rachel Stewart. The exact place of his birth and the given name of his father have also not been found.

Prior to his marriage to Nancy Hale, in the 1850 United States Federal Census Daniel Stewart was recorded as living with Nancy Hale's sister Mary Jane (Williams) Steward and her husband Eber Steward in Moscow.

Nancy Hale and Daniel Stewart had five children during their marriage.

Sarah Lavonia	b. October 15, 1857	d. October 19, 1936
Delia Mae	b. May 13, 1860	d. November 21, 1932
Mary Elizabeth	b. January 19, 1865	d. September 23, 1939
Cora Belle	b. August 21, 1872	d. January 27, 1946
Maude I.	b. October 4, 1877	d. November 24, 1961

When the 1860 United States Federal Census was taken Nancy Hale, Daniel Stewart and their children were recorded as living in Harmony, Somerset, Maine. Daniel Stewart's occupation was listed as "chair maker".

In June 1863 Daniel Stewart registered for the United States Civil War Draft. In that document Daniel Stewart was recorded as being twenty-eight years old, married and a "cabinet maker" from Harmony.

By the time the 1870 United States Federal Census was taken Nancy Hale, Daniel Stewart and their family had moved to Charles City, Floyd, Iowa.

Nancy Hale, Daniel Stewart and their children were living on Cedar Street in Charles City at the time of the 1880 United States Federal Census. They had moved to 1209 Waller Street in Charles City by the time the 1900 United States Federal Census was taken. In both those census documents Daniel Stewart was listed as working as a "carpenter".

On April 10, 1904 Nancy Hale died in Charles City at the age of sixty-nine. The exact cause of her death has not been found. She was buried in Block 8, Section 51, Row 5, Space 6 at the Riverside Cemetery in Charles City.

When the 1910 United States Federal Census was taken Daniel Stewart was recorded as living with his daughter Maude I. and her husband Edmond P. McCausland at 1206 Waller Street in Charles City. In that census, and in the 1915 Iowa State Census, Daniel Stewart was recorded as working as a "contractor".

On January 17, 1920, at the time of the 1920 United States Federal Census, Daniel Stewart was still living at 1206 Waller Street in Charles City with his then widowed daughter Maude I (Williams) McCausland.

Daniel Stewart died at the age of eighty-four on June 11, 1920 in Charles City. The cause of his death has not been found. He was buried next to his wife Nancy H. in Block 8, Section 51, Row 5, Space 6 at the Riverside Cemetery in Charles City.

Gravestones for Nancy Hale Williams (left) and Daniel Stewart Churchill (right)
(Photographs Courtesy of Kathy Gerkins)

SOURCES:

Nancy Hale Williams
Birth: (1) Original Record of Maine Towns & Cities, Town of Moscow, Page 49, Picton Press, Rockland Maine, Copyright 2005; (2) Listing of family births and deaths from the Gilman L. Williams family archives from the collection of SullyJ.
Death:
Graveyard: Find A Grave, Memorial #33534912.

Daniel Stewart Churchill
Birth: "Iowa Death Index, 1900-1939", MyHeritage.com [online database], Lehi, UT, USA.
Marriage:
Death: (1) "Iowa Death Index, 1900-1939", MyHeritage.com [online database], Lehi, UT, USA; (2) "Iowa, County Death Records, 1880-1992", FamilySearch, (https://familysearch.org/ark;/61903/1:1:QVJP-LXP3).
Graveyard: Find A Grave, Memorial #33534896.

Historical Accounts: (1) 1850 United States Federal Census for Moscow, Somerset, Maine, Pages 248 & 249; (2) 1860 United States Federal Census for Harmony, Somerset, Maine, Page 41; (3) 1870 United States Federal Census for Charles City, Floyd, Iowa, Page 5; (4) 1880 United States Federal Census for Charles City, Floyd, Iowa, Page 48; (5) 1900 United States Federal Census for Charles City, Floyd, Iowa, Page 15A; (6) 1910 United States Federal Census for Charles City, Floyd, Iowa, Page 11A; (7) 1915 Iowa State Census for Charles City, Floyd, Iowa; (8) 1920 United States Federal Census for Charles City, Floyd, Iowa, Page 17A; (9) U. S., Civil War Draft Registration Records, 1863-1865, Third Congressional District, Maine, Page 109.

Allen B. Williams
(1839 - 1904)

Allen B., the eleventh child of Isaac Otis Williams and Rachel S. Heald, was born in Moscow, Somerset, Maine on January 3, 1839.

The 1860 United States Federal Census recorded Allen B., at age twenty-one, living with his brother Ephraim H. and his family and working as a "farm laborer" on Ephraim H.'s farm in Moscow.

At age twenty-two, on September 3, 1861, Allen B. and Loantha G. Stevens, age sixteen, filed their intentions to be married with the Town Clerk of Moscow. The exact date of their subsequent wedding has not been found. Loantha G., born around 1845 in Harmony, Somerset, Maine, was the daughter of Truman Allen Stevens and Mary A. Dore. The exact date of her birth is not known.

Allen B. and Loantha G. had five children during their marriage.

Truman A. S.	b. December 1863	d. 1923
Anna B.	b. 1864	d. May 12, 1884
Edward P.	b. January 11, 1867	d. June 3, 1894
Bertie M.	*b. June 30, 1875*	*d. August 11, 1885*
Leslie Dearborn	b. May 2, 1882	d. January 21, 1953

On December 24, 1863, at age twenty-four, Allen B. enlisted in Company K, 2nd Maine Cavalry Regiment of the Union Army. In his enlistment record he was described as being 5' 7½" tall with a light complexion, gray eyes and brown hair. Allen B. served almost two years and was mustered out holding the rank of Full Corporal on December 6, 1865 at Fort Barrancas in Pensacola, Escambia, Florida.

In the 1870 United States Federal Census, Allen B., Loantha G. and the first four of their children were recorded as living in Skowhegan, Somerset, Maine, with Allen B.'s occupation listed as "working in a saw mill".

By the time the 1880 United States Federal Census was taken, Allen B. and his family had moved to Winslow, Kennebec, Maine where he was working as a "brick mason".

On August 10, 1885 the fourth child of Allen B. and Loantha G, Bertie M., died at the age of ten years thirteen days. The location and cause of his death have not been found. He was buried in the Fort Hill Cemetery in Winslow.

When the 1890 United States Census of Soldiers, Sailors, and Marines, and Widows of the Civil War was taken, Allen B. was recorded as living in

Waterville, Kennebec, Maine with a disability listed as "rheumatism".

On December 27, 1894 Allen B., age fifty-five, and Loantha G., age forty-nine, were divorced in Kennebec County, Maine.

Allen B., and his youngest child Leslie Dearborn, were still living in Waterville when the 1900 United States Federal Census was taken on June 13 of that year.

Three and a half years later, on January 28, 1904, Allen B. was admitted to the U.S. National Homes for Disabled Volunteer Soldiers in Togus, Kennebec, Maine. He died the following day, January 29th, at the age of sixty-five of "diffuse nephritis". His body was subsequently returned to Waterville, but his place of burial is unknown.

Additional information regarding the life and death of Loantha G. has not been found.

SOURCES:

Allen B. Williams
Birth: (1) Original Record of Maine Towns & Cities, Town of Moscow, Page 49, Picton Press, Rockland Maine, Copyright 2005; (2) "Maine, Births and Christenings, 1739-1900," index, FamilySearch, (https://familysearch .org/pal:/MM9.1.1/F477-1XQ); (3) Listing of family births and deaths from the Gilman L. Williams family archives from the collection of SullyJ.
Death: "United States, National Homes for Disabled Volunteer Soldiers, 1866-1938," index and images, FamilySearch, (https://familysearch.org/pal:/MM9.1.1/VH4D-G35).
Graveyard:

Loantha G. Stevens
Birth:
Marriage: (1) Original Record of Maine Towns & Cities, Town of Moscow, Page 113, Picton Press, Rockland Maine, Copyright 2005; (2) "Maine, Marriages, 1771-1907" index, FamilySearch, (https://familysearch.org/pal: /MM9.1.1/F4FK-NQM).
Divorce: "Maine Divorces, 1799-1903" database, Maine Genealogy, citing Maine Divorce Index, 2/16, Maine State Archives.
Death:
Graveyard:

Historical Accounts: (1) 1860 United States Federal Census for Moscow, Somerset, Maine, Page 54; (2) 1870 United States Federal Census for Skowhegan, Somerset, Maine, Page 59; (3) 1880 United States Federal Census for the Winslow, Kennebec, Maine, Page 5; (4) 1900 United States Federal Census for Waterville City, Kennebec, Maine, Page 18; (5) 1890 United States Census of Soldiers, Sailors, and Marines, and Widows of the Civil War; (6) "U.S., Civil War Soldier Records and Profiles, 1861-1865", [database on-line]. Provo, UT, USA: Ancestry.com Operations Inc, 2009.

Benjamin Franklin Atwood
(1814 - 1904)

The second child of Elsa Williams and Benjamin Colby Atwood was Benjamin Franklin (also commonly known as Franklin) who was born on June 6, 1814 in Concord, Somerset, Maine.

On August 25, 1834 Benjamin Franklin, age twenty, and Harriet Abigail Berry, age fifteen, published their intentions to marry with the Town Clerk of Embden, Somerset, Maine. They were married seventeen days later, on September 11th, in Solon, Somerset, Maine. Harriet Abigail was born in Stratham, Rockingham, New Hampshire on May 29, 1819 to George Berry and Nancy Ann Westcott.

Benjamin Franklin and Harriet Abigail had eight children.

Samuel Colby	b. January 16, 1836	d. January 30, 1912
Sophia A.	b. January 29, 1838	d. February 13, 1919
George Berry	*b. January 28, 1840*	*d. October 6, 1864*
Franklin Manley	*b. April 1842*	*d. October 23, 1857*
Sarah Nancy	b. January 20, 1844	d. February 26, 1883
Mary Elizabeth	b. December 14, 1848	d. September 11, 1907
Benjamin Franklin	b. October 22, 1856	d. November 4, 1935
Manley George	b. December 22, 1857	d. February 19, 1926

In the 1840 and 1850 United States Federal Census' Benjamin Franklin, Harriet Abigail and their family were recorded as living in Concord. The 1850 census listed Benjamin Franklin's occupation as "farmer".

The fourth child of Benjamin Franklin and Harriet Abigail, Franklin Manley, (commonly known as Manley) died on October 23, 1857 when he was fourteen years and six months old. The cause and place of his death have not been found. He was buried in the Benjamin Franklin family plot at the Pleasantdale Cemetery in Embden. (Note: There is some question as to the correct spelling of his middle name. Official records reviewed indicate that it was spelled Manley and his gravestone indicates it was Manly)

When the 1860 United States Federal Census was taken Benjamin Franklin, Harriet Abigail and their family were still living in Concord. In that census Benjamin Franklin's occupation was again listed as a "farmer".

On November 23, 1863 Benjamin Franklin and Harriet Abigail's third child George Berry joined Company B, 2nd Maine Cavalry of the Union Army holding the rank of Private. In his enlistment record he was described as being 5' 5" tall with a dark complexion, brown eyes and black hair. George Berry listed his occupation as "teamster". He died less than one year later, on October

6, 1864, of "disease" at Fort Barrancas in Pensacola, Escambia, Florida at age of twenty-four. George Berry had never married or had children. He was buried in the Barrancas National Cemetery; Section 5, Site 565, in Pensacola. There is also a notation of George Berry's death inscribed on the family gravestone at the Pleasantdale Cemetery in Embden although the date of death was incorrectly engraved as October 26th.

Gravestone for Franklin Manley Atwood (left)
(Photograph from the Collection of Jeffrey Nelson Williams and Jacqueline Pon Williams)
Gravestone for George Berry Atwood at the Barrancas National Cemetery (right)
(Photograph Courtesy of Jerry Thomas)

The 1870 and 1880 United States Federal Census' for Concord recorded Benjamin Franklin and Harriet Abigail as still living and farming Concord.

Harriet Abigail died on October 23, 1893, at the age of seventy-four, in Concord. Her cause of death was listed as "morbus addisona". She was buried her son Manley in the family plot with at the Pleasantdale Cemetery in Embden.

The 1900 United States Federal Census recorded Benjamin Franklin living and farming in Concord. Four years later, on Friday, May 20, 1904 Benjamin Franklin died at the age of eighty-nine in Concord of "cancer of the stomach". He was buried on Monday, May 23, 1904 in Embden in his family plot at the Pleasantdale Cemetery with his wife and son.

**Gravestone for Benjamin Franklin Atwood Family (left) and
Detailed Inscription for Benjamin Franklin Atwood & Harriet Abigail Berry (right)**
(Photographs from the Collection of Jeffrey Nelson Williams and Jacqueline Pon Williams)

SOURCES:

Benjamin Franklin Atwood
Birth: (1) Original Record of Maine Towns & Cities, Town of Concord, Page 91, Picton Press, Rockland Maine, Copyright 2005; (2) "Maine, Births and Christenings, 1739-1900," index, FamilySearch, (https://familysearch.org /pal:/MM9.1.1/F4Q4-TLD).
Death: (1) Record of a Death, Maine Vital Records; (2) Death Notice, The Somerset Reporter, Skowhegan, Maine, Thursday, May 26, 1904, Page 4; (3) Gravestone.
Graveyard: (1) "Pleasantdale Cemetery" compiled by Nancy Hamlin Davis and Ruth Hamlin, Old Canada Road Historical Society; (2) Find A Grave, Memorial #15550186.

Harriet Berry
Birth:
Marriage: (1) Original Record of Maine Towns & Cities, Town of Embden, Disk 1 Page 367, Picton Press, Rockland Maine, Copyright 2005; (2) Edmund West, comp., "Family Data Collection - Individual Records", [database on-line], Provo, UT, USA: Ancestry.com Operations Inc, 2000; (3) "South of 'Lost Nation', Northwest Embden's Enchanting Skyland Where Pioneers from Barrington, N. H. Settled" by Ernest G. Walker, Pages 21, 27 & 36, Washington, D. C., July 4, 1939, Retyped in 1994-1995 by Dean Lyons for the Embden Historical Society.
Death: (1) Record of a Death, Maine Vital Records; (2) Gravestone.
Graveyard: (1) "Pleasantdale Cemetery" compiled by Nancy Hamlin Davis and Ruth Hamlin, Old Canada Road Historical Society; (2) Find A Grave, Memorial #15550209.

Franklin Manley Atwood
Birth:
Death: (1) Edmund West, comp., "Family Data Collection - Individual Records", [database on-line], Provo, UT, USA: Ancestry.com Operations Inc, 2000; (2) Gravestone.
Graveyard: (1) "Pleasantdale Cemetery" compiled by Nancy Hamlin Davis and Ruth Hamlin, Old Canada Road Historical Society; (2) Find A Grave, Memorial #118445446.

George Berry Atwood
Birth:
Death: (1) U.S. National Cemetery Internment Control Forms, 1928-1962; (2) National Cemetery Administration; Barrancas National Cemetery, Burial Register, c. 1827-1993; (3) Gravestone.
Graveyard: (1) "U.S. National Cemetery Interment Control Forms, 1928-1962," [database on-line], Provo, UT, USA: Ancestry.com Operations, Inc., 2012; (2) U.S. Veterans Gravesites, c. 1775-2006; (3) Find A Grave, Memorial #303506.

Historical Accounts: (1) 1840 United States Federal Census for Concord, Somerset, Maine; (2) 1850 United States Federal Census for Concord, Somerset, Maine; (3) 1860 United States Federal Census for Concord, Somerset, Maine, Page 63; (4) 1870 United States Federal for Concord, Somerset, Maine, Page 12; (5) 1880 United States Federal for Concord, Somerset, Maine, Page 12; (6) 1900 United States Federal for Concord, Somerset, Maine, Page 7; (7) "Maine, State Archives Collections, 1718-1957," Civil War soldiers index, FamilySearch, (https://familysearch.org/ark:/61903/3.1:33SQ-TJ8).

Mary A. Atwood
(1816 - 1909)

Mary A., the fourth child of Elsa Williams and Benjamin Colby Atwood, was born in Concord, Somerset, Maine on July 14, 1816.

On August 29, 1936, Mary A., then age twenty, and Nathan N. Berry, age twenty-two, filed their intentions to marry with the Town Clerk of Concord. They were married in Embden, Somerset, Maine the following month on September 6th. Nathan N., born on May 22, 1814 in Barrington, Strafford, New Hampshire, was the son of Levi Berry and Margaret Felker Moulton.

Mary A. and Nathan N. had a large family of thirteen children.

Aurelia A.	b. January 1837	d. February 9, 1919
Josephine	*b. May 4, 1838*	*d. May 7, 1838*
Charles	*b. July 1840*	*d. November 30, 1847*
Edwin	*b.1842*	*d. December 11, 1842*
Edwin (a twin)	b. October 1843	d.
Elwin (a twin)	b. October 1843	d. April 14, 1924
Electa S.	b. July 24, 1846	d. June 14, 1892
Baby Girl 1 (a twin)	*b. June 20, 1848*	*d. June 20, 1848*
Baby Girl 2 (a twin)	*b. June 20, 1848*	*d. June 20, 1848*
Charles	*b. Apr 1850*	*d. January 11, 1852*
Clara Ella	*b. 1852*	*d. April 26, 1864*
Charles B. (a twin)	b. October 25, 1856	d. June 10, 1935
Ella Mary (a twin)	b. October 25, 1856	d. December 18, 1934

Josephine the second child Mary A. and Nathan N. died on May 7, 1838 when she was just three days old. The cause and place of her death have not been found. She was buried in Nathan N. Berry family plot in Embden at the Pleasantdale Cemetery.

The 1840 United States Federal Census recorded Mary A., Nathan N. and their children Aurelia A. and Charles living in Concord.

Four of Mary A. and Nathan N.'s children died in the 1840s. Their fourth child, Edwin, was less than one year old when he died on December 11, 1842; Charles, their third child, died November 30, 1847 when he was seven; and twin unnamed baby girls, children number eight and nine, died on June 20, 1848, the day of their birth. The places and causes of death of all four children have not been found. All of these children were buried in their father's family plot at the Pleasantdale Cemetery in Embden.

When the 1850 United States Federal Census was taken in September of that year Mary A., Nathan N. and their children were recorded as still living in

Concord where Nathan N. was "farming".

On January 11, 1852, the tenth child of Mary A. and Nathan N., Charles (the second child they had named Charles), died at the age of twenty-one months. His place and cause of death have also not been found. He too was buried in the Pleasantdale Cemetery at Embden with his brothers and sisters.

Mary A. and Nathan N. were recorded as living in Concord when the 1860 United States Federal Census was taken. Nathan N.'s occupation was still listed as "farmer".

Clara Ella the eleventh child of Mary A. and Nathan N. died on April 26, 1864 when she was age twelve. Like her siblings her cause and place of death are not known. She was buried in the family plot at the Pleasantdale Cemetery in Embden.

The 1870 United States Federal Census for Concord recorded Mary A., Nathan N. and their family still living and farming there.

Nathan N. died of an unknown cause in Concord on August 27, 1874, at the age of sixty. He was buried in his family plot in in Embden at the Pleasantdale Cemetery.

In the 1880 United States Federal Census Mary A. was recorded as still living on the family farm in Concord. And by the time the 1900 United States Federal Census was taken, Mary A., at the age of eighty-three, had moved and was living with her daughter, Ella Mary (Williams) Huggins, and her family in Concord.

Mary A. outlived her husband by more than thirty-four years dying at the age of ninety-two on January 9, 1909 in Concord. The cause of her death was listed as "pneumonia". She too was buried with her husband and seven of their children in Embden at the Pleasantdale Cemetery.

Gravestones for Josephine Berry and Edwin Berry-1 (top left), Charles Berry-1 (top right), Charles Berry-2, Baby Girl Berry 1 & Baby Girl Berry 2 (bottom left) and Clara Ella Berry (bottom right)
(Photographs from the Collection of Jeffrey Nelson Williams and Jacqueline Pon Williams)

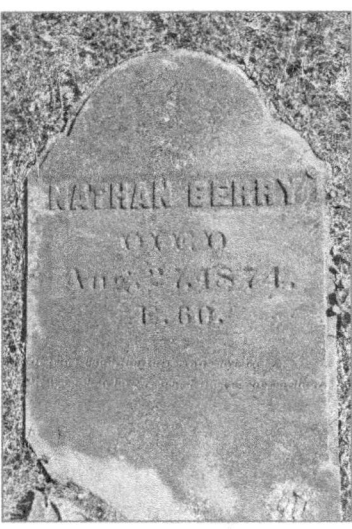

Gravestones for Mary A. Atwood (left) and Nathan N. Berry (right)
(Photographs from the Collection of Jeffrey Nelson Williams and Jacqueline Pon Williams)

SOURCES:

Mary A. Atwood
Birth: (1) Original Record of Maine Towns & Cities, Town of Concord, Page 91, Picton Press, Rockland Maine, Copyright 2005; (2) "Maine, Births and Christenings, 1739-1900," index, FamilySearch, (https://familysearch.org /pal:/MM9.1.1/F4Q4-T25).
Death: (1) Record of a Death, Maine Vital Records; (2) Gravestone.
Graveyard: (1) "Pleasantdale Cemetery" complied by Nancy Hamlin Davis and Ruth Hamlin, Old Canada Road Historical Society; (2) Find A Grave, Memorial #118353075.

Nathan N. Berry
Birth:
Marriage: (1) Original Record of Maine Towns & Cities, Town of Concord, Page 132, Picton Press, Rockland Maine, Copyright 2005; (2) "Maine, Marriages, 1771-1907," index, FamilySearch, (https://familysearch.org/pal: /MM9.1.1/F462-L31); (3) "South of 'Lost Nation', Northwest Embden's Enchanting Skyland Where Pioneers from Barrington, N. H. Settled" by Ernest G. Walker, Washington, D. C., July 4, 1939, Retyped in 1994-1995 by Dean Lyons for the Embden Historical Society.
Death: Gravestone.
Graveyard: (1) "Pleasantdale Cemetery" complied by Nancy Hamlin Davis and Ruth Hamlin, Old Canada Road Historical Society; (2) Find A Grave, Memorial #118352975.

Josephine Berry
Birth:
Death:
Graveyard: (1) "Pleasantdale Cemetery" complied by Nancy Hamlin Davis and Ruth Hamlin, Old Canada Road Historical Society; (2) Find A Grave, Memorial #118353515.

Charles Berry-1
Birth:
Death:
Graveyard: (1) "Pleasantdale Cemetery" complied by Nancy Hamlin Davis and Ruth Hamlin, Old Canada Road Historical Society; (2) Find A Grave, Memorial #118353114.

Edwin, Berry-1
Birth:
Death:
Graveyard: (1) "Pleasantdale Cemetery" complied by Nancy Hamlin Davis and Ruth Hamlin, Old Canada Road Historical Society; (2) Find A Grave, Memorial #118353148.

Baby Girl 1 Berry
Birth:
Death: Gravestone.
Graveyard: (1) "Pleasantdale Cemetery" complied by Nancy Hamlin Davis and Ruth Hamlin, Old Canada Road Historical Society; (2) Find A Grave, Memorial #118353619.

Baby Girl 2 Berry
Birth:
Death: Gravestone.
Graveyard: (1) "Pleasantdale Cemetery" complied by Nancy Hamlin Davis and Ruth Hamlin, Old Canada Road Historical Society; (2) Find A Grave, Memorial #118354199.

Charles Berry-2
Birth:
Death: Gravestone.
Graveyard: (1) "Pleasantdale Cemetery" complied by Nancy Hamlin Davis and Ruth Hamlin, Old Canada Road Historical Society; (2) Find A Grave, Memorial #118353545.

Clara Ella Berry
Birth:
Death: Gravestone.
Graveyard: (1) "Pleasantdale Cemetery" complied by Nancy Hamlin Davis and Ruth Hamlin, Old Canada Road Historical Society; (2) Find A Grave, Memorial #118353693.

Historical Accounts: (1) 1840 United States Federal Census for Concord, Somerset, Maine; (2) 1850 United States Federal Census for Concord, Somerset, Maine; (3) 1860 United States Federal Census for Concord, Somerset, Maine, Page 64; (4) 1870 United States Federal for Concord, Somerset, Maine, Page 11; (5) 1880 United States Federal for Concord, Somerset, Maine, Page 12; (6) 1900 United States Federal for Concord, Somerset, Maine; Page 7.

Jacob Williams Atwood
(1821 - 1900)

The fifth child of Elsa Williams and Benjamin Colby Atwood was Jacob Williams who was born on March 28, 1821 in Concord, Somerset, Maine.

At age twenty, on November 16, 1841, Jacob Williams and Almyra B. Berry, also age twenty, filed their intentions to be married with the Town Clerk of Concord. They were later married in Embden, Somerset, Maine on November 21, 1841 by Christopher Thompson, a Justice of the Peace. Almyra B. (also spelled "Almira B.") was born in Stratham, Rockingham, New Hampshire on December 12, 1820 to George Berry and Nancy Ann Weatherby. She was the sister of Harriet Abigail Berry who was married Jacob Williams' brother Benjamin Franklin Atwood.

Jacob Williams and Almyra B. had a family of eight children.

Lincoln W.	b. January 13, 1842	d. May 13, 1924
Henry H.	*b. July 24, 1843*	*d. September 16, 1859*
Rosina Adelaide	b. March 3, 1845	d. March 15, 1927
Margaret Berry	*b. January 20, 1847*	*d. September 22, 1867*
Oscar Benjamin	b. March 23, 1849	d. April 13, 1922
Stephen Brown	b. October 20, 1851	d. May 2, 1933
Nancy Berry	b. April 15, 1854	d. August 15, 1907
Jacob Howard	b. March 16, 1858	d. January 27, 1946

In the 1850 United States Federal Census Jacob Williams and Almyra B. were recorded as living in Concord, with Jacob Williams' occupation being listed as a "farmer".

The second child, Henry H., of Jacob Williams and Almyra B. died on September 16, 1859 when he was sixteen years old after suffering a "fever" for seven days. He was buried in the Pleasantdale Cemetery in Embden.

When the 1860 United States Federal Census was taken Jacob Williams, Almyra B. and their family were still living and farming in Concord.

On September 22, 1867, Margaret Berry, the fourth child Jacob Williams and Almyra B., died when she was twenty-two years old. No record has been found to indicate that she had ever married or had children. Her cause and place of death have also not been found. Margaret Berry was buried in Embden at the Pleasantdale Cemetery next to her brother.

Jacob Williams, Almyra B. and their family were recorded as living on the family farm in Concord at the time of the 1870 and 1880 United States Federal Census'.

Almyra B. died of a cause not found in Concord on January 9, 1894 at the age of seventy-three. She was buried in the family plot in the Pleasantdale Cemetery in Embden.

Gravestones for Henry H. Atwood (top left) and Margaret Berry Atwood (top right)
(Photographs from the Collection of Jeffrey Nelson Williams and Jacqueline Pon Williams)

Gravestone for Almira B. Berry (bottom)
(Photograph Courtesy of Rick Rollins)

Jacob Williams lived over six years longer than his wife. In the 1900 United States Federal Census, taken on June 23rd and 25th of that year Jacob Williams was listed as living with his son Jacob Howard and his family in Concord. Jacob Williams died on September 22, 1900 at the Maine Insane Hospital in Augusta, Kennebec, Maine. His cause of death was listed as "senile dementia". Jacob Williams' place of burial is unknown.

SOURCES:

Jacob Williams Atwood
Birth: (1) Original Record of Maine Towns & Cities, Town of Concord, Page 91, Picton Press, Rockland Maine, Copyright 2005; (2) "Maine Births and Christenings, 1739-1900," database, FamilySearch, (https://familysearch.org/ark/61903/1.1:/F4Q4-TLF).
Death: Record of a Death, Maine Vital Records.
Graveyard:

Almyra B. Berry
Birth:
Marriage: (1) Original Record of Maine Towns & Cities, Concord, Page 138, Picton Press, Rockland Maine, Copyright 2005; (2) Original Record of Maine Towns & Cities, Embden, Disk 1 Page 361, Picton Press, Rockland Maine, Copyright 2005; (3) "South of 'Lost Nation', Northwest Embden's Enchanting Skyland Where Pioneers from Barrington, N. H. Settled" by Ernest G. Walker, Page 36, Washington, D. C., July 4, 1939, Retyped in 1994-1995 by Dean Lyons for the Embden Historical Society.
Death: Record of a Death, Maine Vital Records; (2) Gravestone.
Graveyard: (1) "Pleasantdale Cemetery" complied by Nancy Hamlin Davis and Ruth Hamlin, Old Canada Road Historical Society; (2) Find A Grave, Memorial #151019988.

Henry H. Atwood
Birth: Edmund West, comp., *"Family Data Collection - Individual Records"*, [database on-line], Provo, UT, USA: Ancestry.com Operations Inc, 2000.
Death: (1) U.S. Census Mortality Schedules, Maine, 1850-1880; Archive Collection: 2; Census Year: 1859; Census Place: Concord, Somerset, Maine; Page: 4; (2) Edmund West, comp., *"Family Data Collection - Individual Records"*, [database on-line], Provo, UT, USA: Ancestry.com Operations Inc, 2000; (3) Gravestone.
Graveyard: (1) "Pleasantdale Cemetery" complied by Nancy Hamlin Davis and Ruth Hamlin, Old Canada Road Historical Society; (2) Find A Grave, Memorial #149338427.

Margaret Berry Atwood
Birth: Edmund West, comp., *"Family Data Collection - Individual Records"*, [database on-line], Provo, UT, USA: Ancestry.com Operations Inc, 2000.
Death: Gravestone.
Graveyard: (1) "Pleasantdale Cemetery" complied by Nancy Hamlin Davis and Ruth Hamlin, Old Canada Road Historical Society; (2) Find A Grave, Memorial #149338566.

Historical Accounts: (1) 1850 United States Federal Census for Concord, Somerset, Maine; (2) 1860 United States Federal Census for Concord, Somerset, Maine, Page 64; (3) 1870 United States Federal for Concord, Somerset, Maine, Page 12; (4) 1880 United States Federal for Concord, Somerset, Maine, Page 12; (5) 1900 United States Federal for Concord, Somerset, Maine, Page 8.

Stillman Howard Atwood
(1824 - 1908)

Stillman Howard, the sixth child of Elsa Williams and Benjamin Colby Atwood, was born in Concord, Somerset, Maine on January 28, 1824.

In the 1850 United States Federal Census Stillman Howard was recorded as living with his parents in Concord and working as a "farmer".

On December 21, 1851, then age twenty-seven, Stillman Howard was married to Sarah Jane Greer, age twenty-two, in Waltham, Middlesex, Massachusetts by Reverend N. J. Merrill. Stillman Howard was working as a "laborer" in Boston at the time of his marriage. Sarah Jane, born on December 11, 1829 in Morrill, Waldo, Maine, was the daughter of Nathaniel S. Greer and Mary Jane Knowlton.

Stillman Howard and Sarah Jane had three children.

Charles Henry T.	b. September 12, 1853	d. April 21, 1921
Emily Celestia	*b. September 21, 1855*	*d. May 11, 1858*
Georgia Mae	b. January 18, 1862	d. May 3, 1946

The 1850's was a period when Stillman Howard and Sarah Jane were living in Boston. In 1853, when their son Charles Henry Thornton was born they were living in Central Square and Stillman Howard was working as a "trader". When Emily Celestia was born in 1855 (although she was born in Concord, Somerset, Maine) they were living at 129 Saratoga Street in Boston and Stillman Howard was working as a "shipwright".

Emily Celestia, the second child of Stillman Howard and Sarah Jane, died on May 11, 1858 when she was two years, seven months and twenty days old. The cause and place of her death are unknown, although her burial card indicates that her body was brought from Concord. She was buried in Lot 674 at the Southside Cemetery in Skowhegan, Somerset, Maine.

By the time the 1860 United States Federal Census was taken Stillman Howard, Sarah Jane and their son, Charles Henry Thornton, had moved to Embden, Somerset, Maine, with Stillman Howard's occupation being listed as a "farmer".

In the 1870 and 1880 United States Federal Census', Stillman Howard and Sarah Jane were recorded as still living and farming in Embden.

Stillman Howard and Sarah Jane had moved to Skowhegan, Somerset, Maine by the time the 1900 United States Federal Census was taken. Stillman Howard's occupation was again listed as "farmer".

Sometime after the 1900 United States Federal Census was taken, Stillman Howard and Sarah Jane moved across the country to Eugene, Lane, Oregon. It is presumed they moved there to be near their children, Charles Henry Thornton and Georgia Mae (Atwood) Tobey, who were both living in Eugene at that time.

Stillman Howard died at the home of his daughter Georgia Mae in Eugene on November 28, 1908 at the age of eighty-four. The cause of his death was listed as "apoplexy and paralysis". He was buried in the Eugene Pioneer Cemetery in Eugene in Section B, Block 376, Plot 4.

In his Last Will and Testament Stillman Howard left the sum of $5.00 to his son Charles Henry Thornton and his remaining estate to his wife and daughter to "share and share alike".

The 1910 United States Federal Census recorded Sarah Jane as living with her daughter, Georgia Mae (Atwood) Tobey and her husband at 527 High Street in Eugene. A little more than three years later, Sarah Jane was listed as still living at 527 High Street in Eugene when the 1912 Lane County Directory was published.

Sarah Jane died in Eugene, at the home of her daughter, on February 18, 1912 at the age of eighty-two. Her cause of death was recorded as "general breaking down". Sarah Jane's funeral, conducted by Reverend H. S. Wilkinson of the Methodist Church, was held at her daughter's home in Eugene at 10:00 on Tuesday, February 20th. She was buried next to Stillman Howard in Section B, Block 376, Plot 5 at the Eugene Pioneer Cemetery in Eugene.

Gravestone for Emily Celestia Atwood
(Photograph Courtesy of Gail Kelly)

Gravestones for Stillman Howard Atwood (top) and Sarah Jane Greer (bottom)
(Photographs Courtesy of Grundbrecan)

SOURCES:

Stillman Howard Atwood
Birth: (1) Original Record of Maine Towns & Cities, Town of Concord, Page 91, Picton Press, Rockland Maine, Copyright 2005; (2) "Maine, Births and Christenings, 1739-1900," index, FamilySearch, (https://familysearch.org /pal:/MM9.1.1/F4Q4-TLV); (3) Gravestone.
Death: (1) "Oregon, Death Index, 1898-2008," [database on-line]. Provo, UT, USA: Ancestry.com Operations Inc, 2000; (2) Obituary, The Eugene Guard, Eugene, Oregon, Saturday, November 28, 1908, Page 9; (3) Eugene Pioneer Cemetery Records, www.eugenepioneercemetery.com; (4) Gravestone.
Graveyard: (1) Eugene Pioneer Cemetery Records, www.eugenepioneercemetery.com; (2) Find A Grave, Memorial #48851102.

Sarah Jane Greer
Birth: (1) "Maine, Births and Christenings, 1739-1900," index, FamilySearch, (https://familysearch.org/pal: /MM9.1.1/F4ST-SZK); (2) Gravestone.
Marriage: "Massachusetts, Marriages, 1841-1915," database with images, FamilySearch, (https://familysearch. org/ark:/61903/1:1: N4ZX-P1T), Marriage Register for the Town of Waltham, Middlesex, Massachusetts for the Year 1851.
Death: (1) "Oregon, Death Index, 1898-2008," [database on-line]. Provo, UT, USA: Ancestry.com Operations Inc, 2000; (2) Obituary, The Eugene Guard, Eugene, Oregon, Monday, February 19, 1912, Page 5; (3) Eugene Pioneer Cemetery Records, www.eugenepioneercemetery.com; (4) Gravestone.
Graveyard: (1) Eugene Pioneer Cemetery Records, www.eugenepioneercemetery.com; (2) Find A Grave, Memorial #48851096.

Emily Celestia Atwood
Birth: "Massachusetts Births, 1841-1915," database with images, FamilySearch, (https://familysearch.org/ark: /61903/1:1: FXDT-CMW), Birth Register for the City of Boston, Middlesex, Massachusetts for the year 1855.
Death: Burial Records for Southside Cemetery, Skowhegan, Maine, www.cemeteryfind.com.
Graveyard: (1) Burial Records for Southside Cemetery, Skowhegan, Maine, www.cemeteryfind.com; (2) Find A Grave, Memorial #144537439.

Historical Accounts: (1) 1850 United States Federal Census for Concord, Somerset, Maine; (2) 1860 United States Federal Census for Embden, Somerset, Maine, Page 57; (3) 1870 United States Federal for Embden, Somerset, Maine, Page 9; (4) 1880 United States Federal for Embden, Somerset, Maine, Page 8; (5) 1900 United States Federal for Skowhegan, Somerset, Maine, Page 10; (6) 1910 United States Federal for Eugene, Lane, Oregon, Page 7B; (7) Probate Notification, Morning Register, Eugene, Oregon, Wednesday, December 2, 1908, Page 5; (8) 1912 Lane County Oregon Directory, Eugene, Oregon, Page 45.

William King Atwood
(1830 - 1899)

The eighth child of Elsa Williams and Benjamin Colby Atwood was William King. He was born in 1830 at Concord, Somerset, Maine.

In the 1850 United States Federal Census, William King was recorded as living in Concord with his parents and working as a "farmer".

At age twenty-six, on June 28, 1856, William King was married to Alma Haines, age fifteen, in Concord. Alma was born in Somerset County, Maine on September 1, 1840. The place of her birth and the names of her parents have not been found.

William King and Alma had one child together.

William Marshall   b. 1858   d.

Alma died in Concord on October 15, 1858 at the age of eighteen of a cause not found. She was buried in the Pleasantdale Cemetery in Embden, Somerset, Maine.

Gravestone for Alma Haines
(Photograph from the Collection of Jeffrey Nelson Williams and Jacqueline Pon Williams)

On July 29, 1859, nine months after Alma's death, William King, then age twenty-nine, married his second wife Esther Tuttle Moulton, age twenty. They were married by William Abbott at his home in New Portland, Somerset, Maine. Esther Tuttle was the daughter of Nathaniel Berry Moulton and William

King's cousin, Abigail Meriam Williams. She was born in Concord on May 10, 1839.

William King had an additional three children with his second wife, Esther Tuttle.

Emma C.	b. September 1860	d. December 5, 1893
Etta May	b. August 8, 1863	d. October 25, 1954
Everett Morrill	b. August 28, 1882	d. February 16, 1966

In the 1860 United States Federal Census, William King and Esther Tuttle were recorded as living in Concord with William King working as a "farmer".

Sometime after the birth of their second daughter, William King and Esther Tuttle moved to Bristol, Grafton, New Hampshire where they were listed as living in the 1870 United States Federal Census. At that time William King's occupation was listed as "carpenter".

Records regarding the life and death of William Marshall, the only child William King had with his first wife Alma, beyond the 1870 census have not been found. Therefore, the discussion of his life will end here.

When the 1880 and 1885 City Directories for Concord, Merrimack, New Hampshire were published William King, Esther Tuttle and their two daughters were listed as living at 3 Thorndike Street in Concord. William King was listed as working as a "carpenter" in both those directories.

The 1891 Concord City Directory recorded William King and Esther Tuttle as living at 65 South Main Street. By the time the1895 Concord City Directory was published they had again moved and were listed as living at 28 Perley Street. In both those directories William King was still listed as working as a "carpenter".

William King died at the age of sixty-nine in Concord, Merrimack, New Hampshire on October 22, 1899. The cause of his death was listed as "pneumonia". He was buried in the Blossom Hill Cemetery in Concord, New Hampshire.

Shortly after William King's death, Esther Tuttle moved with her son, Everett Morrill, to Lawrence, Essex, Massachusetts where they were listed as living in the 1900 and 1910 United States Federal Census'.

On May 8, 1913, Esther Tuttle died of "apoplexy" in Bristol, Grafton, New Hampshire at age seventy-three. She was buried with her husband in the Blossom Hill Cemetery in Concord, New Hampshire.

SOURCES:

William King Atwood
Birth:
Death: "New Hampshire Death and Disinterment Records, 1754-1947," [database on-line], Provo, UT, USA: Ancestry.com Operations, Inc., 2013.
Graveyard: "New Hampshire Death and Disinterment Records, 1754-1947," [database on-line], Provo, UT, USA: Ancestry.com Operations, Inc., 2013.

Alma Haines
Birth:
Marriage: Original Record of Maine Towns & Cities, Town of Concord, Page 187, Picton Press, Rockland Maine, Copyright 2005.
Death: "Pleasantdale Cemetery" complied by Nancy Hamlin Davis and Ruth Hamlin, Old Canada Road Historical Society.
Graveyard: (1) "Pleasantdale Cemetery" complied by Nancy Hamlin Davis and Ruth Hamlin, Old Canada Road Historical Society; (2) Find A Grave, Memorial #118490681.

William Marshall Atwood
Birth:
Death:
Graveyard:

Esther Tuttle Moulton
Birth: Original Record of Maine Towns & Cities, Concord, Page 98, Picton Press, Rockland Maine, Copyright 2005.
Marriage: (1) Original Record of Maine Towns & Cities, Town of Concord, Page 196, Picton Press, Rockland Maine, Copyright 2005; (2) Original Record of Maine Towns & Cities, Town of Concord, Page 200, Picton Press, Rockland Maine, Copyright 2005; (3) "Maine, Marriages, 1771-1907" index, FamilySearch, (https://familysearch.org/pal:/MM9.1.1 /F4FW-C2Z).
Death: "New Hampshire Death and Disinterment Records, 1754-1947," [database on-line], Provo, UT, USA: Ancestry.com Operations, Inc., 2013.
Graveyard: "New Hampshire Death and Disinterment Records, 1754-1947," [database on-line], Provo, UT, USA: Ancestry.com Operations, Inc., 2013.

Historical Accounts: (1) 1850 United States Federal Census for Concord, Somerset, Maine; (2) 1860 United States Federal Census for Concord, Somerset, Maine, Page 64; (3) 1870 United States Federal Census for Bristol, Grafton, New Hampshire, Page 12; (4) 1900 United States Federal for Lawrence, Essex, Massachusetts, Page 8; (5) 1910 United States Federal for Lawrence City, Essex, Massachusetts, Page 7; (6) 1880 Concord, New Hampshire, City Directory, Page 22; (7) 1885 Concord, New Hampshire, City Directory, Page 44; (8) 1891 Concord, New Hampshire, City Directory, Page 68; (9) 1895 Concord, New Hampshire, City Directory, Page 80.

Dorcas Brown Williams
(1817 - 1862)

The first child of Ebenezer Williams and his first wife Mahala Richards was Dorcas Brown who was born on July 10, 1817 in Maine. The exact place of her birth has not been found.

On September 7, 1834, at age seventeen, Dorcas Brown and John H. Jones, age twenty-three, filed their intentions to be married with the Town Clerk of Houlton, Aroostook, Maine. They were subsequently married on September 23, 1834 in Hodgdon, Aroostook, Maine by Cirain Esty, a Justice of the Peace. John H. was born in 1811 in Maine. The exact date and place of his birth as well as the names of his parents have not been found.

Dorcas Brown and John H. had six children.

Julia Eliza	b. April 23, 1836	d. January 18, 1886
Susan S.	b. August 4, 1838	d. May 28, 1921
Charles W.	*b. July 1840*	*d. October 28, 1846*
Phoebe W.	b. 1843	d.
John A.	b. 1845	d. August 24, 1864
Charles Watson	b. September 27, 1852	d. December 31, 1909

The third child of Dorcas Brown and John H., Charles W., died at the age of six years and three months old on October 28, 1846. The cause and place of his death have not been found. He was buried in Section 3, Block 2, Grave 33 of the Evergreen Cemetery in Houlton.

Gravestone for Charles W. Jones
(Photograph Courtesy of Duke Thatcher)

In the 1850 United States Federal Census, Dorcas Brown, John H. and four of their children were recorded as living in Houlton. John H.'s occupation was listed as a "farmer" in that census.

Dorcas Brown died of a "cancer" in Houlton on May 26, 1862 at the age of forty-four. She was buried in Section 3, Block 2, Grave 33 of the Evergreen Cemetery in Houlton.

In 1870 John H. filed a "Claim for Father's Pension" as a dependent of his son John A. who died while serving in the Union Army during the Civil War. John H. was not a healthy man at that time as evidenced by a letter dated January 4, 1870 from his personal physician, Dr. Ezekiel D. French, stating that "for six or eight years past he (John H.) has been generally broken down in health and at times he has been confirmed invalid". Dr. French further stated that John H. "suffered from phtisie and seated cough, his stomach and bowels disarranged, is crippled by rheumatism, and by disease of the head rendered very deaf".

When the 1870 United States Federal Census was taken John H. and his sixth child, Charles Watson, were living in Houlton with his daughter, Susan S. (Jones) Merriam, and her family. John H. was recorded as working on their farm.

Additional information regarding his life and death of John H. has not been found.

Gravestone for Dorcas Brown Williams
(Photograph Courtesy of Duke Thatcher)

SOURCES:

Dorcas Brown Williams
Birth:
Death: (1) Case Files of Approved Pension Applications of Widows and Other Veterans of the Army and Navy Who Served Mainly in the Civil War and the War with Spain, compiled 1861-1934; (2) Gravestone.
Graveyard: Find A Grave, Memorial #22904723.

John H. Jones
Birth:
Marriage: (1) Original Record of Maine Towns & Cities, Town of Houlton, Page 17, Copyright 2005, Picton Press, Rockland Maine, Copyright 2005; (2) Testament of Marriage provided by Cirain Esty, Justice of the Peace and certified by the Town Clerk of Hodgdon, Aroostook, Maine, www.fold3.com.
Death:
Graveyard:

Charles W. Jones
Birth:
Death: Gravestone.
Graveyard: Find A Grave, Memorial #22904797.

Historical Accounts: (1) 1850 United States Federal Census for Houlton, Aroostook, Maine; (2) 1860 United States Federal Census for Houlton, Aroostook, Maine, Page 43; (3) 1870 United States Federal Census for Houlton, Aroostook, Maine, Page 16; (4) Testament of Health dated January 4, 1870 provided by Dr. Ezekiel D. French and certified by John P. Donworth, Justice of the Peace, www.fold3.com.

Truman Allen Williams
(1819 - 1894)

Truman Allen, the second child of Ebenezer Williams and his first wife Mahala Richards, was born on July 25, 1819 in Hodgdon, Aroostook, Maine.

On February 25, 1842, at age twenty-two, Truman Allen and Eliza Jane Smith, age nineteen, filed their intentions to be married with the Town Clerk of Hodgdon. Eliza Jane, the daughter of Hugh Smith and Isabella Hood, was born May 31, 1822 in Fredericton, York, New Brunswick, Canada. The exact date and place of Truman Allen and Eliza Jane's subsequent marriage has not been found.

Truman Allen and Eliza Jane had a family of five children.

Benjamin Franklin	b. 1842	d.
Lucia P.	b. October 21, 1846	d. May 22, 1920
Nelson H.	b. October 1849	d. April 12, 1906
Otis P.	b. May 1852	d. November 24, 1914
Moses H.	b. October 1856	d. March 24, 1910

In 1842 Truman Allen left Hodgdon and moved his family to Township 11, Range 1 in Aroostook, Maine where he cleared a plot of forested land to make a home for Eliza Jane and himself.

When the 1850 and 1860 United States Federal Census' were taken, Truman Allen, Eliza Jane and their family were recorded as living in Township 11, Range 1. In those census documents Truman Allen's occupation was listed as a "farmer".

Like his father Ebenezer Williams, Truman Allen held elected office in Cary Plantation, Aroostook, Maine (which included Township No. 11, Range 1). On June 30, 1859 he was chosen First Assessor of Cary Plantation. He was reelected as Second Assessor on March 31, 1860 and on March 25, 1861 he was chosen as Third Assessor. And then on March 27, 1865, Truman Allen was elected to the position of Plantation Clerk, a position he held off and on for several years. Additionally, the Cary Plantation Town Records reflect that Truman Allen's home was used for official town meetings throughout the 1860's.

In the 1870 and 1880 United States Federal Census' Truman Allen and his family were recorded as still living and farming in Township 11, Range 1.

Eliza Jane died of "dropsy" at the age of sixty-nine on May 3, 1892 in Cary Plantation, Aroostook, Maine. The place of her burial has not been found.

A little more than two years later, on November 11, 1894, Truman Allen, age seventy-five, also died in Cary Plantation. His cause of death was listed as "old age". As with his wife, Truman Allen's place of burial is not known.

SOURCES:

Truman Allen Williams
Birth:
Death: Record of a Death, Maine Vital Records.
Graveyard:

Eliza Jane Smith
Birth:
Marriage: "Maine, Marriages, 1771-1907," index, FamilySearch, (https://familysearch.org/pal:/MM9.1.1/F4FD-WWB).
Death: Record of a Death, Maine Vital Records.
Graveyard:

Historical Accounts: (1) 1850 United States Federal Census for Township 11, Range 1, Aroostook, Maine; (2) 1860 United States Federal Census for Township 11, Range 1, Aroostook, Maine, Page 12; (3) 1870 United States Federal Census for Township 11, Range 1, Aroostook, Maine, Page 3; (4) 1880 United States Federal Census for Township 11, Range 1, Aroostook, Maine, Page 10; (5) Original Record of Maine Towns & Cities, Cary Plantation, Pages 9, 10, 19 & 24, Picton Press, Rockland Maine, Copyright 2005; (6) "History of Aroostook" compiled and written by Hon. Edward Wiggin, Page 271, Star-Herald Press, Presque Isle, Maine, 1922.

Willis Richard Williams
(1821 - 1897)

The third child of Ebenezer Williams and his first wife, Mahala Richards, was Willis Richard. He was born on April 21, 1821 in Maine. The exact location of his birth is not known.

By the time he was twenty-nine, Willis Richard, along with his brother Alden F., were living in Dedham, Hancock, Maine, as recorded in the 1850 United States Federal Census.

Sometime between 1850 and 1867, Willis Richard moved to Michigan Bluff in Placer County, California, where his brother Moses House was also living. In the California Great Register of Placer County for 1867, Willis Richard, age forty-five, was listed as working as a "miner".

By the time the 1870 United States Federal Census was taken, Willis Richard had moved back to Maine and was recorded as living with his brother Alden F. and his family in Howard, Piscataquis, Maine. In that census he was listed as working as a "carpenter".

Between 1870 and 1879 Willis Richard returned to Michigan Bluff where he continued to work in the mining camps. He was listed as living in Michigan Bluff in the California Great Registers of Placer County for the years 1879, 1888, 1890 and 1894; as well as in the 1880 United States Federal Census. Willis Richard was described in the California Great Registers to be around 6' to 6'1" tall with blue eyes.

In the 1896 California Voter Register of Placer County, Willis Richard was recorded as being inflicted with "paralysis of the lower limbs" and living in the town of Auburn.

On May 1, 1897, at the age of seventy-six, Willis Richard died in the Placer County Hospital in Auburn of a cause not found. No record has been found to indicate that Willis Richard had ever married or had children. His body was returned to Michigan Bluff where he was buried in the Odd Fellows Cemetery.

SOURCES:

Willis Richard Williams
Birth:
Death: Placer Herald, 1863-1915, Births, Marriages, Deaths and Misc. Notes, www.placer.ca.gov.
Graveyard: Find A Grave, Memorial #110224949.

Historical Accounts: (1) 1850 United States Federal Census for Dedham, Hancock, Maine; (2) 1870 United States Federal Census for Dedham, Hancock, Maine, Page 4; (3) 1880 United States Federal Census for Michigan Bluff, Placer, California, Page 1; (4) 1867 California Great Register of Placer County, Page 46; (5) 1879 California Great Register of Placer County, Page 43; (6) 1888 California Great Register of Placer County, Page 52; (7) 1890 California Great Register of Placer County, Page 43; (8) 1894 California Great Register of Placer County, Page 57; (9) 1896 California Voter Register of Placer County, Auburn N. 3 Precinct, Page 11.

Alden F. Williams
(1825 - 1903)

Alden F., the fifth child of Ebenezer Williams and his first wife Mahala Richards was born in 1825 in Embden, Somerset, Maine.

In the 1850 United States Federal Census, Alden F. was listed as living and working in Dedham, Hancock, Maine along with his brother, Willis Richard.

Sometime after that Alden F. married Maria B. Green. The date and location of their marriage is unknown. Maria B. was the daughter of James S. Green and Abiah Hines. She was born on September 23, 1834 in Dixmont, Penobscot, Maine.

Alden F. and Maria B. had six children during their marriage.

Chester Orlando	b. June 27, 1853	d.
Minnie J.	b. March 25, 1857	d. May 4, 1927
Eva M.	*b. 1859*	*d.*
Phebe	*b. 1860*	*d.*
William Bryant	b. May 10, 1863	d. January 31, 1939
Fred	*b. 1877*	*d.*

By the time the 1860 United States Federal Census was taken, Alden F., Maria B. and their family were listed as living in the 7th Ward in Bangor, Penobscot, Maine.

Eva M., the third child of Alden F. and Maria B., was listed in the 1860 census which was taken on June 27th of that year but was not listed in any subsequent census documents. It is presumed that she died sometime after that date, but no official record of her death or burial has been found.

In the 1870 United States Federal Census Alden F. and his family were listed as having moved to Howard, Piscataquis, Maine where his occupation was recorded as a "farmer".

The fourth child of Alden F. and Maria B., Phebe, was recorded in the 1870 census, but also has not been listed in any subsequent census document. As such it is believed that she died sometime between the taking of the 1870 and the 1880 United States Federal Census'. Like her sister Eva M., no record of her death or burial has been found.

Alden F., Maria B. and their family had relocated to Monson, Piscataquis, Maine by the time the 1880 United States Federal Census was taken. Alden F. was then working as a "cabinet maker".

Fred, the sixth child of Alden F. and Maria B. was recorded as being three years old at the time of the 1880 United States Federal Census. As with two of his sisters before him, any record of his life and death subsequent to that census has not been found. As such it is presumed that he died sometime after that census was taken.

On November 16, 1896 Maria B. died at the age of sixty-two in Guildford, Piscataquis, Maine. The cause of her death was listed as "neurasthenia". The location of Maria B.'s burial has not been found.

Alden F. was listed as living with his son William Bryant and his family in Guildford at the time of the 1900 United States Federal Census.

At age seventy-five, Alden F. was married to his second wife, the widow Mercy A. (Jackson) Sawyer, on December 8, 1900 in Bangor by H. J. Preble, a Justice of the Peace. Mercy A., then age sixty, was born in Rome, Kennebec, Maine in 1840 to John E. Jackson and Rhoda Whitehouse. At the time of that marriage Alden F. was working as a "mechanic".

Three years later, Alden F., then age seventy-eight, died on November 11, 1903 in Guilford. His cause of death was listed as "uremia". His place of burial is also unknown.

Additional information on the life and death of Mercy A. has not been found.

SOURCES:

Alden F. Williams
Birth:
Death: Record of a Death, Maine Vital Records.
Graveyard:

Maria B. Green
Birth:
Marriage:
Death: Record of a Death, Maine Vital Records.
Graveyard:

Eva M. Williams
Birth:
Death:
Graveyard:

Phebe Williams
Birth:
Death:
Graveyard:

Fred Williams
Birth:
Death:
Graveyard:

Mercy A. Jackson
Birth:
Marriage: (1) Record of a Marriage, Maine Vital Records; (2) "Maine, Marriage Index, 1892-1985," [database on-line], Provo, UT, USA: Ancestry.com Operations Inc, 2000.
Death:
Graveyard:

Historical Accounts: (1) 1850 United States Federal Census for Dedham, Hancock, Maine; (2) 1860 United States Federal Census for 7th Ward, Bangor, Penobscot, Maine, Page 78; (3) 1870 United States Federal Census for Howard, Piscataquis, Maine, Page 4; (4) 1880 United States Federal Census for Monson, Piscataquis, Maine, Page 35; (5) 1900 United States Federal Census for Guilford, Piscataquis, Maine, Page 8.

Moses Henry Williams
(1830 - 1895)

The sixth child of Ebenezer Williams and his first wife, Mahala Richards, Moses Henry, was born on July 20, 1830 in Hodgdon, Aroostook, Maine.

In the 1850 United States Federal Census Moses Henry was listed as living with his father and his father's second wife in Township 11, Aroostook, Maine. His occupation at that time was listed as "farmer".

Moses Henry moved across the country to Michigan Bluff, Placer, California in 1852 participating in the California Gold Rush. During his time there Moses Henry, a "carpenter" by trade, built a home for Leland Stanford who owned and ran the local mercantile store. (As a side note Leland Stanford went on to become the Governor of California and a highly successful businessman.) Moses Henry left California and returned to Maine in 1856 traveling there by ship via Cape Horn.

At age twenty-five, on May 17, 1856, Moses Henry was married to Elizabeth Ann Longley, age twenty-four, in Calais, Washington, Maine. Elizabeth Ann, the daughter of Abraham Longley and Elizabeth Harthon, was born in Orient, Aroostook, Maine on February 19, 1832.

Moses Henry Williams and Elizabeth Ann Longley
(Photographs Courtesy of Rod Headington)

Moses Henry and Elizabeth Ann had seven children.

Leni Leota	b. March 29, 1857	d. October 26, 1924
Ida Viola	b. April 1, 1858	d. August 16, 1895
Frederick George	*b. March 16, 1860*	*d. April 24, 1876*
Lilla Rosalie	b. July 06, 1861	d. April 18, 1927

Marian L.	b. June 14, 1863	d. January 17, 1926
Anna Fay	b. December 1865	d. December 11, 1918
Ella Amelia	b. September 20, 1870	d. October 1, 1935

Shortly after their marriage Moses Henry and Elizabeth Ann moved back across the county to Michigan Bluff, California where in 1857 Moses Henry was credited with building the first covered bridge across the American River.

On May 2, 1857 Moses Henry placed an ad in the Placer Herald newspaper offering a building and lot for sale, known as the Union Hotel, located on Main Street in Michigan Bluff.

In the California Great Register of Placer County for 1867 and the 1870 United States Federal Census, Moses Henry was listed as working as a "carpenter"

Frederick George, the third child of Moses Henry and Elizabeth Ann, died in Michigan Bluff when he was sixteen years old on April 24, 1876. The cause of his death has not been found. His was buried in the Odd Fellows Cemetery in Michigan Bluff.

Gravestone for Frederick George Williams
(Photograph Courtesy of Rod Headington)

The 1880 United States Federal Census and the California Great Registers of Placer County for 1879, 1890, 1892 and 1894, listed Moses Henry, Elizabeth Ann and their children as living in Michigan Bluff. In the California Great

Registers Moses Henry was recorded as being 6′ 2″ tall with brown eyes. His occupation in those documents was listed as "carpenter".

Moses Henry died "suddenly" of a cause not found in Michigan Bluff on September 26, 1895 at the age of sixty-five. He was buried near his son in the Odd Fellows Cemetery in Michigan Bluff.

The Mountain Lodge, No. 14 of the International Order of Odd Fellows (I.O.O.F.) published a tribute to Moses Henry in the October 26, 1895 edition of the Placer Herald. Among the accolades, the tribute indicated that the "Lodge be draped in mourning for thirty days" to honor their beloved brother.

In the 1900 United States Federal Census Elizabeth Ann was recorded as living in Township 6, Placer, California and working as a "lodging housekeeper". The 1910 United States Federal Census for Township 6 listed her as living on the "West side of Town Michigan Bluff" with no occupation.

Elizabeth Ann outlived Moses Henry by almost eleven years. She passed away in Michigan Bluff at the age of eighty-four on May 9, 1916. The cause of her death has not been found. She too was buried in the Odd Fellows Cemetery in Michigan Bluff.

Gravestones for Moses Henry Williams and Elizabeth Ann Longley
(Photographs Courtesy of Rod Headington)

SOURCES:

Moses Henry Williams
Birth: Gravestone.
Death: (1) Obituary, The Placer Herald, Rocklin, California, Saturday, September 28, 1895, Page 4; (2) The Placer Herald, 1863-1915, Births, Marriages, Deaths and Misc. Notes, www.placer.ca.gov; (3) Gravestone.
Graveyard: Find A Grave, Memorial #27248257.

Elizabeth Ann Longley
Birth: Gravestone.
Marriage: "Maine, Marriages, 1771-1907," index, FamilySearch, (https://familysearch.org/pal:/MM9.1.1/F46K-D61).
Death: (1) Death Notice, The Placer Herald, Rocklin, California, Saturday, May 13, 1916, Page 3; (2) Gravestone.
Graveyard: Find A Grave, Memorial #27248358.

Frederick George Williams
Birth: Gravestone.
Death: (1) The Placer Herald, 1863-1915, Births, Marriages, Deaths and Misc. Notes, www.placer.ca.gov; (2) Gravestone.
Graveyard: Find A Grave, Memorial #61286345.

Historical Accounts: (1) 1850 United States Federal Census for Township No. 11, Aroostook, Maine; (2) 1870 United States Federal Census for Township No. 6, Placer, California, Page 9; (3) 1880 United States Federal Census for Michigan Bluff, Placer, California, Page 2; (4) 1867 California Great Register of Placer County, Page 46, , "California, Voter Registers, 1866-1898," [database on-line]., Provo, UT, USA: Ancestry.com Operations, Inc., 2011; (5) 1879 California Great Register of Placer County, Page 43, "California, Voter Registers, 1866-1898," [database on-line]., Provo, UT, USA: Ancestry.com Operations, Inc., 2011; (6) 1890 California Great Register of Placer County, Page 43, , "California, Voter Registers, 1866-1898," [database on-line]., Provo, UT, USA: Ancestry.com Operations, Inc., 2011; (7) 1892 California Great Register of Placer County, Page 61, , "California, Voter Registers, 1866-1898," [database on-line]., Provo, UT, USA: Ancestry.com Operations, Inc., 2011; (8) 1894 California Great Register of Placer County, Page 57, , "California, Voter Registers, 1866-1898," [database on-line]., Provo, UT, USA: Ancestry.com Operations, Inc., 2011; (9) 1900 United States Federal Census for Township No. 6, Placer, California, Page 3; (10) 1910 United States Federal Census for Township No. 6, Placer, California, Page 1.; (11) Advertisement, The Placer Herald, Rocklin, California, Saturday, May 2, 1857, Page 2; (12) In Memoriam, The Placer Herald, Rocklin, California, Saturday, October 26, 1895, Page 1; (13) Obituary for Ella Amelia Williams, Auburn Journal, Auburn, California, Thursday, October 10, 1935, Page 12.

Chandler John Williams
(1844 - 1908)

The second child of Ebenezer Williams and his second wife Martha Ann Colwell was Chandler John (also sometimes known as John Chandler) who was born on March 15, 1844 in Township 11, Range 1, Aroostook, Maine.

Chandler John Williams
(Photograph Courtesy of Chandler Williams)

In the 1860 United States Federal Census Chandler John was listed as living with his father and mother in Township 11. Then age sixteen, his occupation was listed as "farmer".

On April 17, 1862, Chandler John enlisted in Company H, 17th Maine Volunteer Infantry Regiment of the Union Army. In his enlistment records he was described as being 5' 10" tall with gray eyes, dark hair and having a fair complexion. During his time in the army Chandler John also served in Company I of the 15th Maine Volunteer Infantry Regiment. He was mustered out due to a disability at a Camp near Falmouth, Stafford, Virginia on February 19, 1863 holding the rank of Private. During his military service Chandler John suffered from deafness as a result of a bursting shell and applied for his military pension on September 12, 1868.

By the time the 1870 United States Federal Census was taken, Chandler John's father had passed and at age twenty-six, Chandler John was listed as living with his mother in Township 11 and working as a "farm laborer".

Chandler John, age twenty-eight, married Clara Morse, age twenty, in Danforth, Washington, Maine on March 29, 1872. The officiant for their marriage was Joseph B. Foss, a Trail Justice. Clara, the daughter of Eliphalet

Morse and Lucinda Dudley, was born in Danforth on March 15, 1852. No record has been found to indicate that Chandler John and Clara had any children during their marriage. Just how long their married lasted is unknown, however it is known that Chandler John and Clara were legally divorced in Aroostook County in February of 1883.

On May 31, 1880, then age thirty-six, Chandler John was married to his second wife Eva H. Floyd, age twenty-five, in Danforth by Reverend E. A. Glidden. Nine days later when the 1880 United States Federal Census was taken, Chandler John and Eva H. were recorded as living in Danforth with Chandler John working as a "farmer". Eva H., the daughter of Daniel Floyd and Hannah Cossar, was born in Carroll Plantation, Penobscot, Maine on April 26, 1855. Chandler John and Eva H. did not have any children together.

As noted above, Chandler John was not legally divorced from his first wife Clara when he married Eva H. However, it is presumed that sometime before June 2, 1883, when Eva H. married George H. Hoxie in Bangor, Penobscot, Maine, Chandler John and Eva H. were divorced, or due to Chandler John's legal marital status had their marriage annulled. The specific date and place of that event has not been found.

On December 18, 1884 Chandler John, age forty, and Amanda Gillis, age twenty, filed their intentions to be married with the Town Clerk of Danforth. They were subsequently married in Danforth on December 23, 1884 by a Minister of the Gospel. Amanda was born on July 25, 1864 in Forest City, Washington, Maine to John Gillis and an unknown mother.

**Chandler John Williams, Mansfield Harrison Williams, Beecher Clifton Williams,
Amanda Gillis Williams and Bessie Marion Williams (left to right)**
(Photograph Courtesy of Chandler Williams)

Chandler John and his third wife Amanda had five children together.

Mansfield Harrison	b. November 25, 1885	d. January 12, 1968
Beecher Clifton	b. October 7, 1887	d. November 25, 1953
Bessie Marion	b. July 17, 1891	d. July 2, 1981
Harold C.	b. July 27, 1897	d. April 18, 1948
Ellis M.	b. August 7, 1900	d. August 1935

In the 1900 United States Federal Census Chandler John, Amanda and their family were listed as living in Danforth. Chandler John's occupation was listed as "insurance agent".

On June 23, 1908, at age sixty-four, Chandler John died in Danforth of "Bright's disease". He was buried in Section A, Lot 2 of the Danforth Cemetery in Danforth (also known as the Maple Cemetery).

As recorded in the 1910 United States Federal Census Amanda continued living in Danforth. She died on March 22, 1916 at age fifty-one, just six weeks after moving to Weston, Aroostook, Maine. Amanda's cause of death was listed as "chronic dyspepsia and melancholia". She was buried with Chandler John in Section A, Lot 2 at the Danforth Cemetery in Danforth.

Gravestone for Chandler John Williams and Amanda Gillis
(Photograph Courtesy of Chandler Williams)

SOURCES:

Chandler John Williams
Birth: (1) "Maine, Veterans Cemetery Records 1676-1918," database with images, FamilySearch, (https://familysearch.org/ark:/61903/1:1: KXQZ-R12); (2) "Maine, Faylene Hutton Cemetery Collection, ca 1780-1900", database with images, FamilySearch, (https://familysearch.org/ark:/61903/1:1:3QS7-L9FQ); (3) Gravestone.
Death: (1) Record of a Death, Maine Vital Records; (2) "Maine, Veterans Cemetery Records 1676-1918," database with images, FamilySearch, (https://familysearch.org/ark:/61903/1:1:KXQZ-R12); (3) Gravestone.
Graveyard: (1) "Maine, Veterans Cemetery Records 1676-1918," database with images, FamilySearch, (https://familysearch.org/ark:/61903/1:1:KXQZ-R12); (2) "Maine, Faylene Hutton Cemetery Collection, ca 1780-1900", database with images, FamilySearch, (https://familysearch.org/ark:/61903/1:1:3QS7-L9FQ).

Clara Morse
Birth: Record of a Death, Maine Vital Records.
Marriage: (1) Original Record of Maine Towns & Cities, Town of Danforth, Picton Press, Rockland Maine, Copyright 2005, Page 9; (2) "Maine, Marriages, 1771-1907," index, FamilySearch, (https://familysearch.org/pal:/MM9.1.1/F46V-LT5).
Divorce: (1) "Maine, Divorces, 1799-1903," database, Maine Genealogy, Maine Supreme Judicial Court Records (Aroostook Co.), 14/400; (2) "Maine, Divorce Records, 1798-1891," [database on-line], Provo, UT, USA: Ancestry.com Operations Inc, 2011.

Eva H. Floyd
Birth: "Massachusetts, Death Records, 1841-1915", [database on-line], Provo, UT, USA: Ancestry.com Operations, Inc., 2013, Return of a Death, Town of Brookline.
Marriage: (1) Original Record of Maine Towns & Cities, Town of Danforth, Picton Press, Rockland Maine, Copyright 2005, Page 18; (2) "Maine, Marriages, 1771-1907," index, FamilySearch, (https://familysearch.org/pal:/MM9.1.1/F46G-GMD).
Divorce:

Amanda Gillis
Birth: (1) Record of a Death, Maine Vital Records; (2) "Maine, Faylene Hutton Cemetery Collection, ca 1780-1900", database with images, FamilySearch, (https://familysearch.org/ark:/61903/1:1:3QS7-L9FQ); (3) Gravestone.
Marriage: (1) Original Record of Maine Towns & Cities, Town of Danforth, Picton Press, Rockland Maine, Copyright 2005, Page 34; (2) "Maine, Marriages, 1771-1907," index, FamilySearch, (https://familysearch.org/pal:/MM9.1.1/F46V-L2Q).
Death: (1) Record of a Death, Maine Vital Records; (2) "Maine, Faylene Hutton Cemetery Collection, ca 1780-1900", database with images, FamilySearch, (https://familysearch.org/ark:/61903/1:1:3QS7-L9FQ); (3) Gravestone.
Graveyard: "Maine, Faylene Hutton Cemetery Collection, ca 1780-1900", database with images, FamilySearch, (https://familysearch.org/ark:/61903/1:1:3QS7-L9FQ).

Historical Accounts: (1) 1860 United States Federal Census for Township No. 11, Aroostook, Maine; Page 12; (2) 1870 United States Federal Census Township No. 11, Aroostook, Maine; (3) 1880 United States Federal Census for Danforth, Washington, Maine, Page 11; (4) 1900 United States Federal Census for Danforth, Washington, Maine, Page 6; (5) 1910 United States Federal Census for Danforth, Washington, Maine, Page 8; (6) 1890 United States Census of Union Veterans and Widows of the Civil War; (7) United States Civil War and Later Pension Index, 1861-1917; (8) "Army Register of Enlistments, 1798-1914, Special Enlistment Categories, 1859-1862, H-Z Duplicates", page 584, www.fold3.com; (9) "Army Register of Enlistments, 1859-1862", page 562, www.fold3.com; (10) "Declaration of a Recruit", National Archives; (11) "Civil War Pensions Index, Maine, Infantry, Regiment 15, Company I", www.fold3.com.

Charles Jones Williams
(1846 - 1928)

Charles Jones, the third child of Ebenezer Williams and his second wife Martha Ann Colwell, was born in Township 11, Range 1, Aroostook, Maine on December 6, 1846.

Like his brother John Chandler, Charles Jones enlisted in the 17th Maine Volunteer Infantry Regiment of the Union Army joining Company E and serving as a Private.

When the 1870 United States Federal Census was taken, Charles Jones, age twenty-four, was listed as living with his mother in Township 11 and working as a "farm laborer".

Charles Jones, age twenty-nine, and Anna D. Vanjoy, age twenty, filed their intentions to marry on November 20, 1876 with the Plantation Clerk of Township 11. The clerk at the time was Charles Jones' half-brother, Truman Allen Williams, from his father's first marriage. Charles Jones and Anna D. were subsequently married in Aroostook County, Maine on December 26, 1876. Anna D. was the daughter of John Vanjoy and Annie Fletcher. The exact location of their marriage is unknown, as well as Anna D.'s date of birth and birthplace. No record has been found of their having children during their marriage.

In the 1880 United States Federal Census Charles Jones and Anna D. were listed as living in Township 11, Range 1 with his occupation listed as "farmer".

Charles Jones and Annie D. were divorced on September 20, 1894 in Aroostook County after almost eighteen years of marriage. Annie D. was married to her second husband, William D. Brown, on September 12, 1897 in Lowell, Middlesex, Massachusetts.

A little over fifteen months after his divorce, on January 7, 1896, Charles Jones, then age forty-nine, was married to his second wife Geneva E. Lancaster, age nineteen, in Houlton, Aroostook, Maine by R. W. Shaw, a Justice of the Peace. Geneva E., the daughter of John Potter Lancaster and Nellie Pottle, was born in Houlton on October 7, 1876. There is no record of Charles Jones and his second wife Geneva E. having any children together.

In the 1900, 1910 and 1920 United States Federal Census' Charles Jones and Geneva E. were recorded as living in Cary Plantation, Aroostook, Maine. Charles Jones' occupation was listed in all three censuses as "farmer".

On December 27, 1928, Charles Jones died at age eighty-six. The place and cause of his death have not been found. He was buried in the Hodgdon Cemetery in Hodgdon, Aroostook, Maine.

The 1940 United States Federal Census documented that Geneva E. continued to live in Cary Plantation. She died on August 25, 1967 at the age of ninety. The cause and place of her death have also not been found. She was buried with her husband in Hodgdon at the Hodgdon Cemetery.

Gravestone for Charles Jones Williams and Geneva E. Lancaster
(Photograph Courtesy of Debbie Glidden)

SOURCES:

Charles Jones Williams
Birth:
Death:
Graveyard: (1) "Maine, Veterans Cemetery Records 1676-1918," database with images, FamilySearch, (https://familysearch.org/ark:/61903/1:1: KXQZ-R11); (2) Find A Grave, Memorial #101233133.

Anna D. Vanjoy
Birth:
Marriage: Original Record of Maine Towns & Cities, Town of Cary Plantation, Picton Press, Rockland Maine, Copyright 2005, Page 159.
Divorce: "Maine, Divorces, 1799-1903", database, Maine Genealogy, (http://mainegenealogy.net), Maine Divorce Index, 2/3.

Geneva E. Lancaster
Birth: Record of Birth, Maine Vital Records.
Marriage: Record of a Marriage, Maine Vital Records.
Death: (1) "Maine Death Index, 1960-1997," (database on-line). Provo, UT, USA: Ancestry.com Operations, Inc., 2002; (2) "U.S., Social Security Death Index, 1935-2014," (database on-line). Provo, UT, USA: Ancestry.com Operations, Inc., 2011.
Graveyard: Find A Grave, Memorial #101234200.

Historical Accounts: (1) 1870 United States Federal Census Township No. 11, Aroostook, Maine, Page 6; (2) 1880 United States Federal Census Township No. 11, Aroostook, Maine, Page 14; (3) 1900 United States Federal Census for Cary Plantation, Aroostook, Maine, Page 1; (4) 1910 United States Federal Census for Cary Plantation, Aroostook, Maine; (5) 1920 United States Federal Census for Cary Plantation, Aroostook, Maine, Page 7; (6) 1940 United States Federal Census for Cary Plantation, Aroostook, Maine Page 1B; (7) United States Civil War and Later Pension Index, 1861-1917.

Cyrus E. Williams
(1850 -)

The fourth child of Ebenezer Williams and his second wife Martha Ann Colwell was Cyrus E. who was born on September 13, 1850 Township 11 Range 1, Aroostook, Maine.

The 1870 and 1880 United States Federal Census', recorded Cyrus E. as living in Township 11 Range 1 with his mother and working as a "laborer".

In the 1900 United States Federal Census Cyrus E., then age fifty, was listed again as living with his mother, in Cary Plantation, Aroostook, Maine, and working as a "farm laborer".

Sometime after the death of his mother, Cyrus E. went to live with his brother Charles Jones and his wife Geneva E. in Cary Plantation as recorded in the 1910 United States Federal Census. Cyrus E. was listed as having no occupation in that census.

At age sixty-nine, Cyrus E. was listed in the 1920 United States Federal Census as living by himself on Calais Road in Cary Plantation. He was again listed as having no occupation.

Additional information on the life, death and place of burial for Cyrus E. is unknown.

SOURCES:

Cyrus E. Williams
Birth:
Death:
Graveyard:

Historical Accounts: (1) 1870 United States Federal Census for Township No. 11, Aroostook, Maine, Page 6; (2) 1880 United States Federal Census for Township No. 11, Aroostook, Maine, Page 10; (3) 1900 United States Federal Census for Cary Plantation, Aroostook, Maine, Page 4; (4) 1910 United States Federal Census for Cary Plantation, Aroostook, Maine, Page 6; (5) 1920 United States Federal Census for Cary Plantation, Aroostook, Maine, Page 5.

Mansfield M. Williams
(1852 - 1918)

The fifth child, Mansfield M., of Ebenezer Williams and his second wife Martha Ann Colwell and was born on December 19, 1852 in Township 11, Range 1, Aroostook, Maine.

When the 1870 United States Federal Census was taken, Mansfield M. was recorded as living with his mother and working on the family farm in Township 11.

Sometime around 1879 Mansfield M. married Aramenta L. Gellerson. The exact date and place of their marriage has not been found. Aramenta, the daughter of Leonard H. Gellerson and Mahala L. White, was born at the Gellerson Settlement in Seldon, Aroostook, Maine on September 10, 1859.

During their marriage Mansfield M. and Aramenta L. had three children together.

Alma	b. 1881	d. January 3, 1963
Winfield A.	*b. February 24, 1884*	*d. February 6, 1903*
Ruby B.	*b. December 1885*	*d. May 29, 1902*

The 1880 United States Federal Census recorded Mansfield M. and Aramenta L. as living with her parents in Weston, Aroostook, Maine. In that census Mansfield M.'s occupation was listed as "laborer".

On May 23, 1891 Aramenta L. died at the age of thirty-two. The place and cause of her death have not been found. She was buried in the Selden Cemetery in Weston.

It is believed that Mansfield M. was married to his second wife Addie Victoria Estabrook in Amity, Aroostook, Maine sometime in late 1893. Addie Victoria, born in Amity on February 15, 1868, was the daughter of Horace S. Estabrook and Susan K. Lyons.

Mansfield M. had an additional seven children with his second wife Addie Victoria.

Earl Harry	b. May 11, 1895	d. June 18, 1960
Grace	*b. June 16, 1896*	*d. June 30, 1896*
Gurney	*b. July 1899*	*d. September 1899*
Floyd Mansfield	b. March 26, 1902	d. September 23, 1993
Mildred Viola	b. February 28, 1904	d. May 25, 1965
Walter R.	b. February 4, 1906	d. May 7, 2004
Zura A.	b. May 15, 1908	d. November 4, 1976

Grace, the second child of Mansfield M. and his second wife Addie Victoria, died on June 30, 1896 at Amity when she was just fifteen days old. The cause of her death was listed as complications from a "premature birth". The place of her burial has not been found.

In September 1899 Gurney, the third child of Mansfield M. and his second wife Addie Victoria, died when he was just two months old. The exact date of his birth and death, as well as the place and cause of his death have not been found. His place of burial is also not known.

Mansfield M., Addie Victoria and their children had moved to Weston, Aroostook, Maine by the time the 1900 United States Federal Census was taken. Mansfield M. was recorded as working as a "farmer" in that census.

At the age of sixteen, Ruby B., the third child of Mansfield M. and his first wife Aramenta L. died of "consumption" in Weston on May 29, 1902. She was buried in the Selden Cemetery in Weston.

The second child of Mansfield M. and his first wife Aramenta L., Winfield A., died in Weston of "lung disease" on February 6, 1903. He was eighteen years old at the time of his death. Winfield A. was also buried in the Selden Cemetery in Weston.

Gravestone and Marker for Ruby B. Williams and Winfield A. Williams
(Photographs Courtesy of Bertram)

In the 1910 United States Federal Census Mansfield M., Addie Victoria and their family were recorded as still living and farming in Weston.

On April 19, 1918 Mansfield M. died at the age of sixty-five. The cause and exact place of his death have not been found. He was buried in Weston in the family plot at the Selden Cemetery.

By the time the1920 United States Federal Census was taken Addie Victoria and her four youngest children had moved to the Gellerson Roads neighborhood in Weston where they we living on a farm with Mansfield M. and Addie Victoria's oldest child Earl Harry Williams and his family.

The 1930 United States Federal Census recorded Addie Victoria living on Seldon Road in Weston. Residing with her were her daughter Mildred Viola Williams and her son, and Addie Victoria's grandson, Manford M. Williams.

When the1940 United States Federal Census was taken, Addie Victoria, then age seventy-two, was recorded as living in the home of her daughter Mildred Viola (Williams) Whitney in Weston.

Addie Victoria died at the age of eighty-three on June 19, 1951 in Danforth, Washington, Maine. The cause of her death has not been found. She too was buried in the family plot at the Selden Cemetery in Weston.

Gravestones for Mansfield M. Williams and Addie Victoria Estabrook
(Photographs Courtesy of Kim Hardy)

SOURCES:

Mansfield M. Williams
Birth:
Death: Gravestone.
Graveyard: Find A Grave, Memorial #114871227.

Aramenta L. Gellerson
Birth: (1) Original Record of Maine Towns & Cities, Town of Weston, Picton Press, Rockland Maine, Copyright 2005, Page 77; (2) "Maine Births and Christenings, 1739-1900," database, FamilySearch, (https://familysearch .org/ark/61903/1.1:/F4SK-2YD)
Marriage:
Death: "Maine, Nathan Hale Cemetery Collection, ca. 1780-1980," database with images, FamilySearch, (https://familysearch.org/ark:/61903/1:1:QVJ5-SFP1).
Graveyard: (1) "Maine, Nathan Hale Cemetery Collection, ca. 1780-1980," database with images, FamilySearch, (https://familysearch.org/ark:/61903/1:1:QVJ5-SFP1); (2) Find A Grave, Memorial #114872235.

Winfield A. Williams
Birth:
Death: (1) Record of Death, Maine Vital Records; (2) "Maine, Nathan Hale Cemetery Collection, ca. 1780-1980," database with images, FamilySearch, (https://familysearch.org/ark:/61903/1:1:QVJ5-SFP1); (3) Gravestone.
Graveyard: (1) "Maine, Nathan Hale Cemetery Collection, ca. 1780-1980," database with images, FamilySearch, (https://familysearch.org/ark:/61903/1:1:QVJ5-SFP1); (2) Find A Grave, Memorial #114872200.

Ruby B. Williams
Birth:
Death: (1) Record of Death, Maine Vital Records; (2) "Maine, Nathan Hale Cemetery Collection, ca. 1780-1980," database with images, FamilySearch, (https://familysearch.org/ark:/61903/1:1:QVJ5-SFP1); (3) Gravestone.
Graveyard: (1) "Maine, Nathan Hale Cemetery Collection, ca. 1780-1980," database with images, FamilySearch, (https://familysearch.org/ark:/61903/1:1:QVJ5-SFP1); (2) Find A Grave, Memorial #114872178.

Addie Victoria Estabrook
Birth:
Marriage:
Death
Graveyard: Find A Grave, Memorial #114871257.

Grace Williams
Birth: Record of Birth, Maine Vital Records.
Death: Record of Death, Maine Vital Records.
Graveyard:

Gurney Williams
Birth:
Death:
Graveyard:

Historical Accounts: (1) 1870 United States Federal Census Township No. 11, Aroostook, Maine, Page 6; (2) 1870 United States Federal Census Amity, Aroostook, Maine, Page 3; (3) 1880 United States Federal Census Weston, Aroostook, Maine, Page 65; (4) 1880 United States Federal Census Amity, Aroostook, Maine, Page 8; (5) 1900 United States Federal Census for Weston, Aroostook, Maine, Page 4; (6) 1910 United States Federal Census for Weston, Aroostook, Maine, Page 6A; (7) 1920 United States Federal Census for Weston, Aroostook, Maine, Page 4B; (8) 1930 United States Federal Census for Weston, Aroostook, Maine, Page 3B; (9) 1940 United States Federal Census for Weston, Aroostook, Maine Page 3.

James Albert Williams
(1854 - 1908)

James Albert was the sixth child of Ebenezer Williams and his second wife Martha Ann Colwell and was born in Township 11, Range 1; Aroostook, Maine on June 2, 1854.

Like his brother, Cyrus E., in the 1870 and 1880 United States Federal Census' James Albert was listed as living in Township 11 Range 1 with his mother and working as a "farmer".

James Albert was listed the 1900 United States Federal Census as still living with his mother, in Cary Plantation, Aroostook, Maine, and working as a "farm laborer".

James Albert died in Cary Plantation on October 8, 1908 at the age of fifty-six having never married or had children. His cause of death was listed as "locomotial ataxia". The place of James Albert's burial is unknown.

SOURCES:

James Albert Williams
Birth: Record of a Death, Maine Vital Records.
Death: Record of a Death, Maine Vital Records.
Graveyard:

Historical Accounts: (1) 1870 United States Federal Census for Township No. 11, Aroostook, Maine, Page 6; (2) 1880 United States Federal Census for Township No. 11, Aroostook, Maine, Page 10; (3) 1900 United States Federal Census for Cary Plantation, Aroostook, Maine, Page 4.

Bethia Perkins Williams
(1824 - 1913)

The first child of Cyrus Williams and his wife Phydelia C. Perkins was Bethia Perkins who was born on April 29, 1824 in Anson, Somerset, Maine.

On December 7, 1845 Bethia Perkins, age twenty-one, and Joseph W. Freeman, age twenty-four, filed their intentions to be married with the Town Clerk of Waterville, Kennebec, Maine. They were subsequently married in Waterville on December 24, 1845 by Pastor Calvin Gardner. Joseph W., the son of Ebenezer Freeman and Lucy White, was born in Hallowell, Kennebec, Maine on July 1, 1821.

Bethia Perkins and Joseph W. had just two children.

Mary Ella	b. February 24, 1847	d. April 23, 1916
Edmund C.	*b. 1848*	*d.*

In the 1850 United States Federal Census, Bethia Perkins, Joseph W. and their two children were listed as living in Waterville. Joseph W.'s occupation was recorded as "inn holder" at that time.

By the time the 1860 United States Federal Census was taken, Bethia Perkins, Joseph W. and their family had moved to Grand Rapids, Wood, Wisconsin. Joseph W., then age thirty-eight, was working as a "merchant".

Additional information on the life and death of the second child, Edmund C., of Bethia Perkins and Joseph W. could not be found after the 1860 United States Federal Census was taken. As such his documented history will end here.

In the 1870 and 1880 United States Federal Census, Bethia Perkins and Joseph W. were still living in Grand Rapids and Joseph W.'s was now working as "teamster/laborer".

Sometime thereafter, Bethia Perkins and Joseph W. moved to Menominee, the county seat of Menominee, Michigan, where they were recorded as living at 1211 Main Street when the 1903 Polk's Directory for Menominee was published.

When the 1910 United States Federal Census was taken Bethia Perkins and Joseph W. were listed as living with their daughter, Mary Ella, and her husband George Woodford at 1211 Main Street in Menominee.

On August 10, 1910, shortly after the 1910 census was taken, Joseph W. died in Menominee of a "senile related disease" at the age of eighty-nine. Joseph W.'s death was also reported in the 1911 R. L. Polk & Company

Directory for Menominee. He was buried in the Woodford Family plot, Section E-3, Lot 17 at the Riverside Cemetery in Menominee.

Bethia Perkins outlived her husband by more than two years. On February 15, 1913 she passed away at the age of eighty-eight in Menominee at the home of her daughter Mary Ella (Freeman) Woodford. The cause of her death was listed as "due to advanced age". Funeral services for Bethia Perkins were held from her daughter's home at 2:30 P.M. on Monday, February 17th with Reverend F. A. Kuder, Pastor of the Menominee Presbyterian Church, officiating. She was buried with her husband in Section E-3, Lot 17 at the Riverside Cemetery in Menominee that same day.

Headstones for Bethia Perkins Williams (left) and Joseph W. Freeman (right)
(Photographs Courtesy of Caroline Kmiecik)

SOURCES:

Bethia Perkins Williams
Birth: Obituary, The Eagle-Star, Marinette, Wisconsin, February 15, 1913, Page 5.
Death: Obituary, The Eagle-Star, Marinette, Wisconsin, February 15, 1913, Page 5.
Graveyard: (1) Cemetery Records, Riverside Cemetery, Menominee, Michigan, Page 10; (2) Obituary, The Eagle-Star, Marinette, Wisconsin, February 15, 1913, Page 5; (3) Find A Grave, Memorial #23786292.

Joseph W. Freeman
Birth: (1) Record of a Birth, Maine Vital Records; (2) "Freeman Genealogy", by Frederick Freeman, Page 152, Published by Franklin Press: Rand, Avery and Company, 1875.
Marriage: City of Waterville, Men's Marriages 1830-1943, Disk 1, Record 4163, Picton Press, Rockland Maine, Copyright 2005.
Death: (1) Michigan Death Records, 1897-1920; (2) Certificate of Death, SeekingMichigan.org.
Graveyard: (1) Cemetery Records, Riverside Cemetery, Menominee, Michigan, Page 10; (2) Find A Grave, Memorial #23786370.

Edmund C. Freeman
Birth:
Death:
Graveyard:

Historical Accounts: (1) 1850 United States Federal Census for Waterville, Kennebec, Maine; (2) 1860 United States Federal Census for Grand Rapids, Wood, Wisconsin, Page 10; (3) 1870 United States Federal Census for Grand Rapids, Wood, Wisconsin, Page 10; (4) 1880 United States Federal Census for Grand Rapids, Wood, Wisconsin, Page 10; (5) 1910 United States Federal Census for Menominee, Menominee, Michigan, Page 3A; (6) 1903 Menominee, Michigan, City Directory, Page 99; (7) 1911 Menominee, Michigan, City Directory, Page 128.

Emily F. Williams
(1826 - 1871)

Emily F., the second child of Cyrus Williams and his wife Phydelia C. Perkins, was born in Anson, Somerset, Maine in 1826. The exact date of her birth has not been found.

In the 1850 and 1860 United States Federal Census' Emily F. was listed as living in Waterville, Kennebec, Maine with her parents at the family owned "boarding house".

When the 1870 United States Federal Census was taken, Emily F. was recorded was as still living with her mother at the family "boarding house" in Waterville. In that census her occupation was listed as "sewing".

Emily F. died on May 19, 1871 at the age of forty-five in Waterville having never married nor ever having children. The cause of her death has not been found. She was buried in her father's, Cyrus Williams, family plot at the Pine Grove Cemetery in Waterville in Lot 175, Grave 3.

Cyrus Williams Family Plot Marker, front view
(Photograph from the Collection of Jeffrey Nelson Williams and Jacqueline Pon Williams)

Cyrus Williams Family Plot Marker, back view (above)
Headstone for Emily F. Williams (below)
(Photographs from the Collection of Jeffrey Nelson Williams and Jacqueline Pon Williams)

SOURCES:

Emily F. Williams
Birth:
Death: "Maine, Faylene Hutton Cemetery Collection, ca. 1780-1990," database with images, FamilySearch, (https://familysearch.org/ark:/61903/1:1:QKM1-WKBQ) - Accession #4176
Graveyard: (1) Pine Grove Cemetery Records, City of Waterville, Kennebec, Maine; (2) "Maine, Faylene Hutton Cemetery Collection, ca. 1780-1990," database with images, FamilySearch, (https://familysearch.org/ark:/61903/ 1:1: QKM1-WKBQ) - Accession #4176: (3) Find A Grave, Memorial #23786370.

Historical Accounts: (1) 1850 United States Federal Census for Waterville, Kennebec, Maine; (2) 1860 United States Federal Census for Waterville, Kennebec, Maine; (3) 1870 United States Federal Census for Waterville, Kennebec, Maine, Page 69.

Louisa F. Williams
(1831 - 1911)

The third child of Cyrus Williams and his wife Phydelia C. Perkins, Louisa F., was born in 1831 in Anson, Somerset, Maine. The exact date of her birth is not known.

On September 27, 1856, at the age of twenty-five, Louisa F. and James A. Goodwin, age thirty-five, filed their intentions to be married with the Town Clerk of Waterville, Kennebec, Maine. They were married two days later, on September 29, 1856, by Reverend Calvin Gardiner at Louisa F. father's, Cyrus Williams, house in Waterville. James A. was born in Medford, Steele, Minnesota in 1821, and according to the 1850 United States Federal Census, had moved to Waterville where he was working as a "tailor" and living in Louisa F.'s father's boarding house. The names of James A.'s parents and the exact date of his birth have not been found.

Shortly after their marriage Louisa F. and James A. moved to Owatonna, Steele, Minnesota where they were recorded as living in the 1860 United States Federal Census.

Louisa F. and James A. had only one child during their marriage.

Helen May b. April 14, 1861 d. February 7, 1938

On October 1, 1861 at Fort Snelling, Hennepin, Minnesota, James A. enlisted in Company E, 4th Regiment of the Minnesota Volunteers of the Union Army. He was mustered into service holding the rank of Sergeant on November 27, 1861. Eight months later on July 1, 1862 he was promoted to the rank of 2nd Lieutenant.

James A. was wounded at the battle of Iuka, Mississippi on September 19, 1862 suffering a gunshot wound to his thigh, which also fractured his femur. Six months later, on April 18, 1863 James A. died in the City General Hospital in Saint Louis, Missouri from complications related to his wounds. His body was returned to Minnesota where he was buried in the Forest Hill Cemetery in Owatonna.

On July 28, 1864, Louisa F. filed for and was approved to receive a widow's pension of $15 per month related to James A.'s death during his military service.

A little over three years after the death of her first husband, Louisa F. was married to her second husband, William S. Jones, on December 3, 1866, by F. A. Noble in Saint Paul, Ramsey, Minnesota. William S., then age thirty-two, was born in the state of New York in 1834. The exact date of his birth and names of William S.'s parents have not been found.

In the 1870 United States Federal Census, Louisa F., William S. and Louisa's daughter from her first marriage, Helen May Goodwin, were recorded as living in Owatonna with William S. working as a "laborer".

By the time the 1880 United States Federal Census for Owatonna was taken, Louisa F. had changed her last name back to Goodwin, was living with her daughter. In that census both Louisa F. and her daughter were listed as working as "dressmakers". It is not known if William S. died or whether he and Louisa F. were divorced.

Sometime between 1880 and 1887, Louisa F. and her daughter Helen May moved to Los Angeles, Los Angeles County, California. When the 1887 Los Angeles City Directory was published Louisa F. and her daughter were listed as living at 44 North Trueman Street and working as "dressmakers".

Louisa F. was listed as living at 123 Griffin Avenue in the 1892 Los Angeles City Directory and then at 232 South Bunker Hill Avenue in the 1897 Los Angeles City Directory. In both of those directories Louisa F. did not have an occupation listed.

On June 7, 1900, when the 1900 census for Los Angeles was taken, Louisa F., age sixty-nine, had moved and was listed as living at 520 Broadway.

The 1902 Los Angeles City Directory, recorded that Louisa F. had moved yet again and was living at the Hollenbeck Home for the Aged in the Boyle Heights neighborhood just east of downtown Los Angeles. She was recorded as still living there when the 1910 Los Angeles City Directory was published and the 1910 United States Federal Census was taken.

On October 19, 1911 Louisa F. died in Los Angeles at the age of eighty of a cause not known. She was buried in the Hollenbeck Home plot at the Evergreen Cemetery in Los Angeles.

Gravestone for James A. Goodwin
(Photograph Courtesy of suecal)

SOURCES:

Louisa F. Williams
Birth:
Death: "California, Death Index, 1905-1939," [database on-line], Provo, UT, USA: Ancestry.com Operations Inc, 2013, Page 4099.
Graveyard: Find A Grave, Memorial #9784265.

James A. Goodwin
Birth:
Marriage: (1) City of Waterville, Men's Marriages 1830-1943, Disk 1, Record 4752, Picton Press, Rockland Maine, Copyright 2005; (2) Application for Widows Pension, Adjutant General's Office, Fold3.com.
Death: (1) U.S. Military Hospitals, Certificate for Government Undertaker, Fold3.com; (2) Gravestone.
Graveyard: (1) "Minnesota Cemetery Inscription Index, Select Counties," (database on-line), Provo, UT, USA: Ancestry.com Operations Inc., 2003; (2) Find A Grave, Memorial #89458703.

William S. Jones
Birth:
Marriage: Marriage License and Certificate, State of Minnesota.
Death:
Graveyard:

Historical Accounts: (1) 1850 United States Federal Census for Waterville, Kennebec, Maine; (2) 1860 United States Federal Census for Owatonna, Steele, Minnesota, Page 70; (3) 1870 United States Federal Census for Owatonna, Steele, Minnesota, Page 19; (4) 1880 United States Federal Census for Owatonna, Steele, Minnesota, Page 14; (5) 1900 United States Federal Census for Los Angeles, California, Page 3; (6) 1910 United States Federal Census for Los Angeles, Los Angeles, California, Page 1B; (7) Application for Widows Pension, Adjutant General's Office, Fold3.com; (8) 1887 Los Angeles, California, City Directory, Page 201; (9) 1892 Los Angeles, California, City Directory, Page 584; (10) 1897 Los Angeles, California, City Directory, Page 389; (11) 1902 Los Angeles, California, City Directory, Page 449; (12) 1910 Los Angeles, California, City Directory, Page 576.

Charles E. Williams
(1835 - 1874)

The fourth child of Cyrus Williams and his wife, Phydelia C. Perkins, was Charles E. who was born in Anson, Somerset, Maine in 1835. The exact date of his birth has not been found.

On May 9, 1857 Charles E., then age twenty-two, and Adelia Rose Wing, age nineteen, filed their intentions to be married with the Town Clerk of Waterville, Kennebec, Maine. The exact date and place of their subsequent marriage is not known. Adelia Rose, born in 1838 in Maine, was the daughter of William B. Wing and Sophia C. Turner. The place and date of Adelia Rose's birth have not been found.

Charles E. and Adelia Rose had two children together.

Fred	b. 1858	d. June 18, 1934
Helen Alberta	b. August 1865	d. June 29, 1912

In the 1860 United States Federal Census, Charles E., Adelia Rose and their first child, Fred, were listed as living in Waterville. Charles E.'s occupation was recorded as "clerk" at that time.

The 1870 United States Federal Census recorded Charles E. Adelia Rose and their two children as still living in Waterville with Charles E. earning his living as "keeping billiards".

Four short years later, in 1874, Charles E. passed away at the young age of thirty-nine. The exact date, place and cause of his death have not been found. He was buried in Lot 440 at the Pine Grove Cemetery in Waterville.

Gravestone for Charles E. Williams
(Photograph from the Collection of Jeffrey Nelson Williams and Jacqueline Pon Williams)

On December19, 1876 Adelia Rose, age thirty-eight, was married to her second husband Edwin F. Young, age thirty-nine, in Waterville by Reverend D. N. Sheldon. The date and place of Edwin F.'s birth, as well as the names of his parents are not known. Adelia Rose and Edwin F. did not have any children of their own during their marriage.

The 1885 Waterville City Directory listed Edwin F. as working as an "engineer" for the Maine Central Railroad and Adelia Rose running a "dining room" in their home at 120 Main Street.

Sometime between 1885 and 1888, Adelia Rose, her second husband Edwin F. Young and her daughter Helen Alberta Williams from her first marriage moved to Pasadena, Los Angeles, California where Edwin F. was recorded in 1888 Great Register for Los Angeles County as having registered to vote on July 18, 1888. In that register his occupation was listed as "engineer".

In the 1900 and 1910 United States Federal Census' Adelia Rose, Edwin F. and Helen Alberta Williams were recorded as living in Pasadena. The 1900 census recorded then living on Craig Avenue where Adelia Rose was "farming". In the 1910 census they were recorded as living at 42 South Catalina Avenue and Edwin F.'s occupation was listed as "egg peddler".

Edwin F. died in Los Angeles County on May 29, 1913 at the age of seventy-two. The cause of his death and the place of his burial have not been found.

When the 1914 Pasadena City directory was published Adelia Rose was listed as being a widow and still living at 42 South Catalina Avenue.

Adelia Rose died at the age of seventy-seven on November 25, 1917 in Newport, Penobscot, Maine. Whether she had moved back to Maine or was just visiting is not known. The cause of her death was listed as "cancer of the stomach". Adelia Rose was buried with her first husband in Lot 440 at the Pine Grove Cemetery in Waterville.

Gravestone for Adelia Rose Wing
(Photograph from the Collection of Jeffrey Nelson Williams and Jacqueline Pon Williams)

SOURCES:

Charles E. Williams
Birth:
Death:
Graveyard: (1) "Maine, Faylene Hutton Cemetery Collection, ca. 1780-1990," database with images, FamilySearch (https://familysearch.org/ark:/61903/1:1:QKM1-WKPD) - Accession #4176; (2) Find A Grave, Memorial #25781701.

Adelia Rose Wing
Birth:
Marriage: City of Waterville, Kennebec, Maine, Men's Marriages, Disk 3, Record 2375, Picton Press, Rockland Maine, Copyright 2005.
Death: Record of a Death, Maine Vital Records
Graveyard: (1) "Maine, Faylene Hutton Cemetery Collection, ca. 1780-1990," database with images, FamilySearch (https://familysearch.org/ark:/61903/1:1:99FQ-3BDR) - Accession #4176; (2) Find A Grave, Memorial #25781751.

Edwin F. Young
Birth:
Marriage: (1) City of Waterville, Kennebec, Maine, Men's Marriages, Disk 3, Record 2692, Picton Press, Rockland Maine, Copyright 2005; (2) "Maine, Marriages, 1771-1907," index, FamilySearch, (https://familysearch.org/pal:/MM9.1.1/F4NS-C3X).
Death: "California, Death Index, 1905-1939," [database on-line], Provo, UT, USA: Ancestry.com Operations Inc, 2013
Graveyard:

Historical Accounts: (1) 1860 United States Federal Census for Waterville, Kennebec, Maine; (2) 1870 United States Federal Census for Waterville, Kennebec, Maine, Page 112; (3) 1900 United States Federal Census for Pasadena, Los Angeles, California, Page 6; (4) 1910 United States Federal Census for Pasadena, Los Angeles, California, Page 2; (5) 1885 Waterville, Maine, City Directory, Page 75; (6) "California, Great Registers, 1866-1910," database, FamilySearch, (https://familysearch.org/ark:/61903/3:1:VYDQ-M1L), 1888 Great Register for Los Angeles County, Page 261; (7) 1914 Pasadena, California, City Directory, Page 445.

Susan H. Williams
(1838 - 1876)

Susan H., born in Waterville, Kennebec, Maine in 1838, was the sixth child of Cyrus Williams and Phydelia C. Perkins. The exact date of her birth has not been found.

Sometime before the 1860 United States Federal Census was taken, Susan H. married George A. Atkins. George A., the son of James Atkins and Deborah Smith, was born in Hallowell, Kennebec, Maine on September 2, 1836.

Susan H. and George A. had only one child together.

William Henry   b. March 24, 1859   d. October 8, 1942

In the 1860 United States Federal Census for Waterville, Susan H. and George A. were listed as living in the "inn" owned by her father Cyrus. George A's occupation was listed as "tends billiard room".

On June 30, 1863 George A., a married man, registered for the United States Civil War Draft. In that document he was listed as living in Hallowell and working as a "mechanic".

The 1870 United States Federal Census recorded George A. as living with his parents in Hallowell and working as a "river man". That same census listed Susan H. and George A.'s son, William Henry, as living with his grandmother Phydelia C. (Perkins) Williams in Waterville and attending school. The location of Susan H. at the time of that census has not been found.

George A. died in 1874 at the estimated age of thirty-eight. His date, place and cause of death are not known. He was buried in the Pine Grove Cemetery in Waterville.

Two years later, on February 5, 1876, Susan H. died in Waterville at the age of thirty-eight. The cause of her death has also not been found. She was buried in the Pine Grove Cemetery in Waterville with her husband.

SOURCES:

Susan H. Williams
Birth:
Death: City of Waterville, Kennebec, Maine, Deaths, 1830-1943, Page 187, Picton Press, Rockland Maine, Copyright 2005.
Graveyard: Find A Grave, Memorial #8099876.

George A. Atkins
Birth: Record of a Birth, Maine Vital Records.
Marriage:
Death:
Graveyard: Find A Grave, Memorial #8099872.

Historical Accounts: (1) 1860 United States Federal Census for Waterville, Kennebec, Maine; (2) 1870 United States Federal Census for Hallowell, Kennebec, Maine; (3) 1870 United States Federal Census for Waterville, Kennebec, Maine, Page 69; (4) "U. S. Civil War Draft Registration Records, 1863-1865 ", [database on-line]. Provo, UT, USA: Ancestry.com Operations Inc, 2010.

Tiley A. Williams
(1843 - 1905)

The eighth child of Cyrus Williams and his wife Phydelia C. Perkins was Tiley A. who was born in 1843 in Waterville, Kennebec, Maine. The day and month of her birth has not been found.

At age twenty-five, Tiley A. and Jesse G. Stover, age twenty-seven, filed their intentions to be married with the Town Clerk of Waterville. They were subsequently married on September 2, 1868 in Waterville Maine by Pastor Z. Thompson. Jesse G., born on January 25, 1837 in Thomaston, Knox, Maine, was the son of Christopher Stover and Permelia Gahan. During their marriage Tiley A. and Jesse G. did not have any children. However, Jesse G. did have a daughter Lizzie M. Stover from his first marriage.

In the 1870 United States Federal Census, Tiley A. and Jesse G. were recorded as living at the boarding house in Waterville maintained by her mother Phydelia C. In that census Jesse G.'s occupation was listed as "sash and blind maker".

When the 1880 United States Federal Census was taken, Tiley A. and Jesse G. still were living in Waterville where Jesse G. was working as a "machinist".

The 1885 and 1887 Waterville City Directories listed Jessie G. living at 84 Silver Street and working as a "carpenter".

Jesse G. died in 1887 at the age of forty-six. The exact date, cause and place of his death have not been found. He was buried in the Cyrus Williams family plot, Lot 175, Grave 6, at the Pine Grove Cemetery in Waterville.

Prior to their marriage, on May 25, 1861, Jesse G. had enlisted in Company A of the Massachusetts 2nd Infantry Regiment of the Union Army. He served three years during the United States Civil War and was mustered out on May 23, 1864 holding the rank of Sergeant. Because of his service during the Civil War Tilly A. was entitled to receive his military pension which she claimed shortly after his death.

Tiley A. outlived her husband by eighteen years and was working as a "seamstress" when she died of "pulmonary tuberculosis" on January 21, 1905 in Waterville at the age of sixty-two. She was also buried in the Cyrus Williams family plot in Lot 175, Grave 5 at the Pine Grove Cemetery in Waterville.

Cyrus Williams Family Plot Marker, front view (top) and back view (middle)
Headstones for Tiley A. Williams (bottom left) and Jesse G. Stover (bottom right)
(Photographs from the Collection of Jeffrey Nelson Williams and Jacqueline Pon Williams)

SOURCES:

Tiley A. Williams
Birth:
Death: Record of a Death, Maine Vital Records.
Graveyard: (1) Pine Grove Cemetery Records, City of Waterville, Kennebec, Maine; (2) Find A Grave, Memorial #25781658.

Jesse G. Stover
Birth:
Marriage: (1) City of Waterville, Kennebec, Maine, Men's Marriages, 1830-1943, Disk 3, Record 1002, Picton Press, Rockland Maine, Copyright 2005; (2) "Maine, Marriages, 1771-1907," index, FamilySearch (https://familysearch.org/pal:/MM9.1.1/F4NS-GV4).
Death: (1) "Maine, Veterans Cemetery Records, 1676-1918," database with images, FamilySearch, (https://familysearch.org/ark:/61903/1:1: KXQZ-L4S); (2) Gravestone.
Graveyard: (1) Pine Grove Cemetery Records, City of Waterville, Kennebec, Maine; (2) "Maine, Veterans Cemetery Records, 1676-1918," database with images, FamilySearch, (https://familysearch.org/ark:/61903/1:1: KXQZ-L4S); (3) Find A Grave, Memorial #21409569.

Historical Accounts: (1) 1850 United States Federal Census for South Thomaston, Lincoln, Maine; (2) 1870 United States Federal Census for Waterville, Kennebec, Maine, Page 69; (3) 1880 United States Federal Census for Waterville, Kennebec, Maine, Page 48; (4) "U.S., Civil War Pension Index: General Index to Pension Files, 1861-1934", [database on-line]. Provo, UT, USA: Ancestry.com Operations Inc, 2000: (5) 1885 Waterville, Maine, City Directory, Page 68; (6) 1887 Waterville, Maine, City Directory, Page 68; (7) "U.S., Civil War Soldier Records and Profiles, 1861-1865", [database on-line]. Provo, UT, USA: Ancestry.com Operations Inc, 2009.

Cyrus Henri Williams
(1847 - 1905)

Cyrus Henri., the ninth child of Cyrus Williams and his wife, Phydelia C. Perkins, was born on March 5, 1847 in Waterville, Kennebec, Maine.

On August 2, 1868 Cyrus Henri, age twenty-one, was married to Hannah M. Dearborn, age twenty-two, by A. J. Buker, a Clergyman in Fairfield, Somerset, Maine. Hannah M., born in Fairfield in 1846, was the daughter of Joseph Dearborn and Lovina Chase. The exact date of her birth is not known.

Cyrus Henri and Hannah M. had one child together.

Nita Emily   b. December 22, 1875   d. February 18, 1935

In the 1870 United States Federal Census Cyrus Henri and Hannah M. were recorded as living in Fairfield. Cyrus Henri's name was listed as "Henry" and his occupation was listed as "tin man".

By the time the 1880 United States Federal Census was taken, Cyrus Henri and Hannah M. had moved to Waterville. They were still living in Waterville, at 35 Oakland Street, at the time of the 1900 United States Federal Census. In both the 1880 and 1900 census documents, Cyrus Henri was listed as working as a "tin smith".

On February 26, 1905, at the age of fifty-seven, Cyrus Henri died of "Bright's disease" in Waterville. He was buried in his father's, Cyrus Williams, family plot, Lot 175, at the Pine Grove Cemetery in Waterville.

Hannah M. outlived her husband by a little over four years, passing away in Waterville on April 16, 1909 at the age of sixty-three. In her obituary the cause of her death was listed as "cancer of the throat". Hannah M.'s funeral was held at 1:00 P.M. on Sunday April 18th at the Universalist Church in Waterville. The Reverend F. E. Barton officiated. She was buried alongside her husband in Lot 175, the Cyrus Williams family plot, at the Pine Grove Cemetery in Waterville.

Headstones for Cyrus Henri Williams (left) and Hannah M. Dearborn (right)
(Photographs from the Collection of Jeffrey Nelson Williams and Jacqueline Pon Williams)

Cyrus Williams Family Plot Marker, front view (top) and back view (bottom)
(Photographs from the Collection of Jeffrey Nelson Williams and Jacqueline Pon Williams)

SOURCES:

Cyrus Henri Williams
Birth: Record of a Death, Maine Vital Records.
Death: (1) Record of a Death, Maine Vital Records; (2) City of Waterville, Maine, Deaths, 1830-1943, Disk 4, Record 1865, Picton Press, Rockland Maine, Copyright 2005.
Graveyard: (1) Pine Grove Cemetery Records, City of Waterville, Kennebec, Maine; (2) Find A Grave, Memorial #22407560.

Hannah M. Dearborn
Birth:
Marriage: (1) Record of a Marriage, Maine Vital Records; (2) "Maine, Marriage Index, 1670-1921," [database on-line], Lehi, UT, USA: Ancestry.com Operations Inc, 2016.
Death: Obituary, Waterville Morning Sentinel, Waterville, Maine, Saturday, April 17, 1909, Page 5.
Graveyard: (1) Pine Grove Cemetery Records, City of Waterville, Kennebec, Maine; (2) Find A Grave, Memorial #22407621.

Historical Accounts: (1) 1860 United States Federal Census for Fairfield, Somerset, Maine, Page 59; (2) 1870 United States Federal Census for Fairfield, Somerset, Maine, Page 53; (3) 1880 United States Federal Census for Waterville, Kennebec, Maine, Page 10; (4) 1900 United States Federal Census for Waterville, Kennebec, Maine, Page 34.

Atwell R. Williams
(1819 - 1898)

The first child of Francis Llewellyn and Nancy D. Hayward was Atwell R. who was born on January 1, 1819 in Embden, Somerset, Maine.

In January 1844 at the age of twenty-five, Atwell R. married Thankful L. Small, age twenty-two, at The Forks, Somerset, Maine. The exact day of the month is not known. Thankful L., the daughter of Thomas Small and Rachel Ball, was born on August 19, 1821 in Moscow, Somerset, Maine.

Atwell R. and Thankful L. had a large family of thirteen children.

Charles	*b. October 16, 1844*	*d.*
Lewis	b. November 12, 1845	d. 1924
Susan	*b. 1846*	*d.*
Albert	b. September 1848	d. 1935
Mary	*b. 1849*	*d.*
Flavilla	*b. 1852*	*d.*
Julia	*b. 1854*	*d.*
Lorena C.	b. April 1857	d. 1928
Ruel A.	b. 1858	d. May 26, 1925
Etta A.	b. March 7, 1859	d. April 29, 1906
John	*b. 1859*	*d.*
Lucy P. H.	b. March 28, 1861	d. January 9, 1912
Oliver Y.	b. June 13, 1863	d. October 13, 1938

When the 1850 United States Federal Census was taken, Atwell R., Thankful L. and four of their first five children, Charles, Lewis, Albert and Mary, were listed as living in The Forks, Somerset, Maine. Atwell R. was working as a "laborer" at the time. Their third child Susan wasn't listed in that census, it is presumed that she was visiting with another relative at that time.

The 1860 United States Federal Census recorded that Atwell R., Thankful L. and their children, Susan, Albert, Mary, Flavilla, Julia and John, as living in Caratunk, Somerset, Maine. Atwell R.'s occupation was listed as a "mill man" in that census.

For six of Atwell R. and Thankful L.'s children, Charles, Susan, Mary, Flavilla, Julia and John, the only information found regarding their existence was recorded in the1850 and 1860 United States Federal Census'. No additional information about their lives and deaths has been found. As such their documented history will end here.

When the 1870 United States Federal Census was taken Atwell R., Thankful L., Lewis, Ruel A., Lucy P. H. and Oliver Y. were recorded as living in Caratunk. Atwell R.'s occupation at that time was listed as "farmer".

During the early 1870's, the Town Records of Caratunk reflect that Atwell R. often served as the moderator for the town meetings. Additionally, on June 20, 1874, the records show that Atwell R. sold a "light red five-year-old cow" to W. C. Young for the sum of sixteen dollars and forty-five cents. Both Atwell R. and Thankful L. signed the Town Register for that sale.

On August 22, 1875, Thankful L. died at the age of fifty-four. The place and cause of her death has not been found. She was buried in the Webster Cemetery in Caratunk.

In the 1880 United States Federal Census Atwell R. was still living in Caratunk and working as a "farmer". His son, Albert, and his family were listed as living with him at that time.

Atwell R. died eighteen years later, at the age of seventy-nine, on October 4, 1898 in Caratunk. His cause of death was listed as "dropsy from the heart". Atwell R. was buried in the Webster Cemetery in Caratunk next to his wife.

Gravestones for Atwell R. Williams (left) and Thankful L. Small (right)
(Photographs from the Collection of Jeffrey Nelson Williams and Jacqueline Pon Williams)

SOURCES:

Atwell R. Williams
Birth: (1) Original Record of Maine Towns & Cities, Caratunk Plantation, Page 56, Picton Press, Rockland Maine, Copyright 2005; (2) Original Record of Maine Towns & Cities, Town of Moscow, Page 43, Picton Press, Rockland Maine, Copyright 2005; (3) "Maine, Births and Christenings, 1739-1900," index, FamilySearch, (https://familysearch.org/pal: /MM9.1.1/F4QC-SLB).
Death: (1) Record of a Death, Maine Vital Records; (2) Gravestone.
Graveyard: (1) "Maine Old Cemetery Association Special Publication Number 12, Edition No. 1: Series 1, 2 and 3", Page 526, Picton Press, Rockland, Maine, Copyright 2006; (2) Find A Grave, Memorial #52750202.

Thankful L. Small
Birth: (1) Original Record of Maine Towns & Cities, Town of Moscow, Page 11, Picton Press, Rockland Maine, Copyright 2005; (2) "Maine Births and Christenings, 1739-1900," database, FamilySearch, (https://familysearch. org/ark/61903/1.1:/FW77-R3V)
Marriage: Original Record of Maine Towns & Cities, Bangor, Disk 2, Page 477, Picton Press, Rockland Maine, Copyright 2005
Death: Gravestone.
Graveyard: (1) "Maine Old Cemetery Association Special Publication Number 12, Edition No. 1: Series 1, 2 and 3", Page 526, Picton Press, Rockland, Maine, Copyright 2006; (2) Find A Grave, Memorial #52750213.

Charles Williams
Birth: "Maine, Births and Christenings, 1739-1900," index, FamilySearch, (https://familysearch.org/pal:/MM9.1.1 / F4QC-SGM).
Death:
Graveyard:

Susan Williams
Birth:
Death:
Graveyard:

Mary Williams
Birth:
Death:
Graveyard:

Flavilla Williams
Birth:
Death:
Graveyard:

John Williams
Birth:
Death:
Graveyard:

Historical Accounts: (1) 1850 United States Federal Census for No. 1, R5, The Forks, Somerset, Maine; (2) 1860 United States Federal Census for Caratunk, Somerset, Maine, Page 63; (3) 1870 United States Federal Census for Caratunk, Somerset, Maine, Page 7; (4) 1880 United States Federal Census for Caratunk, Somerset, Maine, Page 4; (5) Original Record of Maine Towns & Cities, Caratunk Plantation, Page 163, Picton Press, Rockland Maine, Copyright 2005.

Harriet H. Williams
(1820 - 1899)

On August 27, 1820, Harriet H., the second child of Francis Llewellyn and his wife Nancy D. Hayward, was born in Embden, Somerset, Maine.

In the 1850 and 1860 United States Federal Census Harriet H. was recorded as living with her parents in Caratunk, Somerset, Maine.

The 1870 United States Federal Census recorded Harriet H. living with her mother and brother Horace S. on Horace S.'s farm in Caratunk.

When the 1880 United States Federal Census was taken Harriet was living with her brothers, Horace S. and Jason P., on Horace S.'s farm in Caratunk and "keeping house".

Harriet died, at the age of seventy-eight, a State Pauper on February 25, 1899 in Moscow, Somerset, Maine having never married and without issue. Her cause of death was recorded as "enterocolitis". She was buried in the Sugartown/Baker Cemetery in Moscow.

SOURCES:

Harriet H. Williams
Birth:
Death: Record of a Death, Maine Vital Records.
Graveyard: Find A Grave Memorial #105373931.

Historical Accounts: (1) 1850 United States Federal Census for No. 1, R4, Somerset, Maine; (2) 1860 United States Federal Census for Caratunk, Somerset, Maine, Page 63; (3) 1870 United States Federal Census for Caratunk, Somerset, Maine, Page 1; (4) 1880 United States Federal Census for Caratunk, Somerset, Maine, Page 4; (5) "Embden Town of Yore" by Ernest George Walker, Page 128, Published by Independent-Reporter Company, Skowhegan, Maine, 1929.

Clarissa Hayward Williams
(1821 - 1898)

Clarissa Hayward., the third child of Francis Llewellyn and his wife Nancy D. Hayward, was born on December 15, 1821 in Embden, Somerset, Maine.

On April 6, 1847, at the age of twenty-five, Clarissa Hayward was married to Robert E. Love age twenty-two, at The Forks Plantation, Somerset, Maine. Robert E., the son of John Love and Elizabeth Stanley, was born on January 24, 1824 in Murragh, Cork, Ireland and immigrated to the United States on March 9, 1840.

Clarissa Hayward and Robert E. had a family of seven children.

Elizabeth Jane	b. September 8, 1849	d. July 4, 1936
David	b. April 29, 1851	d. December 26, 1930
Robert E., Jr.	b. August 22, 1853	d. January 1, 1937
John H.	b. February 25, 1856	d. August 29, 1930
Clarissa	b. January 6, 1858	d. September 6, 1940
Charles	*b. September 24, 1860*	*d. April 19, 1864*
Jason W.	b. January 8, 1863	d. September 10, 1923

In the 1850 and 1860 United States Federal Census', Clarissa Hayward and Robert E. were listed as living in The Forks, Somerset, Maine and Robert E. was working as a "farmer".

On April 4, 1864 Robert E., having become a naturalized United States citizen on September 19, 1860, enlisted in Company G, 31st Maine Infantry Regiment of the Union Army as a Private. He was mustered out as a Full Corporal on July 15, 1865.

Charles, the sixth child of Clarissa Hayward and Robert E., died on April 19, 1864 when he was three years seven months old. The cause and place of his death have not been found. He was buried in the Webster Cemetery in Caratunk, Somerset, Maine.

Around 1866, after the death of their son Charles, Robert E., Clarissa Hayward, and their family moved to Getty, Stearns, Minnesota. Later that year Robert E. died on December 21, 1866 at the age of forty-two. The exact place and cause of his death are not known. He was buried in Oakland Cemetery in Sauk Centre, Stearns, Minnesota.

The 1870 and 1880 United States Federal Census' recorded Clarissa Hayward and her children as still living in Getty, Stearns, Minnesota.

On January 16, 1890 Clarissa Hayward filed to receive her late husband's military pension related to his service during the United States Civil War.

When the 1895 Minnesota State Census was taken Clarissa Hayward was recorded as living in Burtrum, Todd, Minnesota with her daughter Elizabeth Jane (Love) Diamond and her family. Three years later, on September 17, 1898, Clarissa Hayward, at the age of seventy-six, died of "old age" at the home of her daughter Elizabeth Jane in Burtrum. She was buried with her husband in the Oakland Cemetery in Sauk Centre.

Gravestone for Charles Love
(Photograph Courtesy of Tim Cooper and Grace Elkins)

Gravestones for Clarissa Hayward Williams (left) and Robert E. Love (right)
(Photographs Courtesy of Carmen Gardiner)

SOURCES:

Clarissa Hayward Williams
Birth: Edmund West, comp., "Family Data Collection - Individual Records", [database on-line]. Provo, UT, USA: Ancestry.com Operations Inc., 2000.
Death: (1) Edmund West, comp., "Family Data Collection - Individual Records", [database on-line]. Provo, UT, USA: Ancestry.com Operations Inc., 2000; (2) Obituary, Little Falls Herald, Little Falls, Minnesota, Friday, September 30, 1898, page 5.
Graveyard: Find A Grave Memorial #49022697.

Robert E. Love
Birth: "U. S. Naturalization Record Indexes, 1791-1992," (database on-line), Provo, UT, USA: Ancestry.com Operations Inc., 2010.
Marriage:
Death: Gravestone.
Graveyard: Find A Grave, Memorial #52855646.

Charles Love
Birth:
Death: Gravestone.
Graveyard: (1) "Maine Old Cemetery Association Special Publication Number 12, Edition No. 1: Series 1, 2 and 3", Page 517, Picton Press, Rockland, Maine, Copyright 2006; (2) Find A Grave, Memorial #52855646.

Historical Accounts: (1) 1850 United States Federal Census for No. 1, R6, Somerset, Maine; (2) 1860 United States Federal Census for The Forks, Somerset, Maine, Page 65; (3) 1870 United States Federal Census for Getty, Stearns, Minnesota; (4) 1880 United States Federal Census for Getty, Stearns, Minnesota, Page 4; (5) 1895 Minnesota States Census for Burtrum, Todd, Minnesota, Page 14; (6) U. S. Naturalization Record Indexes, 1791-1992; (7) "American Civil War Soldiers," [database on-line], Provo, UT, USA: Ancestry.com Operations Inc, 2000; (8) "U.S., Civil War Pension Index, 1861-1934", [database on-line]. Provo, UT, USA: Ancestry.com Operations Inc, 2000; (9) "U.S., Civil War Soldier Records and Profiles, 1861-1865", [database on-line]. Provo, UT, USA: Ancestry.com Operations Inc, 2009.

Charles W. Williams
(1823 - 1892)

The fourth child of Francis Llewellyn and Nancy D. Hayward was Charles W. who was born on October 23, 1823 in Embden, Somerset, Maine.

At the age of twenty-four, Charles W. and Deborah Wyman, age twenty-nine, of Solon, Somerset, Maine filed their intentions to be married on February 11, 1848 with the Solon Town Clerk. The date and place of their subsequent marriage have not been found. Additionally, the names of Deborah's parents, as well as the date and location of her birth, have also not been found.

Charles W. and Deborah had four children during their marriage.

Nancy	b. January 27, 1849	d. March 24, 1918
Arina	b. May 17, 1850	d. March 27, 1899
Francis	b. 1853	d. January 6, 1919
James	*b. 1857*	*d. 1864*

The 1860 United States Federal Census recorded Charles W., Deborah and their four children living in The Forks, Somerset, Maine where Charles W. was "farming".

James, the fourth child of Charles W. and Deborah, was seven years old when he died in 1864. The exact place, cause and date of his death have not been found. He was buried in the Charles W. Williams family plot in the Bean Cemetery at The Forks.

In the1870 and 1880 United States Federal Census' Charles W., Deborah and their family were listed as still living and farming in The Forks.

Deborah died in 1885 at the age of sixty-six. The exact date, place and cause of her death are also not known. She was buried at The Forks in the family plot in the Bean Cemetery.

Charles W. outlived Deborah by seven years, passing away in Madison, Somerset, Maine on July 17, 1892 at the age of sixty-eight. According to the death record, he died suddenly which was most likely caused by "heart disease". He, too, was buried in his family plot in the Bean Cemetery at The Forks.

Gravestone for Deborah Wyman and her son James Williams (left)
(Photograph Courtesy of Wayne Hoar)

Gravestone for Charles W. Williams (right)
(Photograph Courtesy of William Frawley)

SOURCES:

Charles W. Williams
Birth:
Death: Record of a Death, Maine Vital Records.
Graveyard: (1) "The Forks – Bean Cemetery (Mountain Road)" From data collected by Leona Sterling and Mildred Smith, 1938, Record 24, Old Canada Road Historical Society; (2) Find A Grave Memorial #52843582.

Deborah Wyman
Birth:
Marriage: (1) Original Records of Solon, Page 94, Picton Press, Rockland Maine, Copyright 2005; (2) "Maine, Marriages, 1771-1907," index, FamilySearch, (https://familysearch.org/pal:/MM9.1.1/F4FB-GBYF).
Death:
Graveyard: (1) "The Forks – Bean Cemetery (Mountain Road)" From data collected by Leona Sterling and Mildred Smith, 1938, Record 22, Old Canada Road Historical Society; (2) Find A Grave, Memorial #52843681.

James Williams
Birth:
Death:
Graveyard: (1) "The Forks – Bean Cemetery (Mountain Road)" From data collected by Leona Sterling and Mildred Smith, 1938, Record 23, Old Canada Road Historical Society; (2) Find A Grave, Memorial #77215232.

Historical Accounts: (1) 1850 United States Federal Census for No. 1, R6, Somerset, Maine; (2) 1860 United States Federal Census for The Forks, Somerset, Maine, Page 67; (3) 1870 United States Federal Census for The Forks, Somerset, Maine, Page 2; (4) 1880 United States Federal Census for The Forks, Somerset, Maine, Page 12.

Horace S. Williams
(1825 -)

Horace S. was the fifth child of Francis Llewellyn and his wife, Nancy D. Hayward. He was born on August 15, 1825 in Caratunk, Somerset, Maine.

In the 1850 United States Federal Census, at the age of twenty-four, Horace S. was listed as living in a hotel located in No. 1, Range 4 East Kennebec, Somerset, Maine and working as a "laborer".

The 1860 United States Federal Census listed Horace S. as living with his father and mother in Caratunk and working as a "farmer".

When the 1870 United States Federal Census was taken, Horace S. was listed as the "head of the house" living in Caratunk with his mother and his sister, Harriet H. His occupation was again listed as "farmer".

At the age of fifty-four, Horace S. had his brother, Jason P., and his sister, Harriet H., living with him when the 1880 United States Federal Census for Caratunk was taken. He was still working as a "farmer"

Shortly after that census was taken, Horace S. married Ann Jane Kennedy (also known as Jane Ann), who was around age twenty. The place and date of their marriage have not been found. Ann Jane, born in Frampton, Quebec, Canada in August of 1861, was the daughter of Thomas Kennedy and Bridget Gorman. The exact date of her birth is not known.

Horace S. and Ann Jane had two children together.

Florence Maude	b. December 1880	d. October 1, 1962
Ervin Andrew	b. July 18, 1884	d. May 17, 1962

It is believed that Horace S. passed away sometime around between 1883 and 1885. The exact date and place of his death, as well as his burial place, are unknown.

On November 30, 1885 Ann Jane was married to her second husband, Charles E. Pierce in Caratunk by Ephraim Witham, a Justice of the Peace. Charles E., the son of Reuben B. Pierce and Lydia M. Chase, was born on December 25, 1860 in Bingham, Somerset, Maine. Ann Jane and Charles E. went on to have a family of their own.

Ann Jane died in 1932 and was buried in the Charles E. Pierce family plot at the Moscow Union Cemetery in Moscow, Somerset, Maine. The cause, place and date of her death are unknown.

Gravestone for Ann Jane Kennedy
(Photograph Courtesy of maine)

SOURCES:

Horace S. Williams
Birth: Original Record of Maine Towns & Cities, Town of Caratunk, Page 56, Picton Press, Rockland, Maine, Copyright 2005.
Death:
Graveyard:

Ann Jane Kennedy
Birth: "Quebec, Canada, Vital and Church Records (Drouin Collection), 1621-1968," [database on-line], Provo, UT, USA: Ancestry.com Operations, Inc., 2008, Frampton, Quebec, 1861.
Marriage:
Death:
Graveyard: (1) "Moscow Union Cemetery" by Nancy Hamlin Davis and Ruth Hamlin, Record 477, Old Canada Road Historical Society; (2) Find A Grave, Memorial #82140502.

Charles E. Pierce
Birth:
Death:
Marriage: (1) Original Record of Maine Towns & Cities, Town of Caratunk, Page 213, Picton Press, Rockland, Maine, Copyright 2005; (2) "Maine, Marriages, 1771-1907," index, FamilySearch, (https://familysearch.org/pal: /MM9.1.1/F4FQ-YZN).
Graveyard: "Moscow Union Cemetery" by Nancy Hamlin Davis and Ruth Hamlin, Record 476, Old Canada Road Historical Society.

Historical Accounts: (1) 1850 United States Federal Census for No. 1, R4, East Kennebec, Somerset, Maine; (2) 1860 United States Federal Census for Caratunk, Somerset, Maine, Page 62; (3) 1870 United States Federal Census for Caratunk, Somerset, Maine, Page 1; (4) 1880 United States Federal Census for Caratunk, Somerset, Maine, Page 4.

Jason P. Williams
(1828 - 1903)

On June 20, 1828, Jason P., the sixth child of Francis Llewellyn and his wife Nancy D. Hayward, was born in Embden, Somerset, Maine.

In the 1850 and 1860 United States Federal Census', Jason P. was listed as working as a "laborer" and living on his parents' farm in Caratunk, Somerset, Maine.

By the time the 1870 United States Federal Census was taken Jason P. had moved to Bingham, Somerset, Maine and was working as a "farmer". His brother, Cyrus P., and his family were listed as living with him at that time.

The 1880 United States Federal Census recorded that Jason P. had moved back to Caratunk and was living with his brother, Horace S., and his sister, Harriet H., and working as a "laborer".

Jason P. was living in Moscow, Somerset, Maine as a boarder at the time the 1900 United States Federal Census was taken.

Like his sister Harriet H., Jason P. died a State Pauper on December 13, 1903 in Moscow having never married and without issue. His cause of death was recorded as "chronic ulcer of leg". The location of his place of burial is unknown.

SOURCES:

Jason P. Williams
Birth:
Death: Record of a Death, Maine Vital Records.
Graveyard:

Historical Accounts: (1) 1850 United States Federal Census for No. 1, R4, Somerset, Maine; (2) 1860 United States Federal Census for Caratunk, Somerset, Maine, Page 61; (3) 1870 United States Federal Census for Bingham, Somerset, Maine, Page 27; (4) 1880 United States Federal Census for Caratunk, Somerset, Maine, Page 4; (5) 1900 United States Federal Census for Moscow, Somerset, Maine, Page 5; (6) "Embden Town of Yore" by Ernest George Walker, Page 128, Published by Independent-Reporter Company, Skowhegan, Maine, 1929.

Nancy Jane Williams
(1831 - 1891)

The seventh child of Francis Llewellyn and Nancy D. Hayward was Nancy Jane (also known as Jane) who was born on November 13, 1831 in Caratunk, Somerset, Maine.

It is believed that sometime in 1848 Nancy Jane, age sixteen, was married to Louis Vigue age twenty-six. The exact place and date of their marriage have not been found. Louis, (sometimes spelled Lewis) was born on July 4, 1822 in Sault Ste. Marie, Ontario, Canada. The names of his parents have also not been found.

Nancy Jane and Louis had two children during their marriage.

Horace W.	b. October 1848	d. June 15, 1885
Ida J.	b. March 13, 1866	d. July 2, 1947

On July 26, 1862, Louis enlisted in Company A, 19th Maine Infantry Regiment of the Union Army as a Private. He was mustered-in in Bath, Sagadahoc, Maine the following month, on August 5th. In his Volunteer Enlistment papers Louis was described as being 5' 7" tall with blue eyes, brown hair and having a light complexion.

The Adjutant General's Condensed Morning Report for Company A, 19th Maine Infantry Regiment dated December 1, 1863 listed Louis as having been wounded at Gettysburg, Pennsylvania and in the hospital. On March 15, 1864 Louis was transferred into the Maine Volunteer Reserve Corps. Louis was discharged from service in Washington, District of Columbia on July 1, 1865 still holding the rank of Private.

In the 1880 United States Federal Census Nancy Jane, Louis and their children were recorded as living in Mayfield, Somerset, Maine. Louis' occupation at the time of that census was listed as "farmer".

Nancy Jane died, at the age of fifty-nine, on February 15, 1891. The place and cause of her death have not been found. She was buried in the Bingham Village Cemetery in Bingham, Somerset, Maine.

The 1900 United States Federal Census recorded Louis as living on Ferry Street in Solon, Somerset, Maine. In that census his granddaughter Jennie M. Padham was listed as living with him.

Louis outlived his wife by more than twenty years. He died at the home of his granddaughter Alice Grace (Padham) Jackson in Solon on January 16, 1912 at the age of eighty-nine. His death record indicated that his cause of death was "chronic interstitial nephritis". He was buried in Bingham at the Bingham Village Cemetery alongside his wife.

Gravestone for Nancy Jane Williams and Louis (Lewis) Vigue
(Photograph from the Collection of Jeffrey Nelson Williams and Jacqueline Pon Williams)

SOURCES:

Nancy Jane Williams
Birth:
Death: (1) "Maine, Nathan Hale Cemetery Collection, ca. 1780-1980," database with images, FamilySearch, (https://familysearch.org/ark:/61903/1:1:QVJ5-MH2R); (2) Gravestone.
Graveyard: (1) "Maine Old Cemetery Association Special Publication Number 12, Edition No. 1: Series 1, 2 and 3", Page 330, Picton Press, Rockland, Maine, Copyright 2006; (2) "Bingham Village Cemetery" by Nancy Hamlin Davis and Ruth Hamlin, Record 617, Old Canada Road Historical Society; (3) "Maine, Nathan Hale Cemetery Collection, ca. 1780-1980," database with images, FamilySearch, (https://familysearch.org/ark:/61903/1:1:QVJ5-MH2R); (4) Find A Grave, Memorial #52875819.

Louis Vigue
Birth: (1) "Maine, Nathan Hale Cemetery Collection, ca. 1780-1980," database with images, FamilySearch, (https://familysearch.org/ark:/61903/1:1:QVJ5-MH2R); (2) Gravestone.
Marriage:
Death: (1) Record of a Death, Maine Vital Records; (2) Death Notice, The Independent Reporter, Skowhegan, Maine, January 18, 1912, Page 10; (3) "Maine, Nathan Hale Cemetery Collection, ca. 1780-1980," database with images, FamilySearch, (https://familysearch.org/ark:/61903/1:1:QVJ5-MH2R); (4) Gravestone.
Graveyard: (1) "Maine Old Cemetery Association Special Publication Number 12, Edition No. 1: Series 1, 2 and 3", Page 330, Picton Press, Rockland, Maine, Copyright 2006; (2) "Bingham Village Cemetery" by Nancy Hamlin Davis and Ruth Hamlin, Record 616, Old Canada Road Historical Society; (3) Find A Grave, Memorial #52875401.

Historical Accounts: (1) 1880 United States Federal Census for Mayfield, Somerset, Maine, Page 3; (3) 1900 United States Federal Census for Solon, Somerset, Maine, Page 4; (3) "Maine, Civil War Enlistment Papers, 1862-1865," database with images, FamilySearch (https://familysearch.org/ark:/61903/1:1:Q2QB-NX41); (4) "U.S., Adjutant General Military Records, 1631-1976," [database on-line]. Provo, UT, USA: Ancestry.com Operations, Inc., 2011., Page 538; (5) 1890 Veterans Schedules for Bingham, Somerset, Maine, Page 1; (6) "Maine, State Archive Collections, 1718-1957," database with images, FamilySearch, (https://familysearch.org/ark:/61903/1:1:33SQ-G58D).

Francis Llewellyn Williams, Jr.
(1834 - 1916)

Francis Llewellyn, Jr., the eighth child of Francis Llewellyn and Nancy D. Hayward, was born in Caratunk, Somerset, Maine on October 13, 1834.

On August 18, 1863 Francis Llewellyn, Jr., then age twenty-eight, enlisted in the19[th] Maine Infantry Regiment, Company C of the Union Army as a Private. On his enlistment record he was described as being 5' 8¼" tall, with sandy hair, blue eyes and a sandy complexion. After serving in the infantry for twenty-one months he was transferred into Company C, 1st Heavy Artillery Regiment on May 31, 1865. Shortly thereafter, on June 7, 1865, he was honorably discharged from the Army at Washington, District of Columbia.

It is believed that sometime in 1865, after his discharge from the Army, Francis Llewellyn, Jr., age thirty or thirty-one, was married to Flora Withee, age nineteen. The exact date and location of their marriage has not been found. Flora, born December 6, 1845 in Bingham, Somerset, Maine, was the daughter of Nathaniel Withee and Zilpha Smith.

Francis Llewellyn, Jr. and Flora had a family of six children.

Eugene Bolton	b. July 31, 1866	d. December 17, 1919
Israel Austin	b. January 27, 1868	d. 1938
Everett Ansel	b. November 10, 1869	d. 1946
Nathaniel Withee	b. September 9, 1876	d. 1946
Guy Freeman	b. April 23, 1879	d. January 25, 1919
Zelphia M.	b. February 18, 1882	d. February 22, 1929

In the 1870, 1880, 1900 and 1910 United States Federal Census', Francis Llewellyn, Jr., Flora and their children were listed as living in Bingham. Francis L. Jr.'s occupation in all of the aforementioned censuses was recorded as "farmer".

On January 5, 1916, at the age of eighty-one, Francis Llewellyn, Jr. died at his home east of Bingham of "heart failure". Funeral services were held at his home on Friday January 7th and were conducted by Reverend T. B. Hatt. He was buried on January 8, 1916 in the Bingham Village Cemetery in Bingham.

After Francis Llewellyn, Jr.'s death, on March 28, 1916, Flora applied to receive his military pension.

Flora was recorded in the 1920 and 1930 United States Federal Census' as living with her son, Nathaniel W., and his family in Bingham.

Additional information regarding the life and death of Flora has not been found, although it is believed she is buried alongside her husband in the Bingham Village Cemetery in Bingham.

Gravestone for Francis Llewellyn Williams, Jr. and Flora Withee
(Photograph from the Collection of Jeffrey Nelson Williams and Jacqueline Pon Williams)

SOURCES:

Francis Llewellyn Williams, Jr.
Birth: (1) Original Record of Maine Towns & Cities, Town of Caratunk, Page 56, Picton Press, Rockland Maine, Copyright 2005; (2) "Maine, Veterans Cemetery Records 1676-1918," database with images, FamilySearch, (https://familysearch.org/ark:/61903/1:1:KXQZ-TW1); (3) Gravestone.
Death: (1) Record of a Death, Maine Vital Records; (2) "Maine, Veterans Cemetery Records 1676-1918," database with images, FamilySearch, (https://familysearch.org/ark:/61903/1:1:KXQZ-TW1); (3) Obituary, The Independent Reporter, Skowhegan, Maine, January 12, 1916, Page 10; (4) Gravestone.
Graveyard: (1) "Maine Old Cemetery Association Special Publication Number 12, Edition No. 1: Series 1, 2 and 3", Page 334, Picton Press, Rockland, Maine, Copyright 2006; (2) "Bingham Village Cemetery" by Nancy Hamlin Davis and Ruth Hamlin, Record 617, Old Canada Road Historical Society; (3) "Maine, Veterans Cemetery Records 1676-1918," database with images, FamilySearch, (https://familysearch.org/ark:/61903/1:1:KXQZ-TW1); (4) Find A Grave, Memorial #52835306.

Flora Withee
Birth: (1) Original Record of Maine Towns & Cities, Town of Bingham, Page 88, Picton Press, Rockland Maine, Copyright 2005; (2) Gravestone.
Marriage:
Death:
Graveyard: (1) "Maine Old Cemetery Association Special Publication Number 12, Edition No. 1: Series 1, 2 and 3", Page 330, Picton Press, Rockland, Maine, Copyright 2006; (2) "Bingham Village Cemetery" by Nancy Hamlin Davis and Ruth Hamlin, Record 616, Old Canada Road Historical Society; (3) Find A Grave, Memorial #52875401.

Historical Accounts: (1) 1860 United States Federal Census for Bingham, Somerset, Maine, Page 26; (2) 1870 United States Federal Census for Bingham, Somerset, Maine, Page 27; (3) 1880 United States Federal Census for Bingham, Somerset, Maine, Page 1; (4) 1900 United States Federal Census for Bingham, Somerset, Maine, Page 6; (5) 1910 United States Federal Census for Bingham, Somerset, Maine, Page 7; (6) 1920 United States Federal Census for Bingham, Somerset, Maine, Page 5A; (7) 1930 United States Federal Census for Bingham, Somerset, Maine, Page 15B; (8) "United States Census of Union Veterans and Widows of the Civil War, 1890," database with images, FamilySearch (https://familysearch.org/ark:/61903/3:1:939V-RSN7), Page 2; (9) "American Civil War Soldiers," [database on-line], Provo, UT, USA: Ancestry.com Operations Inc, 2000; (10) "Maine, State Archive Collections, 1718-1957," database with images, FamilySearch (https://familysearch.opr/ark:/61903/3:1:33SQ-G58D).

Cyrus P. Williams
(1836 - 1911)

The ninth child, Cyrus P., of Francis Llewellyn and Nancy D. Hayward, was born in Caratunk, Somerset, Maine on March 20, 1836.

Cyrus P. Williams
(Photograph Courtesy of Judith Otis Watt)

In the 1860 United States Federal Census Cyrus P., at the age of twenty-one, was listed as living with his parents in Caratunk and working as a "farm laborer".

On May 15, 1861 Cyrus P. was married to Susan Cordelia Spaulding, age twenty, in Caratunk by Joseph Clark, a Justice of the Peace. Susan Cordelia (also known as Delia), born in Maine on April 29, 1841, was the daughter of Joseph Spaulding and Alice B. Wyman. The exact location of her birth has not been found.

Cyrus P. and Susan Cordelia had two children during their marriage.

Nellie V.	b. March 29, 1862	d. January 25, 1884
Fred P.	b. July 6, 1865	d. January 4, 1919

The 1870 United States Federal Census recorded Cyrus P. and Susan Cordelia as living with his brother, Jason P. Williams, in Bingham, Somerset, Maine and where Cyrus P. was working as a "farm laborer".

By the time the 1880 United States Federal Census was taken, Cyrus P., Susan Cordelia and their children were living in Moscow, Somerset, Maine. At that time Cyrus P.'s occupation was again listed as "farmer".

Cyrus P. and Susan Cordelia were divorced in December 1890 in Somerset County Maine. In 1891 Susan Cordelia went on to marry Francis Williams, the son of Cyrus P.'s brother, Charles W. Williams.

In the 1900 United States Federal Census, Cyrus P. was recorded as living in Caratunk at the hotel owned by Abba Webster and working as a "servant".

When the 1910 United States Federal Census was taken, Cyrus P. had moved to Solon, Somerset, Maine and was living as a boarder in the home of Ansen Sally.

Cyrus P. died less than a year later, on April 8, 1911, in Solon at the age of seventy-five. His cause of death was listed as "prostatitis followed by cystitis". Cyrus P.'s place of burial is unknown.

Susan Cordelia, Cyrus P.'s ex-wife, died of "angina pectoris" in Madison, Somerset, Maine on April 29, 1921 at the age of eighty. Her burial place is also unknown.

SOURCES:

Cyrus P. Williams
Birth: Original Record of Maine Towns & Cities, Caratunk Plantation, Page 56, Picton Press, Rockland Maine, Copyright 2005.
Death: Record of a Death, Maine Vital Records.
Graveyard:

Susan Cordelia Spaulding
Birth:
Marriage: (1) Original Record of Maine Towns & Cities, Caratunk Plantation, Page 87, Picton Press, Rockland Maine, Copyright 2005; (2) "Maine, Marriages, 1771-1907," index, FamilySearch, (https://familysearch.org/pal:/MM9.1.1 /F4FQ-Y8J).
Divorce: (1) "Maine, Divorces, 1799-1903," database, Maine Genealogy, Maine Supreme Judicial Court Records (Somerset Co.), 23/306 (docket no. 444); (2) "Maine, Divorce Records, 1798-1891," [database on-line], Provo, UT, USA: Ancestry.com Operations Inc, 2011.
Death: Record of a Death, Maine Vital Records.
Graveyard:

Historical Accounts: (1) 1860 United States Federal Census for Caratunk, Somerset, Maine, Page 63; (2) 1870 United States Federal Census for Bingham, Somerset, Maine, Page 27; (3) 1880 United States Federal Census for Moscow, Somerset, Maine, Page 5; (4) 1900 United States Federal Census for Caratunk, Somerset, Maine, Page 5; (5) 1910 United States Federal Census for Solon, Somerset, Maine, Page 6A.

Lewis Kingman Williams
(1838 - 1907)

Lewis Kingman was the tenth and youngest child of Francis Llewellyn and his wife, Nancy D. Hayward. He was born on June 27, 1838 in Caratunk, Somerset, Maine.

At the age of twenty-three, on October 20, 1860, Lewis Kingman was married in Caratunk to Susan Davis Cates, age twenty-one, by Joseph Clark, a Justice of the Peace. Susan Davis, born on February 9, 1839 in Caratunk, was the daughter of Horace Cates and Elmira Small.

During their marriage Lewis Kingman and Susan Davis had a family of six children.

Leonard C.	b. February 6, 1863	d. June 17, 1942
Franklin Lewis	b. October 13, 1864	d. November 18, 1933
Mary E.	b. February 12, 1866	d. April 21, 1944
Idris F.	b. July 22, 1868	d. December 18, 1944
Vertie H. (a twin)	b. December 13, 1872	d. March 20, 1875
Vernon C. (a twin)	b. December 13, 1872	d. 1955

In the 1870 United States Federal Census, at the age of twenty-one, Lewis Kingman, Susan Davis and their children were recorded as living in Moscow, Somerset, Maine. Lewis Kingman's occupation in that census was listed as "farmer".

The fifth child of Lewis Kingman and Susan Davis, Vertie H., died on March 20, 1875 when he was two years and three months old. The cause of his death has not been found. He was buried in the Webster Cemetery in Caratunk.

By the time the 1880 United States Federal Census was taken Lewis Kingman, Susan Davis and their children had moved to Vassalboro, Kennebec, Maine. Lewis Kingman was listed working in a "woolen mill" in that census.

Sometime between the time when the 1880 and 1900 United States Federal Census' were taken, Lewis Kingman and his family moved to Madison, Somerset, Maine. In the 1900 United States Federal Census of Madison Lewis Kingman was recorded as working as a "carpenter".

On April 28, 1907 Lewis Kingman died in Madison at the age of sixty-eight. His cause of death was listed as "cancer of the stomach". He was buried in his family plot, Lot 314, at the Forest Hill Cemetery in Madison.

When the 1910 and 1920 United States Federal Census' were taken Susan Davis was living with her son Vernon Charles and his family in Madison.

A little more than thirteen and one-half years after her husband passed away, Susan Davis died in Madison on January 19, 1921 at the age of eighty-one. Her cause of death was recorded as "dilation of the heart with chronic bronchitis". Susan was buried at the Forest Hill Cemetery in Madison with her husband in the Lewis Kingman Williams family plot, Lot 314.

Gravestone for Vertie H. Williams (top)
Lewis Kingman Williams Family Plot Marker (bottom)
(Photographs from the Collection of Jeffrey Nelson Williams and Jacqueline Pon Williams)

Headstones for Lewis Kingman Williams (left) & Susan Davis Cates (right)
(Photographs from the Collection of Jeffrey Nelson Williams and Jacqueline Pon Williams)

SOURCES:

Lewis Kingman Williams
Birth: (1) Record of a Death, Maine Vital Records; (2) Gravestone.
Death: (1) Record of a Death, Maine Vital Records; (2) Gravestone.
Graveyard: (1) Records for Forest Hill Cemetery managed by the Town of Madison, Maine; (2) "Forest Hill Cemetery", updated by Dassie Jackson and Lena Arno in 2002 and 2003, page 163, Madison Historical Society; (3) Find A Grave, Memorial #52511811.

Susan Davis Cates
Birth: (1) Record of a Death, Maine Vital Records; (2) Gravestone.
Marriage: Original Record of Maine Towns & Cities, Caratunk Plantation, Page 87, Picton Press, Rockland Maine, Copyright 2005.
Death: (1) Record of a Death, Maine Vital Records; (2) Gravestone.
Graveyard: (1) Records for Forest Hill Cemetery managed by the Town of Madison, Maine; (2) "Forest Hill Cemetery", updated by Dassie Jackson and Lena Arno in 2002 and 2003, page 163, Madison Historical Society; (3) Find A Grave, Memorial #52511773.

Vertie H. Williams
Birth:
Death: Gravestone.
Graveyard: Find A Grave, Memorial # 52482864.

Historical Accounts: (1) 1850 United States Federal Census for No. 1 Range 6 East Kennebec River, Somerset, Maine; (2) 1870 United States Federal Census for Moscow, Somerset, Maine, Page 2; (3) 1880 United States Federal Census for Vassalboro, Kennebec, Maine, Page 10; (4) 1900 United States Federal Census for Madison, Somerset, Maine, Page 4; (5) 1910 United States Federal Census for Madison, Somerset, Maine, Page 20; (6) 1920 United States Federal Census for Madison, Somerset, Maine, Page 11A.

Sophronia Sawyer Williams
(1826 - 1926)

Sophronia Sawyer was the second child of Jacob Williams, Jr. and Parmelia H. Savage. She was born in Embden, Somerset, Maine on April 21, 1826.

On May 29, 1846 Sophronia Sawyer, age twenty, and Samuel D. Butler filed their intentions to be married in Lincoln, Penobscot, Maine. The date and place of their subsequent marriage, as well as Samuel D.'s date and place of birth and the names of his parents, have not been found.

Sophronia Sawyer and Samuel D. had four children during their marriage.

Elsie R.	b. June 1850	d.
Lucinda O.	b. 1852	d. October 1858
Emma S.	b. 1856	d. March 1864
Linda E.	b. 1858	d. December 1861

The 1850 United States Federal Census recorded Sophronia Sawyer and Samuel D. living in Shirley, Piscataquis, Maine where Samuel D. was working as a "farmer".

Sometime after the 1850 census was taken Sophronia Sawyer, Samuel D. and their daughter Elsie R. moved to Illinois. The name of the town and county they moved to has not been found.

In late September or early October 1858, the second child of Sophronia Sawyer and Samuel D., Lucinda O., died at the age of six years. The exact cause, date and place of her death has not been found. She was buried in Section 16, Lot 12 SE½, Grave 1 at the Greenwood Cemetery in Rockford, Winnebago, Illinois on October 2, 1858.

After the birth of their third daughter Linda in 1858 and the death of their second child Lucinda O., Sophronia Sawyer, Samuel D. and their children moved west to Chico, Butte, California. They were recorded as living and farming there on June 23, 1860 when the 1860 United States Federal Census for Chico was taken. Within a month of that census being taken they moved back to Illinois where they were recorded as living in Rockford on July 25, 1860, the date the 1860 United States Federal Census of Rockford was taken. Samuel D.'s occupation was again listed as "farmer" in Rockford census.

Two of Sophronia Sawyer and Samuel D.'s children died in the 1860s of causes not found. Linda E. died in December of 1861 when she was three years old and Emma S. died in March of 1864 at the age of seven years. Although the exact dates of their deaths are not known, the dates of their burial have been found. Both children were buried with their sister in Rockford in Section 16,

Lot 12 SE½ at the Greenwood Cemetery. Linda E. was buried in Grave 2 on December 6, 1861 and Emma S. was buried on March 12, 1864 in Grave 3.

Additionally, sometime between the taking of the 1860 census and May 1865 either Sophronia Sawyer and Samuel D. were divorced or Samuel D. died. Whichever occurred, documentation of that event has not been found. Nor has any documentation been found relating to Samuel D.'s life after the date of the 1860 census.

Sophronia Sawyer, at the age of thirty-nine, was married to her second husband James Dame, age forty-four, in Winnebago County, Illinois on May 13, 1865. The exact place of their marriage is not known. James, the son of James Dame and Ursula Mitchell, was born on May 1, 1821 in Montville, Waldo, Maine.

During their marriage Sophronia Sawyer and James had two children together.

Charles Edward	b. April 30, 1866	d. June 15, 1939
Willie	*b. April 1869*	*d. September 1869*

The second child of Sophronia Sawyer and her second husband James, Willie, died in Rockford at the age of five months in September 1869. The cause and date of his death are not known. He was buried in in Section 16, Lot 12 SE½, Grave 4 at the Greenwood Cemetery in Rockford on September 16th.

When the 1870 United States Federal Census and the 1872 Rockford City Directory were published Sophronia Sawyer, James, their son Charles Edward and Sophronia Sawyer's daughter Elsie R. from her first marriage were living at 806 Peach Street in Rockford. In both those documents James was listed as working as a "carpenter".

The 1880 United States Federal Census recorded Sophronia Sawyer, James and their son Charles Edward living on Mulberry Street in Rockford. James was still working as a "carpenter" at the time of that census.

On December 11, 1896 James, age seventy-two- died in "in his chair", which he had been confined to for two months, at 1:00 A.M. at the old Tucker House on South Main Street in Rockford. The cause of his death was reported to be "dropsy". His funeral was held at the Court Street M.E. Church on Wednesday, December 13th at 2:30 P.M. with Reverend W. O. Shepard officiating. James was buried in Section 4, Lot 19 N¼, Grave 2 at the Greenwood Cemetery in Rockford that same day.

During his 41 years of living in Rockford James had held the position of

Constable, Sheriff, City Marshall and Coroner.

In the 1900 United States Federal Census Sophronia Sawyer was recorded as lodging at 302 South Church Street in Rockford and working as a "milliner".

The 1905 Rockford City Directory recorded that Sophronia Sawyer had moved and was then living at 309 North Horseman Street in Rockford.

Sophronia Sawyer was recorded as living in the Jennie Snow Home for the Aged located at 525 Kent Street in Rockford when the 1910 and 1920 United States Federal Census' were taken.

On April 21, 1926 the Rockford Republic newspaper published an article honoring Sophronia Sawyer's one hundredth birthday.

Seven months later, on November 19, 1926, Sophronia Sawyer died in her one hundredth year at the Jennie Snow Home after a brief illness. Her funeral service was held at 3:30 P.M. on Saturday November 20th at the Jennie Snow Home with Reverend Charles Parker Connolly officiating. She was buried with her second husband in Section 4, Lot 19 N¼, Grave 3 at the in the Greenwood Cemetery in Rockford on the day of her funeral.

SOURCES:

Sophronia Sawyer Williams
Birth: (1) Application for Burial Permit, Greenwood Cemetery, Rockford, Winnebago, Illinois, (2) "Illinois, Deaths and Stillbirths Index, 1916-1947," [database on-line], Provo, UT, USA: Ancestry.com Operations Inc, 2011; (3) Newspaper Article, Rockford Republic, Rockford, Illinois, April 21, 1926, Page 11; (4) Obituary, Rockford Republic, Rockford, Illinois, November 19, 1926, Page 1; (5) Obituary, Daily Register and Gazette, Rockford, Illinois, April 21, 1926, Page 1.
Death: (1) Application for Burial Permit, Greenwood Cemetery, Rockford, Winnebago, Illinois, (2) "Illinois, Deaths and Stillbirths Index, 1916-1947," [database on-line], Provo, UT, USA: Ancestry.com Operations Inc, 2011; (3) "Illinois Deaths and Stillbirths, 1916-1947", index, FamilySearch, (https://familysearch.org/pal:/ MM9.1.1/NQYN-3W7); (4) Obituary, Rockford Republic, Rockford, Illinois, November 19, 1926, Page 1; (5) Obituary, Daily Register and Gazette, Rockford, Illinois, April 21, 1926, Page 1.
Graveyard: (1) Burial Records, Greenwood Cemetery, Rockford, Winnebago, Illinois; (2) Obituary, Rockford Republic, Rockford, Illinois, November 19, 1926, Page 1; (3) Obituary, Daily Register and Gazette, Rockford, Illinois, April 21, 1926, Page 1. (4) Find A Grave, Memorial # 171781620.

Samuel D. Butler
Birth:
Marriage: Copy of an Old Record of a Marriage, Maine Vital Records.
Death:
Graveyard:

Lucinda O. Butler
Birth:
Death: Burial Records, Greenwood Cemetery, Rockford, Winnebago, Illinois.
Graveyard: Burial Records, Greenwood Cemetery, Rockford, Winnebago, Illinois.

Emma S. Butler
Birth:
Death: Burial Records, Greenwood Cemetery, Rockford, Winnebago, Illinois.
Graveyard: Burial Records, Greenwood Cemetery, Rockford, Winnebago, Illinois.

Linda E. Butler
Birth:
Death: Burial Records, Greenwood Cemetery, Rockford, Winnebago, Illinois.
Graveyard: Burial Records, Greenwood Cemetery, Rockford, Winnebago, Illinois.

James Dame
Birth: Obituary, Daily Register and Gazette, Rockford, Illinois, December 11, 1893, Page 5.
Marriage: "Illinois, County Marriage Records, 1800-1940," [database on-line], Lehi, UT, USA: Ancestry.com Operations Inc, 2016.
Death: Obituary, Daily Register and Gazette, Rockford, Illinois, December 11, 1893, Page 5.
Graveyard: Burial Records, Greenwood Cemetery, Rockford, Winnebago, Illinois.

Willie Dame
Birth:
Death: Burial Records, Greenwood Cemetery, Rockford, Winnebago, Illinois.
Graveyard: Burial Records, Greenwood Cemetery, Rockford, Winnebago, Illinois.

Historical Accounts: (1) 1850 United States Federal Census for Shirley, Piscataquis, Maine; (2) 1860 United States Federal Census for Chico, Butte, California, Page 30; (3) 1860 United States Federal Census for Rockford, Winnebago, Illinois, Page 2; (4) 1870 United States Federal Census for Rockford, Winnebago, Illinois, Page 17; (5) 1880 United States Federal Census for Rockford, Winnebago, Illinois, Page 40; (6) 1900 United States Federal Census for Rockford, Winnebago, Illinois, Page 11; (7) 1910 United States Federal Census for Rockford, Winnebago, Illinois, Page 34; (8) 1920 United States Federal Census for Rockford, Winnebago, Illinois, Page 1A; (9) 1872 Rockford, Illinois, City Directory, Page 99; (10) 1905 Rockford, Illinois, City Directory, Page 161.

Elbridge S. Williams
(1832 - 1862)

The fourth child of Jacob Williams, Jr. and Parmelia H. Savage was Elbridge S. who was born in 1832 in Somerset County, Maine. The exact date and place of his birth have not been found.

When the 1850 United States Federal Census was taken for Bingham, Somerset, Maine, Elbridge S. was recorded as living with his parents and working as a "farmer".

In the 1860 United States Federal Census, Elbridge S., then age twenty-eight, was recorded as living in Ward 5 of Boston, Suffolk, Massachusetts at the home of David Boothby Dyer who would become his future father-in-law. Elbridge S.'s occupation was listed as "cabinet maker".

Elbridge S. enlisted in Major Cook's Massachusetts 1st Light Artillery Battery of the Union Army in Boston on April 20, 1861. He was mustered out at Camp Clare in Baltimore, Maryland on August 3, 1861 holding the rank of Private.

On August 19, 1861, Elbridge S., age twenty-nine, was married to Julia Blanchard Dyer, age twenty-two, in Boston by Phineas Stowe, a Minister of the Gospel. Julia Blanchard, born on October 29, 1839 in Baldwin, Cumberland, Maine, was the daughter of David Boothby Dyer and Catherine Hill Bryant. Elbridge S. and Julia Blanchard did not any children during their marriage.

Shortly after their marriage Elbridge S. and Julia Blanchard moved to Rochester, Winsor, Vermont where on December 1, 1861 Elbridge S. enlisted in the Union Army once again. He joined the 2nd Battery of the Vermont Light Artillery under Captain P. E. Holcomb holding the rank of Sergeant Major. In his enlistment documents Elbridge S. was described as being 5' 5¼" tall, with blue eyes, light hair and a light complexion. His occupation at that time was listed as a "mechanic".

On, or about, March 15, 1862 the 2nd Battery of the Vermont Light Artillery was encamped on the west end of Ship Island off the Gulf Coast of Mississippi when a fierce storm hit blowing down their tents and flooding them out. As a result of his exposure to the storm Elbridge S. became seriously ill and was unable to perform his duties. On July 22, 1862, a little over four months later, at Camp Parapet in Shrewsbury, Jefferson Parrish, Louisiana Elbridge S. received a disability discharge from the Army as he was suffering from chronic "phthisis pulmonalis".

Shortly after his discharge from the Army, on August 4, 1862, Elbridge S.

boarded the ship Merchant of Providence sailing from New Orleans, Orleans Parrish, Louisiana to New York City, New York. Twenty-two days into the voyage, on August 26, 1862, Elbridge S. died from "chronic diarrhea", a side effect of his phthisis pulmonalis. He was buried at sea the following day, August 27th at 12:00 o'clock midnight.

After the death of her husband Julia Blanchard applied for her widow's pension under the Pension Act of 1862. On May 27, 1863 she was awarded a pension of $8.00 per month retroactive back to August 26, 1862.

On December 9, 1869 Julia Blanchard, age thirty, was married to her second husband George Leander Dodge, age thirty-six, in Medfield, Norfolk, Massachusetts. George Leander was born in Newport Corner, Hants, Nova Scotia, Canada in 1833 to Caleb and Mary Ann Dodge. Julia Blanchard and George Leander had one daughter during their marriage.

George Leander died in Medfield of "septicemia" on August 26, 1888 at the age of fifty-five. He was buried in Medfield at the Vine Lake Cemetery in Section 12.

When the 1905 and 1915 New York State Census' were taken, Julia Blanchard was recorded as living at 414 St. Nicholas Avenue in Manhattan, New York, New York, the home of her daughter Sadie Francis (Dodge) Horgan and her husband.

Julia Blanchard died at her daughter's home in Manhattan, on December 14, 1915 at the age of seventy-six. The cause of her death is not known. Her body was shipped back to Massachusetts where she was buried next to her second husband, George Leander, in Section 12 at the Vine Lake Cemetery in Medfield.

SOURCES:

Elbridge S. Williams
Birth:
Death: (1) Letter from Stephen C. Sprague, Master of the Ship Merchant of Providence, dated September 17, 1862; (2) Affidavit from Oliver F. Bogue given on September 16, 1862 before Ezia June, Justice of the Peace, at Brandon, Rutland, Vermont.
Graveyard: Affidavit from Oliver F. Bogue given on September 16, 1862 before Ezia June, Justice of the Peace, at Brandon, Rutland, Vermont.

Julia Blanchard Dyer
Birth: "New York, New York City Municipal Deaths, 1795-1949," database, FamilySearch, (https://
familysearch.org/ark:/61903/1:1:2WHR-K2L)
Marriage: (1) Marriage Certificate, Commonwealth of Massachusetts, www. Fold3.com; (2) Massachusetts Vital
Records, 1840-1911, Volume 146, Page 75, New England Historic Genealogical Society, Boston, Massachusetts;
(3) Massachusetts, Town and Vital Records, 1620-1968, Marriages registered in the City of Boston for the year
1861.
Death: (1) "New York, New York, Death Index, 1862-1948," (database on-line). Provo, UT, USA: Ancestry.com
Operations, Inc., 2014; (2) "New York, New York City Municipal Deaths, 1795-1949," database, FamilySearch,
(https://familysearch.org/ark:/61903/1:1:2WHR-K2L); (3) Record of Pensioner Dropped, Department of the
Interior, Bureau of Pensions, Certificate 2688; www.Fold3.com.
Graveyard: Find A Grave, Memorial #90969743.

George Leander Dodge
Birth:
Marriage: Massachusetts Vital Records, 1840-1911, New England Historic Genealogical Society, Boston,
Massachusetts (George Leander Dodge).
Death: "Massachusetts, Death Records, 1841-1915", [database on-line], Provo, UT, USA: Ancestry.com
Operations, Inc., 2013.
Graveyard: Find A Grave, Memorial #90969656.

Historical Accounts: (1) 1850 United States Federal Census for Bingham, Somerset, Maine; (2) 1855
Massachusetts State Census for Charlestown Ward, Middlesex, Massachusetts; (3) 1860 United States Federal
Census for Ward 5, Boston, Suffolk, Massachusetts, Page 235; (4) 1880 United States Federal Census for
Farmington, Franklin, Maine, Page 21; (5) 1905 New York State Census for Manhattan, New York, New York,
Page 4; (6) 1915 New York State Census for New York City, New York, New York, Page 5; (7) Company
Muster-in Roll, Cook's Company, Light Artillery, Massachusetts, www.Fold3.com; (8) Company Muster-out Roll,
Cook's Company, Light Artillery, Massachusetts; www.Fold3.com; (9) U. S., Civil War Soldier Records and
Profiles, 1861-1865, (database on-line). Provo, UT, USA: Ancestry.com Operations, Inc., 2009; (10) Battery
Descriptive Book, 2nd Battery, Vermont Light, Artillery; (11) Certificate of Disability for Discharge, Army of the
United States, www.Fold3.com; (12) Mrs. Julia Williams Pension Case File of Approved Applications of Widows
and Other Dependents of Civil War Veterans; www.Fold3.com.

Elsie Atwood Williams
(1835 - 1905)

Elsie Atwood was the fifth child of Jacob Williams, Jr. and his wife, Parmelia H. Savage. She was born on March 27, 1835 in Bingham, Somerset, Maine.

On May 10, 1856, at the age of twenty-two, Elsie Atwood was married to Allen Hallett II, age twenty-three, in Boston, Suffolk, Massachusetts by Reverend S. Streeter of Boston. Allen, born on May 29, 1829 in Hyannis, Barnstable, Massachusetts, was the son of Allen Hallett and Belinda Chase.

Elsie Atwood and Allen had a family of four children.

Melintha Lewis	b. October 9, 1859	d. June 2, 1932
Effie Clyde	b. September 7, 1861	d. October 3, 1929
Frederick Allen	b. January 2, 1866	d. May 4, 1933
Ernest Dean	b. March 27, 1872	d. February 18, 1937

In June of 1863 Allen registered for the United States Civil War Draft in the First Congressional District of the State of Massachusetts. In that document his occupation was listed as "mariner".

The 1865 Massachusetts State Census recorded Elsie Atwood, Allen and their first two children, Melintha Lewis and Effie Clyde, as living in Barnstable, Barnstable County, Massachusetts. Allen's occupation was again listed as "mariner".

At the time of the 1870 and 1880 United States Federal Census', Elsie Atwood, Allen and their children were listed as still living in Barnstable. In those censuses Allen's occupation was recorded as "seaman/sailor".

On August 22, 1895 Allen, then age sixty-six, died of "heart disease" in Barnstable. He was buried in the Oak Grove Cemetery in Hyannis.

When the 1900 United States Federal Census was taken, Elsie Atwood was living with her daughter Melintha (Hallett) Snow and her children on Winter Street in Hyannis.

On February 18, 1905, Elsie Atwood died in Hyannis at the age of sixty-nine. Her cause of death was listed as "pneumonia". She was buried with her husband at the Oak Grove Cemetery in Hyannis on February 22, 1905.

SOURCES:

Elsie Atwood Williams
Birth: "Massachusetts, Death Records, 1841-1915", [database on-line], Provo, UT, USA: Ancestry.com Operations, Inc., 2013.
Death: "Massachusetts, Death Records, 1841-1915", [database on-line], Provo, UT, USA: Ancestry.com Operations, Inc., 2013.
Graveyard: (1) "Massachusetts, Death Records, 1841-1915", [database on-line], Provo, UT, USA: Ancestry.com Operations, Inc., 2013; (2) Find A Grave, Memorial #124720871.

Allen Hallett II
Birth:
Marriage: (1) "Massachusetts, Town and Vital Records, 1620-1988", [database on-line], Provo, UT, USA: Ancestry.com Operations, Inc., 2011, Marriages registered in the City of Boston for the year 1856; (2) "Massachusetts Vital Records, 1840-1915," New England Historic Genealogical Society, Boston, Massachusetts.
Death: "Massachusetts, Death Records, 1841-1915", [database on-line], Provo, UT, USA: Ancestry.com Operations, Inc., 2013.
Graveyard: Find A Grave, Memorial #123733788.

Historical Accounts: (1) 1865 Massachusetts State Census for Barnstable, Barnstable, Massachusetts; (2) 1870 United States Federal Census for Barnstable, Barnstable, Massachusetts, Page 106; (3) 1880 United States Federal Census for Barnstable, Barnstable, Massachusetts, Page 25; (4) 1900 United States Federal Census for Hyannis Village, Barnstable, Massachusetts, Page 18; (5) "U. S. Civil War Draft Registration Records, 1863-1865", [database on-line]. Provo, UT, USA: Ancestry.com Operations Inc, 2010

Leonard H. Williams
(1840 - 1914)

Leonard H., born on July 12, 1840 in Concord, Somerset, Maine, was the seventh child of Jacob Williams, Jr. and his wife, Parmelia H. Savage.

At the age of nineteen, Leonard H. married Sarah Jennie Ladd, age twenty, in Lewiston, Androscoggin, Maine on December 6, 1859. The daughter of John Ladd and Mary A. Fossett, Sarah Jennie (also known as Jennie S.) was born in Hallowell, Kennebec, Maine on February 20, 1839.

During their marriage Leonard H. and Sarah Jennie had one child.

Minnie Maretta   b. *May 26, 1868*   d. *April 19, 1871*

In June of 1863 Leonard H. registered for the United States Civil War Draft in the State of New Hampshire.

The only child of Leonard H. and Sarah Jennie, Minnie Maretta, died at 9 Pembroke Street in Boston on April 19, 1871 when she was just two years, ten months and twenty-four days old. Her cause of death was listed as "influenza of the brain and lungs". She was buried at Forest Hills Cemetery in Boston in Section 25, Grave 978, Field of Manoah.

When the 1880 United States Federal Census and the 1880 Boston City Directory were published, Leonard H. and Sarah Jennie were recorded as living at 58 Forrest Street in Boston, Suffolk, Massachusetts. In the 1880 census Leonard H.'s occupation was listed as "clerk" and in the Boston City Directory he was listed as working as a "bartender at Young's Hotel".

Leonard H. and Sarah Jennie had moved to 21 Savin Street in Boston by the time the 1900 United States Federal Census was taken and the 1900 Boston City Directory was published. That census document recorded Leonard H. had a job as a "foreman" and the Boston City Directory listed Leonard H. as working as a "bartender at the Hotel Thorndike".

The 1910 United States Federal Census and the 1911 Boston City Directory recorded that Leonard H. and Sarah Jennie had moved again and were living at 305 Warren Street in Boston. In the 1910 census Leonard H. listed as working as a "salesman of retail liquors".

On January 8, 1911 Sarah Jennie died at home in Boston of "lobar pneumonia". She was seventy-one years old at the time of her death. Sarah Jennie was buried in Section 25, Grave 978, Field of Manoah at Forest Hills Cemetery in Boston along with her daughter.

Two years later on the anniversary of Sarah Jennie's death, January 8, 1913, Leonard H. placed an "In Memoriam" notice in the Boston Post in loving remembrance of his wife.

Leonard H. died at 78 Montgomery Street in Boston of "carcinoma of the stomach" on September 14, 1914 at the age of seventy-four. He was buried with his wife and daughter in Boston at Forest Hills Cemetery in Section 25, Grave 978, Field of Manoah.

SOURCES:

Leonard H. Williams
Birth: "Massachusetts, Death Records, 1841-1915," images, FamilySearch, (https://familysearch.org/ark:/61903/3:1: S3HY-Y7D).
Death: (1) "Massachusetts, Death Records, 1841-1915," images, FamilySearch, (https://familysearch.org/ark:/61903/3:1: S3HY-Y7D); (2) Death Notice, Boston Journal, Boston, Massachusetts, Wednesday, September 16, 1914, Page 2.
Graveyard: Burial Records, Forest Hills Cemetery, Boston, Massachusetts.

Sarah Jennie Ladd
Birth: (1) Record of Birth, Maine Vital Records; (2) "Maine Birth and Christenings, 1739-1900," database, FamilySearch, (https://familysearch.orgark:/61903/1:1:F4HL-4ZD).
Marriage: "Maine, Marriages, 1771-1907," database, FamilySearch, (https://familysearch.org/ark:/61903/1:1: F4F1-M6P)
Death: "Massachusetts, Death Records, 1841-1915," images, FamilySearch (https://familysearch.org/ark:/61903/3:1: S3HT-62H7-FMK).
Graveyard: Burial Records, Forest Hills Cemetery, Boston, Massachusetts.

Minnie Maretta Williams
Birth: (1) "Massachusetts, State Vital Records, 1841-1920," database with images, FamilySearch, (https://familysearch.org/ark/61903/1.1.:/23BQ-V3W); (2) "Massachusetts Births, 1841-1915," database with images, FamilySearch, (https://familysearch.org/ark:/61903/1:1:FXZJ-PGQ), Births registered in the City of Boston for the Year 1868.
Death: "Massachusetts, Death and Burials, 1795-1910," database, FamilySearch, (https://familysearch.org/ark:/61903 /1:1: FHZW-PZP), Deaths in Boston.
Graveyard: (1) Burial Records, Forest Hills Cemetery, Boston, Massachusetts; (2) Massachusetts, Death and Burials, 1795-1910," database, FamilySearch, (https://familysearch.org/ ark:/61903 /1:1: FHZW-PZP), Deaths in Boston.

Historical Accounts: (1) 1880 United States Federal Census for Boston, Suffolk, Massachusetts, Page 16; (2) 1900 United States Federal Census for Boston, Suffolk, Massachusetts, Page 16; (3) 1910 United States Federal Census for Boston, Suffolk, Massachusetts, Page 4B; (4) "U. S. Civil War Draft Registration Records, 1863-1865", [database on-line]. Provo, UT, USA: Ancestry.com Operations Inc, 2010; (5) In Memoriam, Boston Post, Boston Massachusetts, Wednesday, January 8, 1913, Page 13; (6) 1880 Boston, Massachusetts, City Directory, Page 1019; (7) 1900 Boston, Massachusetts, City Directory, Page 1724; (7) 1911 Boston, Massachusetts, City Directory, Page 1983.

Randall Benjamin Williams
(1844 - 1926)

The eighth child of Jacob Williams, Jr. and his wife, Parmelia H. Savage, was Randall Benjamin (also known as Benjamin Randall). He was born on May 20, 1844 in Bingham, Somerset, Maine.

The 1860 United States Federal Census recorded Randall Benjamin living in Athens, Somerset, Maine with his mother and her second husband John Kinsman and working as a "domestic".

Randall Benjamin was mustered in as a Private into Company K, 10th Regiment Maine Infantry of the Union Army at Athens on October 4, 1861. After serving for nineteen months he was mustered out on May 7, 1863. On April 7, 1865, Randall Benjamin re-enlisted in Union Army for one year joining Company B, 8th Regiment Maine Volunteer Infantry holding the rank of Private. In his re-enlistment papers he was described as being 5′ 11″ tall with blue eyes, brown hair and a fair complexion. Randall Benjamin was discharged on April 6, 1866.

**Civil War veteran Randall Benjamin Williams, from Maine, poses with all his Civil War memorabilia for a 1924 reunion photograph.
He was 80 years old at the time.**
(From the John Mead Gould papers, 1841-1944, David M. Rubenstein Rare Book & Manuscript Library, Duke University)

Sometime between 1862 and 1866 Randall Benjamin was married to Maretta L. Eaton. The exact date and place of their marriage has not been found. Maretta L., the daughter of Timothy Eaton and Lydia Holmes, was born in Athens, Somerset, Maine on September 16, 1846.

Randall Benjamin and Maretta L. had two children during their marriage.

Stella H.	*b. May 1867*	*d. August 29, 1888*
Inez May	b. January 6, 1874	d. September 30, 1957

When the 1870 United States Federal Census was taken, Randall Benjamin was living in a city hotel in Boston, Suffolk, Massachusetts and working as a "steam engineer".

In the 1880 United States Federal Census, Randall Benjamin, Maretta L. and their children were recorded as living in Brewer, Penobscot, Maine. Randall Benjamin's occupation was listed as "laborer".

The 1885, 1890, and 1891 Bangor City Directories listed Maretta L. as being the "proprietor" of the Williams Boarding House on Columbia Street in Bangor, Penobscot, Maine.

On August 29, 1888 Stella H., the first child born to Randall Benjamin and Maretta L. died at the age of twenty-one a spinster and without issue. The exact place and cause of her death has not been found. She was buried in the Oak Hill Cemetery in Brewer.

Gravestone for Stella H. Williams
(Photograph Courtesy of Dale & Patti Mower)

When the 1900 United States Federal Census was taken and the 1901 Bangor City Directory was published Randall Benjamin and Maretta L. were recorded as living at 84 Columbia Street in Bangor, with Randall Benjamin working as a "pipe fitter" and Maretta L. still managing the Williams Boarding House.

Sometime after 1901, Randall Benjamin and Maretta L. moved back to Brewer where they were recorded living at 49 Holyoke Street in the 1910 United States Federal Census. Randall Benjamin, then age sixty-five, was listed as working as a "steam fitter".

On February 2, 1914, Maretta L. died at home in Brewer at the age of sixty-six. Her cause of death was recorded as "malignant disease of the liver and inner bile ducts". She was buried in the Oak Hill Cemetery in Brewer.

When the 1920 United States Federal Census was taken Randall Benjamin, the age seventy-five, was living with his daughter, Inez May (Williams) Barter, and her family in Brewer.

Randall Benjamin outlived his wife by over twelve years, passing away in Brewer at the age of eighty-two on July 26, 1926. The cause of his death is not known. Private funeral services for Randall Benjamin were held at 2:00 P.M. on Wednesday, July 28th in Brewer at his home at 49 Holyoke Street. He was buried in his family plot in Brewer at the Oak Hill Cemetery.

Gravestone for Randall Benjamin Williams and Maretta L. Eaton
(Photograph Courtesy of Dale & Patti Mower)

SOURCES:

Randall Benjamin Williams
Birth: (1) "Maine, Civil War Enlistment Papers, 1862-1865," database with images, FamilySearch, (https://familysearch.org/ark:/61903/1:1: Q2QB-J2ZD); (2) "Maine, Veterans Cemetery Records, 1676-1918," database with images, FamilySearch, (https://familysearch.org/ark:/61903/1:1:KXQZ-TH2); (3) Gravestone.
Death: (1) "Maine, Veterans Cemetery Records, 1676-1918," database with images, FamilySearch, (https://familysearch.org/ark:/61903/1:1:KXQZ-TH2); (2) Death Notice, Bangor Daily News, Bangor, Maine, Tuesday, July 27, 1926, Page 2; (3) Obituary, Bangor Daily News, Bangor, Maine, Tuesday, July 27, 1926, Page 5; (4) Civil War Pensions Index, Fold3.com; (5) Gravestone.
Graveyard: (1) Oak Hill Cemetery records, City of Brewer, Maine; (2) "Maine, Veterans Cemetery Records, 1676-1918," database with images, FamilySearch, (https://familysearch.org/ark:/61903/1:1:KXQZ-TH2); (3) Find A Grave, Memorial #129733891.

Maretta L. Eaton
Birth:
Marriage:
Death: (1) Record of a Death, Maine Vital Records; (2) 1914 Brewer Maine City Directory, Deaths in Brewer.
Graveyard: (1) Oak Hill Cemetery records, City of Brewer, Maine; (2) Find A Grave, Memorial #129734007.

Stella H. Williams
Birth:
Death: Gravestone.
Graveyard: (1) Oak Hill Cemetery records, City of Brewer, Maine; (2) Find A Grave, Memorial #129734023.

Historical Accounts: (1) 1870 United States Federal Census for Boston, Suffolk, Massachusetts, Page 152; (2) 1880 United States Federal Census for Brewer, Penobscot, Maine, Page 36; (3) 1900 United States Federal Census for Bangor, Penobscot, Maine, Page 10; (4) 1910 United States Federal Census for Brewer, Penobscot, Maine, Page 11B; (5) 1920 United States Federal Census for Brewer, Penobscot, Maine, Page 5A; (6) "U. S., Civil War Soldier Records and Profiles, 1861-1865," (database on-line). Provo, UT, USA: Ancestry.com Operations, Inc., 2009; (7) 1890 United States Federal Census Special Schedule, Surviving Soldiers, Sailors, and Marines, and Widows, Etc., Bangor, Penobscot, Maine; (8) Annual Report of the Adjutant General of the State of Maine for the year ending December 31, 1863, Page 366; (9) Index to Compiled Service Records of Volunteer Union Soldiers who served in Organizations from the State of Maine; (10) 1885 Bangor Maine City Directory, Page 339; (11) 1890 Bangor Maine City Directory, Page 246; (12) 1891 Bangor Maine City Directory, Page 256; (13) 1901 Bangor Maine City Directory, Page 267; (14) 1926 Bangor Maine City Directory, Page 532.

Adelaide Pamelia Williams
(1847 - 1932)

Adelaide Pamelia, the ninth child of Jacob Williams, Jr. and his wife Parmelia H. Savage, was born on November 7, 1847 in Bingham, Somerset, Maine.

Sometime before 1870, Adelaide Pamelia was married to William F. Shattuck. William F., born in Solon, Somerset, Maine on March 8, 1841, was the son of Lovell Shattuck and Sarah Wyman.

Adelaide Pamelia and William L. had a family of four children.

Ilione L.	b. January 1870	d.
Leon B.	*b. August 23, 1874*	*d. August 28, 1875*
Florence	*b. April 1879*	*d. August 17, 1883*
William Houghton	b. September 26, 1885	d. August 16, 1959

In the 1870 United States Federal Census, Adelaide Pamelia, William F. and their first child were recorded as living in Solon with William L. listed as working as a "blacksmith".

The second child of Adelaide Pamelia and William F., Leon B., died on August 28, 1875 at the age of one year and five days. The place and cause of his death are not known. He was buried in the Southside Cemetery in Skowhegan, Somerset, Maine in Lot 13.

Gravestone for Leon B. Shattuck, front side (left) and back side (right)
(Photographs Courtesy of Gail Kelly)

By the time the 1880 United States Federal Census was taken William F. was still working as a "blacksmith", but the family had moved and was living in Boston, Suffolk, Massachusetts.

Florence, the third child of Adelaide Pamelia and William F., died of "membranous croup" at 10 Auburn Street in Boston on August 17, 1883 at the age of four years and five months. Her body was transferred back to Maine where she was buried next to her brother Leon B. in Lot 13 at the Southside Cemetery in Skowhegan.

On January 14, 1892, William F. died at the age of fifty in Somerville, Middlesex, Massachusetts. His cause of death was listed as "nephritis cystitis". His remains were transferred to the Southside Cemetery in Skowhegan where he was buried in Lot 13 with his children. William F., a United States Civil War veteran, served as a Private in Company D of the 14th Maine Infantry of the Union Army from March 26, 1862 to April 8, 1865 and therefore was entitled to a military headstone.

Gravestone for William F. Shattuck
(Photograph Courtesy of Gail Kelly)

The 1900 United States Federal Census recorded that Adelaide Pamelia had moved back to Somerset County, Maine where she was living in Skowhegan and working as a "dressmaker".

As the widow of William F., Adelaide Pamelia was approved, on April 19, 1908, to receive his Army pension of $12 per month as allowed under the Pension Act of 1862.

In the 1910, 1920 and 1930 United States Federal Census', Adelaide Pamelia was still living in Skowhegan, Somerset, Maine and working as a "dressmaker". According to the 1929, 1931 and 1932 Skowhegan City Directories she was living at 54 Water Street.

Adelaide Pamelia died at the age of eighty-five at the home of Mr. and Mrs. Charles Currier in Skowhegan on December 18, 1932 after an illness several weeks. The exact cause of her death is not known at this time. Funeral services for Adelaide Pamelia were held at the Currier home at 2:00 P.M. on Tuesday December 20th with Reverend George Merriam officiating. She was also buried in Lot 13 at the Southside Cemetery in Skowhegan.

Headstone for Adelaide Pamelia Williams
(Photograph Courtesy of Gail Kelly)

SOURCES:

Adelaide Pamelia Williams
Birth: Burial Records, Southside Cemetery, Skowhegan, Somerset, Maine, Cemeteryfind.com.
Death: (1) Burial Records, Southside Cemetery, Skowhegan, Somerset, Maine, Cemeteryfind.com; (2) Obituary, Lewiston Daily Sun, Lewiston, Maine, December 19, 1932, Page 9; (3) Obituary, Waterville Morning Sentinel, Waterville, Maine, Monday, December 19, 1932, Page 5.
Graveyard: (1) Burial Records, Southside Cemetery, Skowhegan, Somerset, Maine, Cemeteryfind.com; (2) Find A Grave, Memorial #136446037.

William F. Shattuck
Birth: (1) Original Record of Maine Towns & Cities, Town of Solon, Page 32, Picton Press, Rockland Maine 2005; (2) "Maine, Births and Christenings, 1739-1900," database, FamilySearch, (https://family search.org/ark:/61903/1.1/FW1H-VBM).
Marriage:
Death: (1) "Massachusetts, Death Records, 1841-1915", [database on-line], Provo, UT, USA: Ancestry.com Operations, Inc., 2013, Deaths Registered in the City of Somerville for the Year 1892, Page 352; (2) Burial Records, Southside Cemetery, Skowhegan, Somerset, Maine, Cemeteryfind.com.
Graveyard: (1) Burial Records, Southside Cemetery, Skowhegan, Somerset, Maine, Cemeteryfind.com; (2) Find A Grave, Memorial #13644035.

Leon B. Shattuck
Birth: Burial Records, Southside Cemetery, Skowhegan, Somerset, Maine, Cemeteryfind.com.
Death: Burial Records, Southside Cemetery, Skowhegan, Somerset, Maine, Cemeteryfind.com.
Graveyard: (1) Burial Records, Southside Cemetery, Skowhegan, Somerset, Maine, Cemeteryfind.com; (2) Find A Grave, Memorial #136446037.

Florence Shattuck
Birth: Burial Records, Southside Cemetery, Skowhegan, Somerset, Maine, Cemeteryfind.com.
Death: (1) "Massachusetts, Death Records, 1841-1915", [database on-line], Provo, UT, USA: Ancestry.com Operations, Inc., 2013, Deaths Registered in the City of Boston for the Year 1883, Page 231; (2) Burial Records, Southside Cemetery, Skowhegan, Somerset, Maine, Cemeteryfind.com.
Graveyard: Burial Records, Southside Cemetery, Skowhegan, Somerset, Maine, Cemeteryfind.com.

Historical Accounts: (1) 1870 United States Federal Census for Solon, Somerset, Maine, Page 25; (2) 1880 United States Federal Census for Boston, Suffolk, Massachusetts, Page 33; (3) 1900 United States Federal Census for Skowhegan, Somerset, Maine, Page 18; (4) 1910 United States Federal Census for Skowhegan, Somerset, Maine, Page 14B; (5) 1920 United States Federal Census for Skowhegan, Somerset, Maine, Page 9B; (6) 1930 United States Federal Census for Skowhegan, Somerset, Maine, Page 12A; (7) 1929 City Directory for Skowhegan, Somerset, Maine, Page 309; (8) 1931 City Directory for Skowhegan, Somerset, Maine, Page 563; (9) 1932 City Directory for Skowhegan, Somerset, Maine, Page 558, (10) "U. S., Civil War Soldier Records and Profiles, 1861-1865," (database on-line), Provo, UT, USA: Ancestry.com Operations, Inc., 2009: (11) "United States Veterans Administration Pension Payment Cards, 1907-1933," database with images, FamilySearch, (https://familysearch.org/ark:/61903/1:1:2MKR-RLJ).

Laura Williams
(1830 - 1912)

The second child of Chandler Nason Williams and Rebecca Hunnewell was Laura. She was born on February 10, 1830 in Embden, Somerset, Maine.

Laura, at the age of twenty-two, was married to William Clark, also age twenty-two, on September 16, 1852 in Bingham, Somerset, Maine by Reverend Sydney Turner. William was born on July 14, 1830 to Joseph Clark and Sarah Hunt in Moscow, Somerset, Maine.

Laura and William had six children together.

Benjamin S.	b. July 17, 1853	d. July 20, 1923
Nason C.	b. April 13, 1858	d. November 16, 1891
Carrie (a twin)	*b. February 1860*	*d. October 18, 1863*
Carroll (a twin)	b. February 1860	d. 1935
Willie E.	*b. July 1862*	*d. October 19, 1863*
Sarah	b. 1865	d. 1943

In the 1860 United States Federal Census Laura, William and their first four children were recorded as living in Moscow. William's occupation was listed as "farmer".

William registered for the United States Civil War Draft as a resident of the Maine 3rd Congressional District in June of 1863.

Two of Laura and William's children died in 1863 at a young age within one day of each other. Carrie was three years eight months old when she died on October 18th and Willie E. was sixteen months old when he died on October 19th. The causes of their deaths are not known. They were both buried in their grandfather Joseph Clark's plot in the Baker Cemetery (also known as the Sugartown Cemetery) in Moscow.

Laura, William and their children were still living and farming in Moscow at the time of the 1870 United States Federal Census.

By the time the 1880 United States Federal Census was taken, Laura, William and their family had moved to Concord, Somerset, Maine where William was still "farming".

When the 1900 United States Federal Census was taken Laura and William had once again moved. At that time, they were recorded as were living on North Main Street in Solon, Somerset. Maine with William's occupation again listed as "farmer"

William died in Solon on September 29, 1902 at the age of seventy-two. His cause of death was recorded as "aortic stenosis". William was buried in his family plot at the Village Cemetery in Solon.

Sometime after William's death, Laura moved to Anson, Somerset, Maine where in the 1910 United States Federal Census she was recorded as living with her daughter, Sarah (Clark) Booker, and her family.

Laura died at the age of eighty-two on August 11, 1912 in Anson. Her cause of death was listed as "intestinal obstruction, most likely cancer'. She was buried in Solon in the family plot at the Village Cemetery alongside her late husband William.

Gravestone for Carrie Clark and Willie E. Clark
(Photograph Courtesy of Francine York)

Gravestone for Laura Williams and William Clark
(Photograph from the Collection of Jeffrey Nelson Williams and Jacqueline Pon Williams)

SOURCES:

Laura Williams
Birth: (1) Record of a Death, Maine Vital Records; (2) Gravestone.
Death: (1) Record of a Death, Maine Vital Records; (2) Gravestone.
Graveyard: Find A Grave, Memorial #140895955.

William Clark
Birth: (1) Record of a Death, Maine Vital Records; (2) Gravestone.
Marriage: Original Record of Maine Towns & Cities, Town of Bingham, Page 165, Picton Press, Rockland Maine, Copyright 2005.
Death: (1) Record of a Death, Maine Vital Records; (2) Gravestone.
Graveyard: Find A Grave, Memorial #140895956.

Carrie Clark
Birth:
Death: (1) Record of a Death, Maine Vital Records; (2) "Maine, Deaths and Burials, 1841-1910," database, FamilySearch, (https://family search.org/ark:/61903/1.1: F48J-647); (3) Gravestone.
Graveyard: (1) "Maine Old Cemetery Association Special Publication Number 12, Edition No. 1: Series 1, 2 and 3", Page 1256, Picton Press, Rockland, Maine, Copyright 2006; (2) "Sugartown Cemetery", complied by Nancy Hamlin Davis and Ruth Hamlin, Record 60, Old Canada Road Historical Society.

Willie E. Clark
Birth:
Death: (1) Record of a Death, Maine Vital Records; (2) Gravestone.
Graveyard: (1) "Maine Old Cemetery Association Special Publication Number 12, Edition No. 1: Series 1, 2 and 3", Page 1256, Picton Press, Rockland, Maine, Copyright 2006; (2) "Sugartown Cemetery", complied by Nancy Hamlin Davis and Ruth Hamlin, Record 61, Old Canada Road Historical Society.

Historical Accounts: (1) 1860 United States Federal Census for Moscow, Somerset, Maine, Page 48; (2) 1870 United States Federal Census for Moscow, Somerset, Maine, Page 3; (3) 1880 United States Federal Census for Concord, Somerset, Maine, Page 8; (4) 1900 United States Federal Census for Solon, Somerset, Maine, Page 2; (5) 1910 United States Federal Census for Anson, Somerset, Maine, Page 22A; (6) "U. S. Civil War Draft Registration Records, 1863-1865 ", [database on-line]. Provo, UT, USA: Ancestry.com Operations Inc, 2010, Page 82.

Nason Chandler Williams
(1834 - 1922)

Nason Chandler was the third child born to Chandler Nason Williams and Rebecca Hunnewell. He was born on January 20, 1834 in Embden, Somerset, Maine.

The 1850 United States Federal Census, taken in August of that year, recorded Nason Chandler then age sixteen as living with his parents in Moscow, Somerset, Maine and working as a "farmer".

Shortly after the 1850 census was taken Nason Chandler left home and moved to Boston, Suffolk, Massachusetts where he took a job as a "clerk" in a shipyard.

In 1855 Nason Chandler moved west to California sailing by way of the Isthmus of Panama to San Francisco. From there he made his way to Amador County where in 1866 he was recorded in the California Voter Register as living in Township No. 3.

When the 1870 United States Federal Census was taken, Nason Chandler was still living Township No. 3 in Amador County where he was working as a "miner".

Sometime in 1871 Nason Chandler acquired a "ranch" fourteen miles east of Jackson, Amador, California on the Pine Grove and Antelope toll road.

On May 13, 1874, at the age of forty, Nason Chandler was married to Rosella Worley, age eighteen, in Volcano, Amador, California by L. McLaine, a Justice of the Peace. Jasper Babenek and W. Q. Mason, both from Volcano, served as witnesses to the marriage. Rosella, the daughter of Stephen and Louisiana Worley, was born in Jackson on May 7, 1856.

Nason Chandler and Rosella did not have any children of their own, but they did adopt a daughter.

Hattie Irene (adopted)   b. May 21, 1879   d. February 13, 1937

In the 1890, 1892 and 1896 California Voter Registers, Nason Chandler was described as being 5' 8½" tall with a dark complexion, dark eyes and black hair. During those years Nason Chandler was recorded as working as a "hotel keeper".

The 1900 United States Federal Census' recorded Nason Chandler, Rosella and their adopted daughter Hattie Irene as still living in Township No. 3 and listed Nason Chandler's occupation as "farmer"

On Friday December 7, 1906 the Amador Ledger published a notification that the "U. S. had transferred 160 acres to Nason C. Williams for agricultural land".

Illustration of Nason Chandler Williams' Property
(History of Amador County, California, Thomson & West, 1881)

In the 1910 and 1920 United States Federal Census' Nason Chandler and Rosella were still farming and living in Township No. 3.

Nason Chandler died at the age of eighty-eight on May 2, 1922. The place and cause of his death have not been found. He was buried in Pine Grove Cemetery at Pine Grove, Amador, California.

When the 1930 and 1940 United States Federal Census' were taken, Rosella was living by herself in Township No. 3 and recorded as "head of the house".

Rosella died on August 22, 1940, shortly after the 1940 census was taken. The cause and place of her death are also not known. She was buried in the Pine Grove Cemetery at Pine Grove with her husband.

Gravestone for Nason Chandler Williams and Rosella Worley
(Photograph Courtesy of Marilyn Diaz)

SOURCES:

Nason Chandler Williams
Birth: (1) "California, Pioneer and Immigrant Files, 1790-1950," [database on-line], Provo, UT, USA: Ancestry.com Operations, Inc., 2011; (2) Pine Grove Cemetery Records, Amador County Archives; (3) Gravestone.
Death: (1) Pine Grove Cemetery Records, Amador County Archives; (2) Gravestone.
Graveyard: (1) Pine Grove Cemetery Records, Amador County Archives; (2) Find A Grave, Memorial #22734329.

Rosella Worley
Birth: (1) "California, Death Index, 1940-1997," [database on-line], Provo, UT, USA: Ancestry.com Operations Inc, 2000; (2) Pine Grove Cemetery Records, Amador County Archives; (3) Gravestone.
Marriage: (1) "California County Marriages, 1843-1918," database, FamilySearch, (https://familysearch.org/ark: /61903/1:1:Q24W-LY71); (2) "California, County Birth, Marriage, and Death Records, 1849-1980," [database on-line], Provo, UT, USA: Ancestry.com Operations Inc, 2017; (3) Western States Marriage Record Index, ID #276462; (4) "California, Pioneer and Immigrant Files, 1790-1950," [database on-line], Provo, UT, USA: Ancestry.com Operations, Inc., 2011.
Death: (1) "California, Death Index, 1940-1997," [database on-line], Provo, UT, USA: Ancestry.com Operations Inc, 2000; (2) Pine Grove Cemetery Records, Amador County Archives; (3) Gravestone.
Graveyard: (1) Pine Grove Cemetery Records, Amador County Archives; (2) Find A Grave, Memorial #22734329.

Historical Accounts: (1) 1850 United States Federal Census for Moscow, Somerset, Maine; (2) 1870 United States Federal Census for Township No. 3, Amador, California, Page 9; (3) 1900 United States Federal Census for Township No. 3, Amador, California, Page 8; (4) 1910 United States Federal Census for Township No. 3, Amador, California, Page 4B; (5) 1920 United States Federal Census for Township No. 3, Amador, California, Page 2A; (6) 1930 United States Federal Census for Township No. 3, Amador, California, Page 2A; (7) 1940 United States Federal Census for Township No. 3, Amador, California, Page 3A; (8) 1890 California Voter Register for Amador County, "California, Voter Registers, 1866-1898," [database on-line], Provo, UT, USA: Ancestry.com Operations, Inc., 2011; (9) 1892 California Voter Register for Amador County, "California, Voter Registers, 1866-1898," [database on-line], Provo, UT, USA: Ancestry.com Operations, Inc., 2011; (10) 1898 California Voter Register for Amador County, "California, Voter Registers, 1866-1898," [database on-line], Provo, UT, USA: Ancestry.com Operations, Inc., 2011; (11) History of Amador County California with Illustrations and Biographical Sketches, Thompson & West, Oakland, Cal., 1881, Page 324; (12) Amador Ledger, Friday, December 7, 1906, Page 3.

Milo Reed Williams
(1838 - 1913)

The fifth child of Chandler Nason Williams and Rebecca Hunnewell, Milo Reed, was born on February 21, 1838 in Embden, Somerset, Maine.

In the 1860 United States Federal Census Milo Reed was recorded as living on his father's farm in Moscow, Somerset, Maine and working as a "farm laborer".

On March 24, 1862, at the age of twenty-four, Milo Reed and Caroline Matilda Henderson, age twenty-two, filed their intentions to marry with the Town Clerk of Moscow. The exact date and place of their subsequent marriage has not been found. Caroline Matilda, a school teacher by profession, was the daughter of Joseph Henderson and Mary Wood Tinkham. She was born in February 1840 in Anson, Somerset, Maine. The exact day of her birth is not known.

Milo Reed and Caroline Matilda had a family of six children.

Cora Rebecca*	b. September 7, 1861	d. April 10, 1934
Mary Wood	b. February 28, 1863	d. December 18, 1940
Chandler Nason	b. August 1868	d. May 26, 1932
Joseph Reed	b. August 1873	d. August 2, 1916
Charles Frank	b. May 1877	d.
Caroline Matilda	b. November 11, 1878	d. March 13, 1967

*Note: From the records found it appears that the first child of Milo Reed and Caroline Matilda, Cora Rebecca, was born prior to their being married.

Sometime after their marriage, and before the birth of their second child Mary Wood on February 28, 1863, Milo Reed and Caroline Matilda moved from Maine and lived in the state of Illinois at least until after the birth of Chandler Nason, their third child, in August of 1868.

By the time the 1870 United States Federal Census was taken Milo Reed, Caroline Matilda and their first three children had moved again and were living in Washington Township, Washington, Kansas. Milo Reed's occupation was listed as "farmer" in that census.

When the 1880 United States Federal Census was taken Milo Reed, Caroline Matilda and their children had moved again and were then living in Clear Fork, Marshall, Kansas where Milo Reed was working as a "laborer".

The Great Register for Tulare County, California recorded Milo Reed, as of October 4, 1884, living in the town of Tulare and working as a "blacksmith".

By the time the 1890 Great Register for Tulare County was published Milo Reed was registered as living and working as a "farmer" in Yokohl. And the 1894 Great Register for Tulare County Milo Reed was again listed as living in the town of Tulare. In that document he was described as fifty-four years old, 5' 7½" tall with a dark complexion, brown eyes and dark hair.

Milo Reed was registered in the 1894 and 1896 the Great Register's for Kern County, California as a "miner" and living in the mining town of Goler. He was described in those registers as being 5' 9 to 9½" tall with brown eyes, grey hair and a dark complexion.

At the time of the 1900 and 1910 United States Federal Census' Milo Reed, Caroline Matilda and their children were recorded as again living in Tulare. In those documents Milo Reed's occupation was listed as "farming".

Milo Reed died in Tulare at the age of seventy-five on June 13, 1913. The cause of his death has not been found. He was buried in the Tulare Cemetery in Tulare.

Caroline Matilda outlived her husband by five years, passing away on April 30, 1918 at the age of seventy-eight. Her place and cause of death have also not been found. She too was buried at Tulare in the Tulare Cemetery.

Gravestones for Milo Reed Williams (left) and Caroline Matilda Henderson (right)
(Photographs Courtesy of Steve and Jane Revord)

SOURCES:

Milo Reed Williams
Birth:
Death: "California Death Index 1905-1939," (database on-line), Provo, Utah, USA: Ancestry.com Operations, Inc., 2013, Page 11727.
Graveyard: Find A Grave, Memorial #49432416.

Caroline Matilda Henderson
Birth:
Marriage: (1) Original Record of Maine Towns & Cities, Town of Moscow, Page 114, Picton Press, Rockland Maine, Copyright 2005; (2) "Maine, Marriages, 1771-1907," index, FamilySearch, (https://familysearch.org/pal: /MM9.1.1/F4FK-J6X).
Death: "California Death Index 1905-1939," (database on-line), Provo, Utah, USA: Ancestry.com Operations, Inc., 2013, Page 11696.
Graveyard: Find A Grave, Memorial #49432490.

Historical Accounts: (1) 1860 United States Federal Census for Moscow, Somerset, Maine, Pages 43 & 48; (2) 1870 United States Federal Census for Washington Township, Washington, Kansas, Page 9; (3) 1880 United States Federal Census for Clear Fork Township, Marshall, Kansas, Page 3; (4) 1900 United States Federal Census for Tulare Township, Tulare, California, Page 5; (5) 1910 United States Federal Census for Tulare Township, Tulare, California, Page 4A; (6) 1884 Great Register for Tulare, County, California, "California, Voter Registers, 1866-1898," [database on-line], Provo, UT, USA: Ancestry.com Operations, Inc., 2011; (7) 1890 Great Register for Tulare, County, California, Page 82, "California, Voter Registers, 1866-1898," [database on-line], Provo, UT, USA: Ancestry.com Operations, Inc., 2011; (8) 1892 Great Register for Tulare, County, California, Page 84, "California, Voter Registers, 1866-1898," [database on-line], Provo, UT, USA: Ancestry.com Operations, Inc., 2011; (9) 1894 Great Register for Kern County California, "California, Voter Registers, 1866-1898," [database on-line], Provo, UT, USA: Ancestry.com Operations, Inc., 2011; (10) 1896 Great Register for Kern County California, Goler Precinct, "California, Voter Registers, 1866-1898," [database on-line], Provo, UT, USA: Ancestry.com Operations, Inc., 2011.

Aura Hamblet
(1831 - 1870)

Aura (sometimes spelled Orra) was the first child of Susan Williams and Theodore Hamblet. She was born on August 15, 1831 in Somerset, Maine. The town she was born in has not been found.

In the 1850 United States Federal Census, Aura was living on her father's farm in Madison, Somerset, Maine. Sometime between that census and 1853, Aura married John C. Walker, the son of Samuel Walker and Irinda Cleveland. John C. was born on December 25, 1825 in Anson, Somerset, Maine. The date and place of their marriage has not been found.

During their marriage Aura and John C. had nine children together.

William Theodore	b. March 15, 1854	d. November 4, 1923
Mark M.	*b. 1855*	*d.*
Asher Martin	b. July 15, 1856	d. September 17, 1898
Laura B.	b. August 3, 1858	d. October 13, 1944
Gardner	*b. February 18, 1860*	*d. March 18, 1861*
Sidney Turner	b. April 16, 1861	d. September 30, 1947
Selden	*b. January 1862*	*d. June 1862*
Albert B.	b. May 1866	d. 1937
Georgia M.	d. June 14, 1867	d. December 14, 1905

When the 1860 United States Federal Census was taken, Aura, John C. and their family were living in Solon, Somerset, Maine where John C. was working as a "teamster".

Additional information on the life of Aura and John C.'s second child Mark M. beyond that provided by the 1860 census has not been found. As such his documented history will end here.

Two of Aura and John C.'s children died at young ages. Gardner was thirteen months old when he died on March 8, 1861 and Selden was just five months old when he died in June 1862. The causes and exact places of Gardner and Selden's deaths, as well as the date of Selden's death, have not been found. Both boys were buried in the Village Cemetery in Solon.

By the time the 1870 United States Federal Census was taken Aura, John C. and their family had moved to Brighton, Somerset, Maine and John C. was then working as a "keeper of a hotel".

Aura died a few months later on October 28, 1870 at the age of thirty-nine. The place and cause of her death are not known. She was buried in Solon at the Village Cemetery along with her children, Gardner and Selden.

Gravestones for Gardner Walker & Selden Walker (left) and Aura Hamblet (right)
(Photographs from the Collection of Jeffrey Nelson Williams and Jacqueline Pon Williams)

On April 15, 1872, eighteen months after the death of his first wife, John C. married his second wife Lucinda L. Smith in Wellington, Piscataquis, Maine. The daughter of Gardner Smith and Sydney Grant, Lucinda L. was born in Wellington around 1840. The date of her birth has not been found. Additionally, no record has been found indicating that John C. and Lucinda L. had any children together.

John C. and Lucinda L. were recorded as living in Brighton in the 1880 United States Federal Census and John C. was then working as a "truck man".

Lucinda L. died in Brighton of "consumption" on January 17, 1896 at the age of fifty-six. She was buried in the Walker family plot in the Brighton Village Cemetery in Brighton.

When the 1900 United States Federal Census was taken in June of that year, John C. was living with his daughter, Georgie M. (Walker) Jones, and her family in Brighton. In that census document John C. was recorded as working as a "farm laborer".

On February 18, 1901 at the age of seventy-five, John C. died in Brighton of "dropsy". He was also buried in the Walker family plot in the Brighton Village Cemetery next to his second wife.

Gravestones for John C. Walker (left) and Lucinda L. Smith (right)
(Photographs Courtesy of Gail Kelly)

SOURCES:

Aura Hamblet
Birth:
Death: (1) "Faylene Hutton Cemetery Collection, 1780-1980, Accession #4798", FamilySearch, (https://familysearch.org/ark:/61903/1.1/QKM1-W3YX); (2) Gravestone.
Graveyard: Find A Grave, Memorial #112242522.

John C. Walker
Birth:
Marriage:
Death: (1) Record of a Death, Maine Vital Records; (2) Gravestone.
Graveyard: (1) "Maine Old Cemetery Association Special Publication Number 12, Edition No. 1: Series 1, 2 and 3", Page 344, Picton Press, Rockland, Maine, Copyright 2006; (2) "Brighton Cemetery" complied by Nancy Hamlin Davis and Ruth Hamlin, Old Canada Road Historical Society; (3) Find A Grave, Memorial #82275291.

Mark M. Walker
Birth:
Death:
Graveyard:

Gardner Walker
Birth:
Death: (1) "Faylene Hutton Cemetery Collection, 1780-1980, Accession #4798", FamilySearch, (https://familysearch.org/ark:/61903/1.1/QKM1-W3YX); (2) Gravestone.
Graveyard: Find A Grave, Memorial #112242653.

Selden Walker
Birth:
Death: (1) "Faylene Hutton Cemetery Collection, 1780-1980, Accession #4798", FamilySearch, (https://familysearch.org/ark:/61903/1.1/QKM1-W3YX); (2) Gravestone.
Graveyard: Find A Grave, Memorial #112242791.

Lucinda L. Smith
Birth:
Marriage: (1) Record of a Marriage, Maine Vital Records; (2) "Maine, Marriages, 1771-1907," database, FamilySearch, (https://familysearch.org/ark:/61903/1:1:F4XF-MXC)
Death: Record of a Death, Maine Vital Records.
Graveyard: (1) "Maine Old Cemetery Association Special Publication Number 12, Edition No. 1: Series 1, 2 and 3", Page 344, Picton Press, Rockland, Maine, Copyright 2006; (2) "Brighton Cemetery" complied by Nancy Hamlin Davis and Ruth Hamlin, Old Canada Road Historical Society; (3) Find A Grave, Memorial #82275310.

Historical Accounts: (1) 1850 United States Federal Census for Madison, Somerset, Maine; (2) 1860 United States Federal Census for Solon, Somerset, Maine, Page 48; (3) 1870 United States Federal Census for Brighton, Somerset, Maine, Page 6; (4) 1880 United States Federal Census for Brighton, Somerset, Maine, Page 31; (5) 1900 United States Federal Census for Brighton, Somerset, Maine, Page 12.

Jotham Lowell Hamblet
(1833 - 1913)

The second child of Susan Williams and Theodore Hamblet was Jotham Lowell who was born on March 8, 1833 in Solon, Somerset, Maine.

In his book "History of Cherokee County, Kansas and Representative Citizens" Nathanial Thompson Allison wrote that in his youth Jotham Lowell "...worked with his father in the lumber business, driving a four-horse team between Solon (Somerset, Maine) and the lumber camp. As the trip could be made between Saturday and Monday, it gave him the opportunity to attend school, and he received a superior education".

At age seventeen, when the 1850 United States Federal Census was taken, Jotham Lowell was recorded as living with his father in Madison, Somerset, Maine and working as a "farmer".

Nathanial Thompson Allison also wrote in his book that Jotham Lowell moved to Manhattan, Riley, Kansas in 1853 and while there helped to lay out the town. And in 1855 Jotham Lowell help organize the first Masonic Lodge in Kansas in the county of Wyandotte.

In the 1855 Kansas State Census Jotham Lowell was recorded as living and working as a "farmer" in District 10. Whether that census for District 10 included the town of Manhattan is not known.

On January 12, 1856 Jotham Lowell, at the age of twenty-two, married Emily Adeline Williams, age twenty. The exact location of their marriage has not been found. Emily Adeline, born on February 7, 1836 in Hopkinsville, Christian, Kentucky, was the daughter of William Tucker Williams and Olive M. Shelton.

Jotham Lowell and Emily Adeline had five children during their marriage.

William Lowell	b. August 15, 1858	d. March 2, 1936
Charley	*b. November 2, 1860*	*d. March 3, 1864*
Cora Lee	b. February 5, 1863	d. June 4, 1935
Henry Clay	b. February 25, 1866	d. February 13, 1957
Willis Edwin	b. July 19, 1870	d. November 30, 1938

When the 1860 United States Federal Census was taken Jotham Lowell, Emily Adeline and their first child William Lowell were recorded as living in Lewiston, Androscoggin, Maine where Jotham Lowell was working as a "factory operator". Additionally, in that census Jotham Lowell had dropped the letter "b" from his last name and was then known as Jotham Lowell Hamlet. This is the name he would retain until the end of his life and is also the surname his children used throughout their lives.

Sometime after the 1860 census Jotham Lowell, Emily Adeline and their family moved to Pettis, Platte, Missouri where in October of 1863 Jotham Lowell registered for the Civil War draft. In that document he listed his occupation as "farmer"

The second child of Jotham Lowell and Emily Adeline, Charley, died on March 3, 1864 at the age of three years and four months. The cause and place of his death have not been found. He was buried in the Barry Cemetery at Kansas City, Clay, Missouri.

Jotham Lowell, Emily Adeline and their children were still living and farming in Pettis when the 1870 United States Federal Census was taken.

Nathanial Thompson Allison wrote in his book that while living in Pettis during the Civil War Jotham Lowell joined the "Paw Paw Regiment" which was a local militia consisting of Platte and Clay County men who organized to keep bushwhackers and foragers away from their farms.

According to Nathanial Thompson Allison, Jotham Lowell and Emily Adeline lived in Pettis until 1881 when they decided to move to Cherokee County in Kansas. During the years he lived in Pettis, besides farming, Jotham Lowell also taught for six years at the Brighton schoolhouse.

In the 1885 and 1905 Kansas State Census', and the 1900 United States Federal Census, Jotham Lowell, Emily Adeline and their family were recorded as living in Shawnee, Cherokee, Kansas where Jotham Lowell and his son Henry Clay were "farming".

On February 14, 1908 Emily Adeline died at the age of seventy-three. The place and cause of her death have not been found. She was buried in the Barry Cemetery in Kansas City alongside her son Charley.

The 1910 United States Federal Census recorded Jotham Lowell and his son Henry Clay still living in Shawnee. That census recorded Jotham Lowell with no employment and Henry Clay working as a "shopkeeper".

Jotham Lowell died on February 24, 1913 at the age of seventy-nine. The place and cause of his death are also not known. His funeral was held on February 25th at the Christian Church in Columbus, Cherokee, Kansas with Reverend Goodrick presiding. At his funeral Masonic rites were conducted in his honor by fellow Masons from his Lodge in Galena, Cherokee, Kansas. Jotham Lowell was buried in the Barry Cemetery in Kansas City with his wife and son Charley.

**Gravestone for Jotham Lowell (Hamblet) Hamlet, Emily Adeline Williams
and Charley Hamlet**
(Photograph Taken by Find A Grave Member #47019839)

SOURCES:

Jotham Lowell Hamblet (AKA Jotham Lowell Hamlet)
Birth: (1) "History of Cherokee County, Kansas and Representative Citizens", by Nathanial Thompson Allison,
Pages 623 and 624, Published by Biographical Publishing Company, Chicago, Illinois, 1904; (2) Gravestone.
Death: (1) Obituary, Modern Light, Columbus, Kansas, Thursday, February 27, 1913, Page 6; (2) Gravestone.
Graveyard: Find A Grave, Memorial # 42535395.

Emily Adeline Williams
Birth: Gravestone.
Marriage: (1) Obituary for Jotham Lowell Hamlet, Modern Light, Columbus, Kansas, Thursday, February 27,
1913, Page 6; (2) "History of Cherokee County, Kansas and Representative Citizens", by Nathanial Thompson
Allison, Pages 623 and 624, Published by Biographical Publishing Company, Chicago, Illinois, 1904.
Death: (1) Obituary for Jotham Lowell Hamlet, Modern Light, Columbus, Kansas, Thursday, February 27, 1913,
Page 6; (2) Gravestone.
Graveyard: Find A Grave, Memorial # 42535396.

Charley Hamlet
Birth: Gravestone.
Death: Gravestone.
Graveyard: Find A Grave, Memorial # 42535397.

Historical Accounts: (1) 1850 United States Federal Census for Madison, Somerset, Maine; (2) 1855 Kansas
State Census for District 10; (3) 1860 United States Federal Census for Lewiston, Androscoggin, Maine, Page 69;
(4) 1870 United States Federal Census for Pettis, Platte, Missouri, Page 43; (5) 1885 Kansas State Census for
Shawnee, Cherokee, Kansas, Page 27; (6) 1900 United States Federal Census for Shawnee, Cherokee, Page 5; (7)
1905 Kansas State Census for Shawnee, Cherokee, Kansas, Page 24; (8) 1910 United States Federal Census for
Shawnee, Cherokee, Page 7A; (9) "U. S. Civil War Draft Registration Records, 1863-1865 ", [database on-line].
Provo, UT, USA: Ancestry.com Operations Inc, 2010; (10) "History of Cherokee County, Kansas and
Representative Citizens", by Nathanial Thompson Allison, Pages 623 and 624, Published by Biographical
Publishing Company, Chicago, Illinois, 1904; (11) Newspaper Article for Jotham Lowell Hamlet, Chetopa
Clipper, Chetopa, Kansas, Wednesday, March 5, 1913, Page 4.

Susan Jane Hamblet
(1836 - 1895)

Susan Jane (also known as Jane S.) was the third child of Susan Williams and Theodore Hamblet. She was born on August 26, 1836 in Solon, Somerset, Maine.

The 1850 United States Federal Census recorded Susan Jane as living with her parents in Madison, Somerset, Maine.

It is assumed that sometime after the taking of the 1850 census, but before the birth of their first child in 1858, Susan Jane and James G. Rowell were married. The exact date and place of their marriage has not been found. James G., the son of David Spaulding Rowell and Rachel Jewett, was born in Madison on March 5, 1831.

Susan Jane and James G. had a small family of three children.

Harlow Wood	b. December 12, 1858	d. May 8, 1921
Emma F.	b. October 16, 1860	d. June 10, 1886
Albion K.	b. January 29, 1863	d. November 18, 1938

In the 1860, 1870 and 1880 United States Federal Census', Susan Jane and James G. were recorded as living in Madison with James G.'s occupation being listed as a "farmer".

On December 26, 1895 Susan Jane died at the age of fifty-nine in Madison. Her cause of death was listed as "phthisis pulmonalis". She was buried in Solon at the Village Cemetery.

James G. outlived his wife by almost four years dying in Madison on November 1, 1899 of "apoplexy" at the age of sixty-eight. He was buried in the Village Cemetery in Solon next to his wife.

Gravestones for Susan Jane Hamblet (left) and James G. Rowell (right)
(Photographs from the Collection of Jeffrey Nelson Williams and Jacqueline Pon Williams)

SOURCES:

Susan Jane Hamblet
Birth:
Death: (1) Record of a Death, Maine Vital Records: (2) Gravestone.
Graveyard: Find A Grave, Memorial # 162155361.

James G. Rowell
Birth
Marriage:
Death: (1) Record of a Death, Maine Vital Records; (2) Gravestone.
Graveyard: (1) Record of a Death, Maine Vital Records; (2) Find A Grave, Memorial # 162155362.

Historical Accounts: (1) 1850 United States Federal Census for Madison, Somerset, Maine; (2) 1860 United States Federal Census for Madison, Somerset, Maine; Page 19; (3) 1870 United States Federal Census for Madison, Somerset, Maine, Page 35; (4) 1880 United States Federal Census for Madison, Somerset, Maine, Page 9.

Person Index

WING

WITHAM

www.ingramcontent.com/pod-product-compliance
Lightning Source LLC
Chambersburg PA
CBHW050459270326
41927CB00009B/1815